DIGITAL TRANSFORMATION AND BUSINESS SUSTAINABILITY

Digital transformation brings new opportunities, but also disruption, to the way businesses work. The application of technologies such as blockchain, AI, Internet of Things (IoT) and Big Data has the potential to revolutionize how businesses operate and incorporate sustainable practices within manufacturing processes and supply chains, creating value and redeveloping business models. Digital technologies can also enable more efficient collaboration between various partners across the globe and increase transparency in the supply chain. But while the adoption of new technology can have benefits for businesses, customers and the environment, individual businesses' uptake of new technologies is highly variable, leading to disruption in the supply and value chains.

Digital Transformation and Business Sustainability: From Theory to Practice provides insights into the principle of digital transformation and the key technologies that enable businesses to put the principle into practice. The early chapters set out what digital transformation means for business and how an organization can be ready for it. This book then asks a series of critical questions about digital transformation, such as whether it enables inclusive markets and how compatible it is with digital inclusion and the UN's Sustainable Development Goals. The issue of business sustainability is then addressed in a series of chapters looking at digital transformation and the circular economy.

Featuring diverse cases and examples drawn from across the global economy, and assessing both the theory and practice of digital transformation, this book is an ideal resource for postgraduate students on management courses, professionals on executive education courses, researchers and lecturers.

Dr Geetika Jain is Lecturer in Digital Transformation at Keele Business School, Keele University, UK. Prior to joining Keele Business School, Geetika Jain was a Senior Researcher at the European Blockchain Center, IT University of Copenhagen, Denmark. She was associated with the Danish Skylab Innovation Center as an Expert Researcher. Geetika has gained corporate experience at GE (General Electric), USA, as a strategic consultant. She has a proven record of publication with ABS-3*/3 journals and is an active reviewer of FT50, Academy of Management, ABS and WoS-listed journals and associated with different journals as an editorial board member and guest-edited the journal's special issue.

Malahat Ghoreishi, DSc, is Senior Researcher and Lecturer at LAB University of Applied Sciences, Finland. Her research focuses on digitalization and circular economy, data-driven solutions in circular economy and data-driven and digitally enabled business models in circular economy. She has been involved in several European and Horizon projects as a researcher. She has been involved in several European and Finnish National projects related to circular economy and sustainability.

DIGITAL TRANSFORMATION AND BUSINESS SUSTAINABILITY

From Theory to Practice

Edited by
Geetika Jain and Malahat Ghoreishi

Routledge
Taylor & Francis Group
LONDON AND NEW YORK

Designed cover image: INDU BACHKHETI via Getty Images

First published 2025
by Routledge
4 Park Square, Milton Park, Abingdon, Oxon OX14 4RN

and by Routledge
605 Third Avenue, New York, NY 10158

Routledge is an imprint of the Taylor & Francis Group, an informa business

British Library Cataloguing-in-Publication Data
A catalogue record for this book is available from the British Library

ISBN: 978-1-032-56075-5 (hbk)
ISBN: 978-1-032-56074-8 (pbk)
ISBN: 978-1-003-43374-3 (ebk)

DOI: 10.4324/9781003433743

Typeset in Sabon
by codeMantra

CONTENTS

FIGURES

TABLES

CONTRIBUTORS

Kajal Bhandari, MSc (Tech), is the Strategy and Business Development Manager for Port Solutions at Konecranes, Finland, where she leads strategy and market intelligence to guide the business's long-term vision. She is also pursuing a doctoral degree at LUT University, Finland, specializing in Industrial Engineering and Management. Her research centers on human–machine collaborative systems and their impact across various industries. In recent years, she has collaborated with engineering and technology companies to publish coauthored papers presented at prominent conferences such as IOP Conference Series and the IEEE International Conference on Industrial Engineering and Engineering Management.

Professor Kalyan Ghadei is a distinguished faculty member in the Department of Extension Education at Banaras Hindu University (BHU), Varanasi, Uttar Pradesh. With a strong academic background and extensive experience in the field of extension education, Professor Ghadei has contributed significantly to the development and dissemination of knowledge in rural development, agricultural extension and community education. His research focuses on improving extension services, enhancing rural livelihoods and promoting sustainable agricultural practices. At BHU, he is also involved in guiding students and conducting research projects aimed at addressing real-world challenges in rural India.

Dr Helen Millward is a Lecturer in Marketing in Keele Business School, Keele University, UK. She is a Certified Management Business Educator and an AdvanceHE Fellow. Helen is lead for the Principles of Responsible Management Education at Keele Business School, and she teaches a range of marketing modules at both undergraduate and postgraduate levels. Her research projects surrounding education for sustainable development have previously received funding from Keele University and have been presented at Chartered Association of Business School and AdvanceHE conferences.

Iben Bolund Nielsen, MSc of Global Studies and MBA of International Business and Project Management, is finalizing her PhD in sustainability and circular economy in the Business School at the Lappeenranta-Lahti University of Technology while continuing her 15+ year career in sustainability in various industries across the globe.

Ville Ojanen, DSc (Tech), is a Professor of Industrial Engineering and Management at LUT University, Finland. In the research field of innovation and technology management, he leads a research team, which focuses on the interconnections between industrial renewal and smart manufacturing, digital service business development, as well as sustainability-oriented innovation. In recent years, Professor Ojanen has managed multiple national and international projects, which have included wide collaboration with industrial manufacturing and service firms. In his research fields, he has coauthored papers in leading journals such as *R&D Management*, *Cities*, *Journal of Cleaner Production*, and *International Journal of Human-Computer Interaction*.

Dr Pankaj Kumar Ojha did his MSc (Ag.) in Extension Education from BHU, Varanasi, and PhD in Extension Education from Dr Rajendra Prasad Central Agricultural University, Pusa. He got university Gold Medal in PhD. Besides these, he did Postgraduate Diploma in Rural Development from IGNOU, Postgraduate Diploma in Theatre Communication from BHU, Varanasi, and MBA (HR & IT). He has number of publications to his credit, including edited books (four), research papers, book chapters, review articles, popular articles, etc. He is a Life Member of various professional societies. Presently he is working as an Assistant Professor, Department of Agricultural Extension, Banda University of Agriculture and Technology, Banda, Uttar Pradesh.

Jaakko Palokangas, with over two decades of experience in product and software development, is passionate about improving sustainability, safety and productivity of industrial processes by developing innovative digital and AI solutions. He leads a team of software professionals that develops and maintains digital channels for our distributors and customers, fleet management and real-time systems that automatically sense, think and optimize the performance of machines.

Titta Pitman, MSc, is a corporate professional in marketing management. She is a city council member in Imatra and has served in several boards. Currently, she works as a Junior Researcher and Doctoral Student in the LUT Business School, Finland. She is defending her doctoral thesis "Digital transformation as a driving force in B2B sales management" fall 2024. Her research interests include B2B sales management and leadership development, digital transformation of B2B sales, the B2B sales competencies needed to succeed in today's labor market and sustainability in B2B sales.

Mikko Pynnönen, PhD, is an Associate Professor in LUT Business School (LBS) and holds the title of Docent at LUT University, Finland. He is the leader of the International Business and Entrepreneurship team in LBS. Pynnönen is PI in several research projects in the field of services and business development and his main research interests include value creation and business models in complex business systems.

Dr. Hiranmoy Roy, PhD in Economics, is an Associate Professor in the Department of Economics, School of Humanities and Social Sciences, Hemvati Nandan Bahuguna Garhwal University, Srinagar, Uttarakhand, India. He has been engaged in teaching, research and academic administration for the last 24 years. He has published 50 research papers with reputed journals like *ABDC, Scopus* and other peer-reviewed journals. Published 30 papers in edited volumes. He has also published six books with reputed publishers. Completed research and consultancy projects sanctioned by NITI Aayog (India), World Bank, UGC (India) and Government of Uttarakhand (India).

Fathema Rashid Saba holds an MSc in Business Analytics with distinction from Keele University, marking her second postgraduate degree after completing an MBA in Finance from Shahjalal University of Science & Technology, Bangladesh. With a strong academic background and practical experience, she has spent nine years as a Lecturer at North East University Bangladesh. Fathema is passionate about data-driven decision-making and continues to contribute to the academic and business communities through teaching and research in these fields. And her area of interests are circular economy, sustainability and data-driven decision-making to make the world a better place to live.

Professor Hari P. Sharma is a distinguished academic with over 21 years of teaching and 24 years of research experience. Specializing in Development Economics, Energy Economics and Econometric Modeling, he has received prestigious accolades, including the UGC Fellowship and the Best Research Paper Award from IGBR, USA. He has supervised seven awarded Ph.D. candidates and led impactful research projects funded by organizations like NITI Aayog. He has held significant administrative roles and contributed to numerous publications, workshops and international collaborations, establishing himself as a respected figure in the field of economics.

Parveen Kumar Sharma is a PhD candidate in Economics at DIT University, Dehradun, India, researching renewable energy integration's impact on sustainable development in BRICS nations. He holds an M.A. in Economics from Central University of Jammu and has experience as a Teaching Associate and Research Professor. Proficient in R-Studio, STATA and SPSS, he has published articles, attended international conferences and participated in faculty development programs. His academic pursuits focus on energy economics, sustainable development and practical applications of econometrics.

Jenni Sipilä is an Assistant Professor at LBS and holds the title of Docent at the University of Turku. She received the degree of D.Sc. (Economics and Business Administration) from LUT University in 2018. Her research focuses on consumer behavior, sustainable consumption and sustainability communication and has been published in esteemed journals. She has extensive international experience (University of Mannheim, Stanford University) and has received several awards for her academic activities.

Becky Snelgrove has always been interested in research around teaching and learning, and her current role sees her supporting academics through design of their modules. She has supported the development and subsequent re-running of Keele University's online programs, and has coordinated and led the pilot of many new processes for our learning design support on both online and in-situ programs to support academics in the development of their learning design thinking and skills. Becky also develops and teaches on several modules at both undergraduate and postgraduate levels, including Podcast and Radio Production and Online and Blended Learning Design.

Luke Treves is a Postdoctoral Researcher at LUT University, Business School. He holds a D.Sc. in Business and Economics from LUT University. His research focuses on business model, business model innovation and business strategies, particularly their intersection with Industry 4.0 and 5.0, digital transformation, AI, automation and the IoT. He has participated in numerous research to business projects related to these topics.

INTRODUCTION

Geetika Jain and Malahat Ghoreishi

In 1987, the sustainability concept was defined by the United Nations General Assembly as "meeting the needs of the present without compromising the ability of future generations to meet their own needs" (United Nations General Assembly, 1987). For this reason, environmental and societal issues have gained significant consideration alongside economic issues for all businesses. Organizations must implement sustainability principles at all levels of strategies, operations, and organizational culture to achieve financial and environmental benefits. Embedding sustainability principles increases the productivity and efficiency of the processes, for example, by reducing energy and material extraction and consumption. This way, more sustainable products and services are produced, leading to enhanced financial, societal, and environmental performance (Baumgartner and Rauter, 2017; Pizzi et al., 2020). On the other hand, recent research debates that business sustainability has a positive impact on organizational competitiveness (de Carvalho et al., 2021; Patwa et al., 2020). In this regard, companies gain competitive advantages by implementing innovative solutions and technologies that change how their business operates (Fung et al., 2020). Geng et al. (2020) argue that companies can utilize new technologies and adopt employee reward systems to improve their performance and increase sustainability.

On the other hand, sustainable development is directly related to the new economy model, the circular economy (CE) that has been introduced in contrast to the current linear economy model (Ellen MacArthur Foundation, 2013). The current linear model, which is based on a take-make-use-dispose model, limits the flow of materials while bringing challenges and negative impacts on the environment, economy, and society. In a CE, products and services are designed to maintain their value for a longer period by entering new biological and technical cycles. The CE promotes sustainable development by offering regenerative solutions and offering practices for decreasing and closing the material and energy loops. Shifting towards CE solutions requires a holistic change and rethinking of how the current system works. Implementing CE strategies offers opportunities for developing new and innovative businesses with which companies can enter new markets (Sarfraz et al., 2021). However, implementing sustainability and CE principles

DOI: 10.4324/9781003433743-1

brings complex challenges to companies, specifically regarding to planning, financing, and controlling systems (Dalby et al., 2019).

In recent years, digitalization has been identified as a major driver in business innovation, offering new opportunities for companies while creating value in various aspects. Utilizing digital technologies has transformed the way companies run their business and how they interact with their stakeholders (Chan et al., 2021). According to recent research, digitalization contributes to the improvement of processes and the development of new products and services, which enhances companies' competitive advantages and sustainability (Kristoffersen et al., 2020). In this regard, implementing digital tools can support companies, for example, in sustainability planning and reporting as well as monitoring systems (Baumgartner and Rauter, 2017). According to Broccardo et al. (2023), the essential role of digitalization is to "(i) create opportunities; (ii) support companies at the intra-organizational level-screening and connecting business process activities; and (iii) improve efficiency and effectiveness in a sustainable manner". Therefore, digitalization supports sustainability value by offering new resources and generating new value networks and stakeholders while increasing business performances (Parida and Wincent, 2019; Truant et al., 2021). Furthermore, recent research distinguished the important role of digitalization on societal and environmental aspects of companies' sustainable transitions. The integration of digital technologies in sustainability offers numerous opportunities especially regarding data and information transformation within organization boundaries. Furthermore, as SDG emerges, businesses should rethink the way they create, capture, and deliver value to the end users and customers, in other words, the business model (BM). Recently, many organizations have altered and reframed their BMs based on sustainability goals (Geissdoerfer et al., 2018). In many cases, organizations are required to innovate new BM through the sustainability transition to enter brand-new markets while improving efficiency. New BMs are disruptive innovations that can be enabled by digital capabilities such as data collection, storage, and transfer. In this regard, digital technologies such as big data, the Internet of Things, data analytics, and artificial intelligence have been implemented by businesses to enable new product and service development, resource and process optimization, as well as customer relationships. Therefore, digitalization supports sustainability management and performance by increasing traceability and transparency of processes and operations through data management. According to Broccardo et al. (2023), digitalization impacts the sustainability performance of a business in positive ways, both directly (on profit performance) and indirectly (on financial performance).

Furthermore, from the CE perspective, the role of data has been identified as highly crucial in all circular strategies, especially for developing BMs. Various experts argue that data is at the core of all CE solutions and supports managers in making efficient decisions for their business, for example, regarding resource and energy consumption, product/service design and development, and innovating new BMs (Awan et al., 2021; Järvenpää et al., 2021; Ghoreishi, 2023; Çetin et al., 2023). In the concept of CE, it is highly important to identify the life cycle of the products and services in order to make the right decisions on implementing the most suitable and efficient circular strategies. In this regard, data collection and analysis from the entire life cycle of the product can support slowing and closing the material flows/loops (Luoma et al., 2021). For example, data from customer behavior and experiences could be analyzed and utilized in making decisions regarding the product design, life extension strategies, and offering product–service systems. This type of data can be used to optimize the environmental performance of the CE system and value network. Therefore, we need a circular system consisting of connected products and materials within the entire supply chain. In this sense, the utmost efficient use of CE data can be achieved through suitable digital technologies that can connect product and material flows to enable monitoring, assessing, and optimizing environmental and societal performances (Rajput and Singh, 2019). In addition, to achieve CE-related goals for sustainability, data must be *available*, accessible, and *shared* within the entire value network. Digital technologies can enable the accessibility and sharing of information through digital platforms and data-driven ecosystems to increase businesses' sustainability performance.

The aim of this book is to deepen the understanding of the impacts of utilizing digital technologies and solutions on the sustainable transition of businesses. This book consists of eight chapters.

Chapter 1 - Digital Transformation: Empowering the Circular Economy

Chapter 2 - Artificial Intelligence of Things: Unlocking New Business Sustainability Possibilities or Opening Pandora's Box?

Chapter 3 - Adaptation of Artificial Intelligence by Start-Ups for a Data-Driven Circular Economy: Evidence from Multiple Case Study in Finland

Chapter 4 - Organizational Readiness of a Manufacturing Firm for Sustainable Business Growth with Digital Initiatives: The Role of Sales and Sustainability

Chapter 5 - Interaction between Technological, Economic, and Social Changes

Chapter 6 - Digital Skills Development for Inclusive Digital Transformation

Chapter 7 - Applying Design Sprint Method to Create a Minimum Viable Product with Machine Vision

Chapter 8 - Developing a Digital Sustainable Development Goal Passport for Postgraduate Management Students in a UK Business School

References

Awan, U., Shamim, S., Khan, Z., Zia, N. U., Shariq, S. M., & Khan, M. N., 2021. Big data analytics capability and decision-making: The role of data-driven insight on circular economy performance. *Technological Forecasting and Social Change*, 168, 120766.

Baumgartner, R. J., & Rauter, R. (2017). Strategic perspectives of corporate sustainability management to develop a sustainable organization. *Journal of Cleaner Production*, 140, 81–92. https://doi.org/10.1016/j.jclepro.2016.04.146.

Broccardo, L., Truant, E., & Dana, L. P. (2023). The interlink between digitalization, sustainability, and performance: An Italian context. *Journal of Business Research*, 158, 113621.

Çetin, S., Raghu, D., Honic, M., Straub, A., & Gruis, V. (2023). Data requirements and availabilities for material passports: A digitally enabled framework for improving the circularity of existing buildings. *Sustainable Production and Consumption*, 40, 422–437. https://doi.org/10.1016/j.spc.2023.07.011.

Chan, J. H., Chen, S. Y., Piterou, A., Khoo, S. L., Lean, H. H., Hashim, I. H. M., & Lane, B. (2021). An innovative social enterprise: Roles of and challenges faced by an arts hub in a World Heritage Site in Malaysia. *City, Culture and Society*, 25, 100396. https://doi.org/10.1016/j.ccs.2021.100396.

Dalby, S., Horton, S., Mahon, R., & Thomaz, D. (Eds.). (2019). *Achieving the sustainable development goals: Global governance challenges*. Routledge.

de Carvalho, R. A., da Hora, H., & Fernandes, R. (2021). A process for designing innovative mechatronic products. *International Journal of Production Economics*, 231, 107887.

Ellen MacArthur Foundation. (2013). *Towards the Circular Economy*. Vol. 1. Ellen MacArthur Foundation. https://doi.org/10.1162/108819806775545321.

Fung, Y. N., Chan, H. L., Choi, T. M., & Liu, R. (2020). Sustainable product development processes in fashion: Supply chains structures and classifications. *International Journal of Production Economics*, 231, 107911.

Geissdoerfer, M., Vladimirova, D., & Evans, S. (2018). Sustainable business model innovation: A review. *Journal of Cleaner Production*, 198, 401–416. https://doi.org/10.1016/j.jclepro.2018.06.240.

Geng, D., Lai, K. H., & Zhu, Q. (2020). Eco-innovation and its role in performance improvement among Chinese small and medium-sized manufacturing enterprises. *International Journal of Production Economics*, 231, 107869.

Ghoreishi, M. (2023). The role of digital technologies in a data-driven circular business model: A systematic literature review. *Journal of Business Models*, 11(1), 78–81. https://doi.org/10.54337/jbm.v11i1.7245.

Järvenpää, A. M., Kunttu, I., Jussila, J., & Mäntyneva, M. (2021, April). Data-driven decision-making in circular economy SMEs in Finland. In *The International Research & Innovation Forum* (pp. 371–382). Cham: Springer International Publishing.

Kristoffersen, E., Blomsma, F., Mikalef, P., & Li, J. (2020). The smart circular economy: A digital-enabled circular strategies framework for manufacturing companies. *Journal of Business Research*, 120, 241–261. https://doi.org/10.1016/j.jbusres.2020.07.044.

Luoma, P., Toppinen, A., & Penttinen, E. (2021). The role and value of data in realizing circular business models – A systematic literature review. *Journal of Business Models*, 9, 44–71. https://doi.org/10.5278/jbm.v9i2.3448.

Parida, V., & Wincent, J. (2019). Why and how to compete through sustainability: A review and outline of trends influencing firm and network-level transformation. *International Entrepreneurship and Management Journal*, 15(1), 1–19. https://doi.org/10.1007/s11365-019-00558-9.

Patwa, N., Sivarajah, U., Seetharaman, A., Sarkar, S., Maiti, K., & Hingorani, K. (2020). Towards a circular economy: An emerging economies context. *Journal of Business Research*.

Pizzi, S., Rosati, F., & Venturelli, A. (2020). The determinants of business contribution to the 2030 agenda: Introducing the SDG reporting score. *Business Strategy and the Environment*. https://doi.org/10.1002/bse.2628.

Rajput, S., & Singh, S. (2019). Connecting circular economy and industry 4.0. *International Journal of Information Management*. https://doi.org/10.1016/j.ijinfomgt.2019.03.002.

Sarfraz, M., Ivascu, L., Belu, R., & Artene, A. (2021). Accentuating the interconnection between business sustainability and organizational performance in the context of the circular economy: The moderating role of organizational competitiveness. *Business Strategy and the Environment*, 30, 2108–2118.

Truant, E., Broccardo, L., & Dana, L. P. (2021). Digitalisation boosts company performance: An overview of Italian listed companies. *Technological Forecasting and Social Change*, 173, 121173. https://doi.org/10.1016/j.techfore.2021.121173.

United Nations General Assembly. (1987). *Report of the world commission on environment and development: Our common future*. Oslo: United Nations General Assembly, Development and International Co-operation: Environment.

1

DIGITAL TRANSFORMATION

Empowering the Circular Economy

Fathema Rashid Saba

1   Introduction

Numerous academics contend that several ongoing trends in population, politics, industry, economy, technology, and human behaviour are putting the globe at risk of a catastrophic climate change. Long-term sustainable development has become a major concern for governments, businesses, and scholars around the globe. The relevance of sustainable, regenerative, and restorative corporate operations and activities is emphasised by modern economists and business experts. The circular economy (CE) concept emerged in response to the growing need to decouple economic growth from resource use and environmental effects, and it has gained popularity in recent years (Demestichas and Daskalakis, 2020; Khan, Piprani and Yu, 2022). The CE as a business model has acquired a lot of interest with both practitioners and researchers in many parts of the world. It tries to achieve sustainable symbiosis between economic endeavours and environmental preservation (Murray, Skene and Haynes, 2017).

CE is known as a continuous and regenerating loop of materials and resources that characterise the sustainable economic system (Riesener et al., 2019). The CE system substitutes the 'end-of-life' approach with the principles of reducing, reusing, recycling, and recovering. Majority of the global economic activity still relies on the usage of virgin resources, despite the CE's many benefits. The global circularity has dropped from 9.1% in 2018 to 8.6% in 2020. More than 90% of resources are lost, squandered, or aren't available for reuse for years because they are locked into durable stock-like buildings and machines (www.circularity-gap.world, n.d.). In contrast, in a variety of industries, from manufacturing and supply chain (SC) management to consumer interaction and environmental monitoring, digital transformation uses technology to innovate, streamline processes, and improve connections. A company's operations can significantly change because of the ongoing, complex digital transformation project. Rethinking how we now produce, distribute, and use material is necessary to diminish current 'make-use-dispose' culture. The ongoing digital transformation provides chances to technically make this transition possible. Big data, block chain, cyber-physical systems, and the Internet of

DOI: 10.4324/9781003433743-2

Things (IoT) are some of the technologies that primarily offer real-time data availability, connectivity, and consistency along the value chain. As a result, the digital transformation has the ability to maximise resource utilisation, improve consumption efficiency, and reduce waste to improve the recirculation of product and material streams throughout the product lifecycle (Wilts, 2017).

1.1 Research Questions

Focus of this study is to gather information for a clear understanding of CE and digital transformation, find links between these two, and identify the enablers for CE that are related to digital transformation. Therefore, the research is designed in such a way to identify the studies that cover both these areas. Figure 1.1 depicts the common area between CE and digital transformation that is covered as objective of this study. Thus, to carry on the research, the following research questions (RQs) have been formulated:

RQ 1: How does the existing literature explain the link between digital transformation and CE?
RQ 2: What are the enablers of digital transformation that empower CE?

The reminder of this document is structured as follows: Section 2 presents a literature review. Section 3 presents the methodology employed in this study. Section 4 presents the descriptive analysis of the selected papers. Section 5 is the discussion, which includes a detailed explanation of the findings from analysis along with the limitations of this study and theoretical and managerial implications of the study. Section 6 is the conclusion.

2 Literature Review

This section illustrates the underlying theoretical concepts of this study. This research is mainly based on two topics, which are CE and digital transformation. The knowledge of academics, professionals, and thought leaders who have experimented with digital technology and CE concepts is collected in this literature study. It is prepared carefully and methodically. As we embark on this journey, we are building upon the efforts of

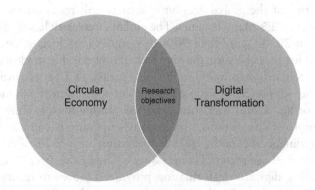

FIGURE 1.1 Links between circular economy and digital transformation.

people who have sought to discover answers to the issues at hand. Both academic and non-academic literature are used to understand CE and digital transformation.

2.1 Circular Economy

The concept of CE is not something new. The idea of CE is based on the theories of industrial ecology and industrial metabolism developed in the 1970s and 1980s through a reevaluation of the industrial processes (D'Amato et al., 2017). The phrase 'CE' initially originated in a Pearce and Turner (1990) study that looked at the connections between economic activity and the environment (Merli, Preziosi and Acampora, 2018). It gained popularity based on the rapid economic development China saw in the 1990s and the scarcity of natural resources that are needed to manufacture products and services (Tavera Romero et al., 2021). Though the concept is not something new, it gained attention from policymakers, academic researchers, governments, and businesses in recent years, and was promoted by various businesses and governments around the world. Because it is seen as a way for businesses to operationalise the much-discussed idea of sustainable development, CE is a topic of significant interest to both academics and practitioners (Murray et al., 2017, cited in Kirchherr, Reike and Hekkert, 2017).

TABLE 1.1 Definitions of circular economy

Definition	Source
"A circular economy describes an economic system that is based on business models which replace the 'end-of-life' concept with reducing, alternatively reusing, recycling and recovering materials in production/distribution and consumption processes, thus operating at the micro level (products, companies, consumers), meso level (eco-industrial parks) and macro level (city, region, nation and beyond), with the aim to accomplish sustainable development, which implies creating environmental quality, economic prosperity and social equity, to the benefit of current and future generations."	Kirchherr et al. (2017)
"A circular economy is a system that promotes the reuse of products and raw materials to maximize the restorative capacity of natural resources. It aims to minimize value destruction and maximize value creation in each link of the system."	Koech and Munene (2019)
"Circular economy is an economic system in which resource input and waste, emission, and energy leakages are minimized by cycling, extending, intensifying, and dematerializing material and energy loops. This can be achieved through digitalization, servitisation, sharing solutions, long-lasting product design, maintenance, repair, reuse, remanufacturing, refurbishing, and recycling."	Geissdoerfer et al. (2020)
"Circular economy is an economic system based on the reusability of products and product components, recycling of materials, and on conservation of natural resources while pursuing the creation of added value in every link of the system."	PBL (2017)
"The circular economy is a model of production and consumption, which involves sharing, leasing, reusing, repairing, refurbishing and recycling existing materials and products as long as possible. In this way, the life cycle of products is extended."	European Parliament (2023)

CE might imply many different things to various people (Kirchherr, Reike and Hekkert, 2017). CE is linked with many other concepts that may not be necessarily circular. These include 'sharing economy' (Frenken and Schor, 2017), 'collaborative economy' (Huber, 2017), and 'circle economy' (PACE, 2020).

The CE is a concept that is being pushed by the EU, numerous national governments, including those of China, Japan, the UK, France, Canada, the Netherlands, Sweden, and Finland, as well as numerous enterprises throughout the world (Korhonen, Honkasalo and Seppälä, 2018).

A CE is an integrated strategy for economic growth that is intended to benefit organisations, society, and the environment. It is regenerative by design and seeks to gradually divorce growth from the consumption of finite resources, in contrast to the linear 'take-make-waste' model (Ellen Macarthur Foundation, 2023). Academicians, business experts, and government agencies defined CE from different perspectives.

Thus, CE is a system that is established based on the concept of repair, reuse, and recycle of products, and gives an opportunity to ensure environmental quality, economic prosperity, and social equality.

CE is considered as a sustainable development because it focuses on economic, social, and environmental aspects. Numerous theories and schools of thinking have influenced the idea of CE. Various disciplines such as design thinking, zero-waste programmes,

TABLE 1.2 Circular economy hierarchy of choices

Strategy	R-imperative	Description
Better product design and production	R0 Refuse	Make the product obsolete by giving up on its purpose or by providing the same purpose with a drastically different product
	R1 Rethink	Increase the frequency with which products are used (by sharing products or introducing multipurpose products to the market, for example)
	R2 Reduce	Using fewer natural resources and commodities will increase the efficiency of product production or consumption
Boost the product's and its components' longevity	R3 Reuse	Using a discarded item that is still in good shape and serves its intended purpose but is being used by another user
	R4 Repair	Repair and maintenance of faulty products so they can be used in accordance with their intended uses
	R5 Refurbish	Update an outdated product by restoring it
	R6 Remanufacture	Utilise discarded product components to create a new item with a different purpose
	R7 Repurpose	Utilise discarded products and their components to create a new item with a different purpose
Efficient use of resources	R8 Recycle	Processing resources to produce the same (high grade) or a lower (low grade) quality
	R9 Recover	Burning materials in a way that recovers energy

Source: PBL (2017)

closed-loop cycles, green operations, Industry 4.0 (I4.0), technology platforms, and cleaner production are associated with the CE.

CE is considered an umbrella concept. Various circularity solutions are available to minimise the utilisation of natural resources and commodities. These could be ranked in order of priority based on how circular they are. Based on PBL (2017), the author created the Table 1.2, which shows the hierarchy of CE choices.

Though 10 R's are used for explaining circularity, these mainly depend on the industry where circularity is implemented. It may vary from industry to industry and country to country. It depends on the nature of business and what targets they want to achieve.

2.2   Digital Transformation

Words like digitisation, digitalisation, and digital transformation are used interchangeably. But it is important to understand the actual meaning of all these terms. Jason Bloomberg mentioned that these terms have distinct meanings (Bloomberg, 2018). Digitisation, in its simplest form, is the conversion of analogue information into zeroes and ones for storage, processing, and transmission by computers. Digitalisation is the transformation of a business model to create new options for value creation and income generation. Academicians, governments, and business experts defined digital transformation in various ways.

I4.0 is an important tool for digital transformation. Advanced digital technologies are the main elements of I4.0. Building blocks of I4.0 are big data and analytics, autonomous robots and vehicles, additive manufacturing (AM), simulation, augmented and virtual reality, horizontal/vertical system integration, the IoT, cloud, fog, and edge technologies, and block chain and cyber security (Rosa et al., 2019).

2.3   CE and Digital Transformation

Given the importance of CE and digital transformation, many scholars discuss these from different perspectives. With time the number of papers are increasing as scholars are focusing more and more on CE and digital transformation. Though many of these are not directly referred to as digital transformation.

Pagoropoulos et al.'s article "The Emergent Role of Digital Technologies in the Circular Economy: A Review" from 2017 acknowledges the convergence of CE and digital technologies as a rapidly expanding research area and examines CE in terms of data architecture and integration infrastructure. Examining how digital technologies facilitate the move to a CE is the main objective. The architecture perspective (data collecting, data analysis, and data integration) is used to identify seven key technologies that will assist this shift. The study primarily focuses on a review of the literature to classify important technologies that have an impact on CEs, but it does not look at specific digital transformation opportunities that support the shift from a linear to a circular system (Pagoropoulos, Pigosso and McAloone, 2017).

"Digital Technologies in Circular Economy Transition: Evidence from Case Studies" by Uçar et al. (2020): The authors mentioned that two main roles of digital technologies are enabler and trigger. This paper is based on three case studies. The enabler role is more dominant than the trigger role. Only in the value proposition does the trigger role exists. The role's supporting functions are data sharing, data storage, and data analysis. The enabler function facilitates channels, cost structure, revenue streams, partners, activities, critical resources, value proposition, and customer relationships. Although the use of

TABLE 1.3 Definitions of digital transformation

Definition	Source
"Digital transformation is concerned with the changes that digital technologies can bring about in a company's business model, products, processes and organizational structure. These changes can be observed in individual and organizational contexts. It reflected in the change of entire business models brought about by digital technologies."	Hess et al. (2016)
[Digital transformation is a] "process through which companies converge multiple new digital technologies, enhanced with ubiquitous connectivity, with the intention of reaching superior performance and sustained competitive advantage, by transforming multiple business dimensions, including the business model, the customer experience (comprising digitally enabled products and services) and operations (comprising processes and decision-making), and simultaneously impacting people (including skills talent and culture) and networks (including the entire value system)."	Ismail, Khater and Zaki (2017)
"Digitization is the conversion of analogue data and processes into a machine-readable format. Digitalization is the use of digital technologies and data as well as interconnection that results in new or changes to existing activities. Digital transformation refers to the economic and societal effects of digitization and digitalization."	OECD (2017)
"Digital transformation is not a software upgrade or a supply chain improvement project. It's a planned digital shock to what may be a reasonably functioning system."	Andriole (2017)
"Digital transformation requires the organization to deal better with change overall, essentially making change a core competency as the enterprise becomes customer-driven end-to-end. Such agility will facilitate ongoing digitalization initiatives but should not be confused with them."	Bloomberg (2018)

digital technologies is increasing in many industries, use of them for CE is still needed exploration in terms of research (Uçar, Dain and Joly, 2020).

"Synergy between Circular Economy and Industry 4.0: A Literature Review" by Tavera Romero et al. (2021) identified various theories and concepts pertaining to CE and I4.0 through a thorough knowledge, analysis, and synthesis process. The study made clear the need for more research on the effects of technology advancements on society and people, as well as how people are being prepared for the shift from a linear economy to a CE.

Exploring how usage-focused business models enable CE through digital transformation. A study by Bressanelli et al. (2018) titled "Exploring How Usage-Focused Business Models Enable Circular Economy through Digital Transformation" looked at how digital technologies contribute to the successful adoption of the CE paradigm in business. The model explains how service business models are made possible by digital technologies (IoT, big data, and analytics) and how this can have a beneficial impact on CE value drivers. The paper effectively examines each technology that makes the business model in issue possible, but it makes no recommendations on how to facilitate the shift and pave the way for a CE.

In the last few years many articles and papers have been published based on digital transformation and CE. Many of these articles mainly focused on developing new models of business where digital transformation could be used for CE. It is time to answer how the CE and digital transformation can work together to restructure sectors and enhance sustainability at a time of fast technical developments and rising environmental concerns?

3   Methodology

This study followed a well-defined literature review model. A systematic literature review (SLR) is a research methodology that is used to collect, identify, and critically evaluate the research works that are currently available, which may include articles, conference papers, books, and so on, by using a systematic procedure (Pati and Lorusso, 2017). This is a valuable tool to view and easily understand the current research trend and existing research of any specified topic (Gil Lamata and Latorre Martínez, 2022). Liberati et al. (2009) mentioned that a systematic review can be explained as a research method and process for identifying and critically appraising relevant research, as well as for collecting and analysing data from said research (Snyder, 2019). The SLR methodology is an exacting and methodical way to review the literature on a certain subject. Many scholars provide different approaches to complete a SLR. SLR system is mainly developed within medical science, which is transparent, systematic, and reproducible. As this system has several advantages, it is gaining popularity among many research areas including business.

A SLR would be conducted as part of this project, in accordance with the recommendations provided by Denyer and Tranfield (2009). As an essential stage in creating theoretical frameworks and conceptual models, a literature review is a great way to synthesise research results, provide evidence at the meta-level, and pinpoint areas that require more study (Snyder, 2019).

This whole study is divided into five phases.

Phase 1: Developing the RQ: Main focus of this study is to gather information for a clear understanding of CE and digital transformation, find links between these two, and identify the enablers for CE that are related to digital transformation. Therefore, the research is designed in such a way to identify the studies that cover both these areas.

Phase 2: Developing review protocol: For getting a good result, it is important to identify the most relevant studies. Issues taken into account for identifying studies are selection of databases and selection of key words. For getting a great outcome, it is important to select appropriate databases, and determine the key words, because these will give an opportunity to gather sufficient and informative information for analysis. Selected key words for inclusion and exclusion criteria are as follows:

A summary of the selection criteria is given below:

The Web of Science (WoS) and ProQuest databases are used to locate the articles of digital transformation and CE. WoS is the primary source of data and ProQuest is used to further increase the data that are not included in WoS. To identify the search terms and key words connected with CE and digital transformation and to locate the relevant studies in the databases of WoS, a string query using Boolean operators and truncated characters was created. The search string used was ('Artificial intelligence' OR 'AI' OR 'Big data' OR 'Machine learning' OR 'Machine intelligence' OR 'Web intelligence' OR 'Artificial

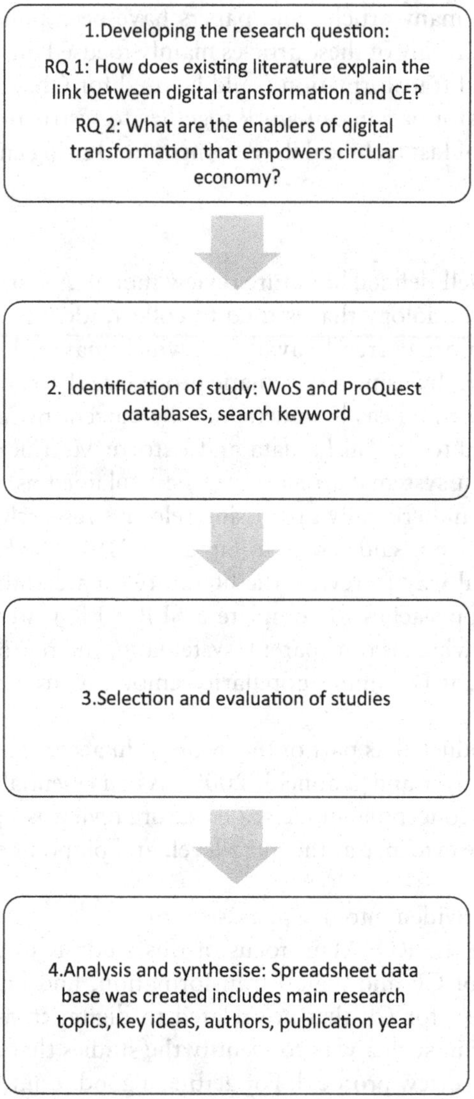

1.Developing the research question:

RQ 1: How does existing literature explain the link between digital transformation and CE?

RQ 2: What are the enablers of digital transformation that empowers circular economy?

2. Identification of study: WoS and ProQuest databases, search keyword

3.Selection and evaluation of studies

4.Analysis and synthesise: Spreadsheet data base was created includes main research topics, key ideas, authors, publication year

5. Finding results and discussion: Descriptive analysis, classification based on research themes, identify the key findings

FIGURE 1.2 Research procedure.

TABLE 1.4 Topic-related key words

Digital-transformation-related key words	CE-related key words
Artificial Intelligence (AI), Big data, Machine learning, Digitalisation, Digital technology, Internet of Things (IoT), Block chain, Cloud computing, Cyber security, Industry 4.0	Circular economy, Circularity, Circular economy principles, Sustainability, Economic, Sustainability, Green economy

TABLE 1.5 Selection criteria

Code	Description	Reason
Language	English	Easy to access and understand
Databases	Scopus, Web of Science	Transparent, focused
Time of publication	2006 to 2022	As earlier works were not that details
Search string	('Artificial intelligence' OR 'AI' OR 'Big data' OR 'Machine learning' OR 'Machine intelligence' OR 'Web intelligence' OR 'Artificial neural network' OR 'Digitalisation technology*' OR 'Digitalisation*' OR 'Internet of thing' OR 'IoT' OR 'Blockchain' OR 'Cloud computing' OR 'Industry 4.0' OR 'Cybersecurity') And ('circular economy*' OR 'CE principle*' OR 'bioeconomy*' OR 'circular design*' OR 'economic sustainability*' OR 'green economy*')	
Inclusion criteria	Papers addressing both circular economy and digital transformation/digital technologies	
Exclusion criteria	Papers purely based on technical knowledge	

neural network' OR 'Digitalisation technology*' OR 'Digitalisation*' OR 'Internet of thing' OR 'IoT' OR 'Blockchain' OR 'Cloud computing' OR 'Industry 4.0' OR 'Cybersecurity') And ('circular economy*' OR 'CE principle*' OR 'bioeconomy*' OR 'circular design*' OR 'economic sustainability*' OR 'green economy*'). For ProQuest, only the key words were used as search terms. Further filters were used to get the desired articles that are more connected in terms of relevance. Such as for area of research, only business economics was selected, and only open-access articles were chosen.

This search query returns 285 articles in WoS and 99 in ProQuest. Mendeley was used to track the articles and stop duplication.

Phase 3: Selection and evaluation of the studies: For final screening, few criteria were selected to identify the appropriate articles for the study. For inclusion, only those articles that addressed CE and digital transformation or digital technologies were selected. Year of publication was selected from 2006 to 2022. Language was selected as English, and 16 no reviews were included. Articles that are purely technical were also excluded. After applying all these criteria, the total number of articles reduced significantly. Only 37 articles were selected from WoS, and 9 from ProQuest. So, a total of 46 articles were selected for thorough reading.

Phase 4: Analysis and synthesis: In this phase, all the selected articles were read thoroughly to identify the key findings based on the objectives determined earlier and to answer the RQs. In this phase, a spreadsheet file was generated that contained information such as authors, year of publication, objectives, and key findings.

Phase 5: Finding results and report writing: In this phase, the result was accumulated after analysis in the previous phase, which is discussed in the report. This is a complex step, which is explained in a separate section.

All these steps helped to finally accumulate all the necessary data and proceed for final analysis and get the findings to fulfil the objectives.

4 Data Analysis

This section is focused on providing a descriptive analysis of the 46 articles that were selected. It explains how the articles were categorised based on research themes, analyses the key findings of each theme, and identifies the findings that can answer the RQs.

4.1 Statistical Descriptions of the Literature

Figure 1.3 depicts the annual distribution of the publication of the articles. Though the timeframe was selected from 2006 to 2022 in initial stage, no significant papers could be found before 2017. Thus, it clearly shows that this is comparatively a new area and gaining attention from scholars in recent years. In just five years, number of publications increased ten fold. It is an anticipation that over time, attention towards CE and digitalisation will increase.

Among the 46 papers, 30 papers were written by 4 or more than 4 authors. Only 1 paper was written by one author. Number of papers prepared by 2 and 3 authors were respectively 6 and 9. This distribution is presented on Figure 1.4.

4.2 Classification and Content Evaluation

After careful reading of the articles, four main themes were selected that are part of digital transformation. These thematic categories are: (1) CE and big data, (2) CE and digital technologies, (3) CE and I4.0, and (4) CE and SC.

TABLE 1.6 Number of selected articles

First screening	384 articles (WoS = 285 articles) (ProQuest = 99 articles)
Final screening	46 articles (WoS = 37 articles) (ProQuest = 09 articles)

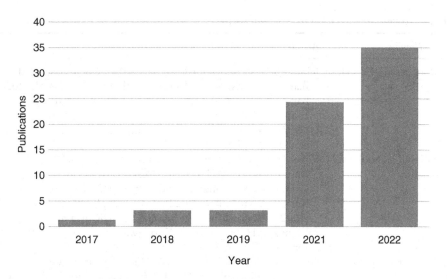

FIGURE 1.3   Annual distribution of articles.

TABLE 1.7 Author analysis

Number of authors	Number of papers
1	1
2	6
3	9
4 or more	30

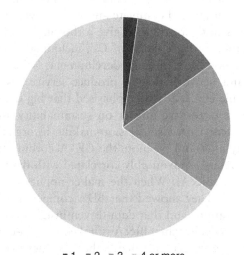

■ 1 ■ 2 ■ 3 ▨ 4 or more

FIGURE 1.4   Author analysis.

TABLE 1.8 Article categorisation by research themes

Research themes	Articles
CE and big data (14 articles)	Jeble et al. (2018), Mamedov et al. (2018), Coble et al. (2018), Bianchini, Rossi and Pellegrini (2019), Chidepatil et al. (2020), Bag et al. (2020), Kristoffersen et al. (2020), Kazancoglu et al. (2021), Awan et al. (2021), Fraga-Lamas, Lopes and Fernández-Caramés (2021), Kristoffersen et al. (2021), Fallahi et al. (2022), Luoma et al. (2022), Agrawal et al. (2021)
CE and digital technologies (13 articles)	Vijverman, Henkens and Verleye (2019), Demestichas and Daskalakis (2020), Liu et al. (2021), Patwa et al. (2020), Chaudhuri, Subramanian and Dora (2022), Pakseresht, Ahmadi Kaliji and Xhakollari (2022), Tavana et al. (2022), Gong et al. (2022), Alonso-Muñoz et al. (2022), Neligan et al. (2022), Heim and Hopper (2022), Kurniawan et al. (2022), Wynn and Jones (2022)
CE and Industry 4.0 (10 articles)	Spring and Araujo (2017), Ćwiklicki and Wojnarowska (2020), Ciliberto et al. (2021), Vacchi et al. (2021), da Silva and Sehnem (2022), Chari et al. (2022), Dwivedi et al. (2022), Dongfang et al. (2022), Hettiarachchi, Seuring and Brandenburg (2022)
CE and supply chain (9 articles)	Dubey et al. (2019), Del Giudice et al. (2020), Rehman Khan et al. (2021), Jinru et al. (2021), Piyathanavong et al. (2022), Liu et al. (2021), Liu et al. (2022), Xin, Lang and Mishra (2022), De Giovanni (2022)

Abbreviation: CE, circular economy.

4.2.1 Studies Focused on Big Data

Big data and their analysis are gaining popularity as they come up with an opportunity to provide a more accurate and complete answer. Agrawal et al. (2021) mentioned emerging research themes in their article to give a thorough understanding of artificial intelligence (AI) application in the context of CE, including industry strategy, sustainable development, CE models, economic development, waste management, system management, logistic and network design, product service system, design strategies, and research models. Jeble et al. (2018) emphasised that big data analytics (BDA) and predictive modelling have a positive impact on sustainability and environment. BDA is a ground-breaking strategy for wise decision-making in organisations that have the potential to dramatically alter and promote the CE. According to Awan et al. (2021), the quality of decision-making is favourably correlated with BDA capacity and Business Intelligence and Analytics (BI&A). When the maker applies data-driven insights, this effect is more pronounced. They showed that BDA competence impacts the calibre of decisions made in organisations and that data-driven insights do not mitigate this relationship. Through data-driven insights, BI&A is linked to high-quality decision-making. These findings give managers crucial information because they may be used as a guide for creating data-driven insights in organisations using the CE paradigm.

Kristoffersen et al. (2021) proposed a conceptual model showing eight business analytic resources that, when combined, create a business analytics capable for the CE and how this relates to businesses' ability to implement the CE, manage resources, and perform competitively. They argued that the role of digital technologies in driving business transitions to the CE is expanding. However, there hasn't been much research on the organisational resources and capacities needed to properly leverage digital technologies for CE, with the focus, instead, predominantly being on the technical aspects of deploying these technologies. Bianchini, Rossi and Pellegrini (2019) have also proposed a business model. It is a brand-new Circular Business Model (CBM) visualisation tool that gets through the major drawbacks of the pre-existing models, which could only teach CE concepts and did not help advance their actual application in industry. Every industrial sector can use the new CBM visualisation tool to identify untapped or hidden circular potential and choose the appropriate CE strategy. However, product companies that switch from linear business model to CBMs face a number of potential financial repercussions because they must invest more money in a stock of goods that will be rented out over time and as a result will experience a slower, more erratic cash flow than they would under linear direct sales of goods. The role of financial actors in circular business ecosystems and alternative financing solutions when transitioning from product-dominant business models to Product-as-a-Service (PaaS) or function-based business models is discussed by Fallahi et al. (2022). They showed a solution that allows for the incorporation of cutting-edge AI modelling for financial risk assessment. They emphasised solutions, management implications, and funding opportunities for CBMs, and they make the case for the significance of various types of data in upcoming company ecosystems.

Millions of people worldwide, particularly in underdeveloped nations, are impacted by the food crisis. There are several reasons that contribute to it, including population growth, land degradation, water scarcity, food waste, and others. Aiming to keep goods and materials in use, eliminate waste and pollution, and renew natural systems, the CE is a methodology that could ensure sustainability. By encouraging sustainable methods of production, consumption, and waste disposal, it can provide solutions to the food crisis. In this context, Kazancoglu et al. (2021) mentioned that the most important factor influencing the development of BDA applications in the Food Supply Chain (FSC) transition from linearity to CE is governmental incentive. Additionally, major BDA drivers in FSC for the transition to CE include organisational commitment, collaborations with SC partners, and operation efficiency.

Compared to other sectors, only the manufacturers of automotive components and related products have made a substantial advancement in digitalisation. Additionally, when making judgements about manufacturing, this industry pays close attention to environmental and social factors. All of this is made possible by the government's, suppliers', and clients' collective participation in achieving sustainable development goals. Bag et al. (2020) presented these in their paper where data was collected from South Africa. The results showed that coercive pressures and mimetic pressures are favourably correlated with physical resources. Coercive and normative pressures also show a favourable correlation with workforce skills. The use of BDA–AI is positively correlated with tangible resources and worker skills.

Fraga-Lamas, Lopes and Fernández-Caramés (2021) found that security, speed, and fragmentation are just a few of the problems that Edge-AI G-IoT systems are up against. However, there are a variety of solutions that can be put into place to deal with these issues, including improved security measures, increased edge computing power, a standardised framework, decentralised storage, and SC visibility and transparency. Edge-AI G-IoT systems can overcome these obstacles and realise their full potential, revolutionising CE.

Luoma et al. (2022) in their study discussed three major findings. Firstly, the framework recognised three variables to be crucial, including company commitment, high consumer awareness, and regulatory push, both for the development of CE and for the role of data therein. This result is in line with past literature, which suggests that businesses, consumers, and policymakers must all work together to create the CE. Secondly, more collaboration is required on sharing, maintaining, and using CE data throughout SCs and value networks in order to achieve broad-based data exploitation in pursuit of firms' and society' transition towards CE. And finally, increasing the openness of corporate operations across the whole value chain and the lifecycle of products is crucial. This desire, which academics recognise as crucial for the shift to a CE, is reflected in the transparency image.

Overall, big data and related elements can play a crucial role to ensure implementation of CE by providing an opportunity for data collaboration, wide data collection range, and implementing CBM. This system could include all the areas of business, such as management, finance, SC management, research, design, and production. Areas such as waste management, product design, and value creation opportunities could be identified by using big data that are key drivers for a sustainable CE. Big data and CE are complementary concepts that each assist and advance the other in the quest for sustainability and resource efficiency. In a CE framework, big data's capacity to gather, process, and analyse massive amounts of information is essential for optimising resource use. This includes SC transparency, which enables stakeholders to monitor and manage the lifecycle of goods and resources, as well as proactive maintenance to increase the useful life of assets. Big data also provides information on consumer behaviour and tastes, aiding in the development of products that adhere to circular principles. By finding inefficiencies and improving recycling procedures, it also contributes to waste reduction.

4.2.2 Studies Focused on Digital Technologies

To create a more sustainable and efficient system, many scholars proposed to combine digital technologies and CE. Digital technologies, which include automated systems, electronic tools, and technical gadgets that generate, process, and store information, are widely acknowledged to be challenging and transforming business models and practises as well as altering the way we live our daily lives (Wynn and Jones, 2022). In order to close loops in the CE, Vijverman, Bieke Henkens and Katrien Verleye (2019) underlined the significance of involving a wide range of players involved in the production and distribution of goods and services, including the end user. Innovative technologies are also suggested as key enablers for including actors in the circular transformation. Examples include the IoT.

Liu et al. (2021) stated that as Block Chain Technology (BT) is still in its early stage, it is difficult to identify SCs that have successfully included this technology to monitor their sustainable actions. As a result, it is important to research the role of clients, members, and local, national, and global obstacles that could prevent the implementation of block chain and harm SC sustainability. As a result, the categories of inter-organisational, intra-organisational, technical, and external barriers are introduced as obstacles to the implementation of BT. These barriers' links between each other were demonstrated by them. It is difficult to use BT because there aren't any proven business models or best practises, so it's critical that practitioners recognise these difficulties early on.

To maintain the rate of production of goods and services to satisfy the constantly rising consumer demand that is stressing the environment and society, CE and the acceptance of its principles globally are more crucial than ever. Patwa et al. (2020) stated the implementation of CE principles in emerging nations, given that these economies face issues that are generally distinct from those of developed economies in terms of the availability of resources, differing government policies, and consumer behaviour. Similarly, Pakseresht, Ahmadi Kaliji and Xhakollari (2022) mentioned few barriers to implementing CE in agri-food sector. These include complex SCs, a lack of technological know-how, a lack of information on products and processes, and issues with quality assurance relating to food safety.

Chaudhuri, Subramanian and Dora (2022) in their article demonstrated that Small and medium-sized enterprises (SMEs) that engaged with CE initiatives that adopted digital technologies demonstrated both exploitations and exploration capabilities; on the other hand, those who only used CE business models without digital technologies demonstrated only exploitation and adaptive capabilities.

Kurniawan et al. (2022) mentioned that the recycling industry has the ability to utilise digitisation to take advantage of CE prospects. Although landfills are a common method of trash disposal, digitalising waste recycling in the marketplace is the way of the future. Digital technology can be used to manage waste effectively, allowing for the creation of "Pay-As-You-Throw" systems, "Know-As-You-Throw" programmes, and the use of "Radio Frequency Identification", which tracks waste fractions at the source.

For digital transformation, crucial topics are "sustainable supply chain management" and "circular economy and industry 4.0 technologies" according to Tavana et al. (2022). Technologies can advance the CE throughout the SC and within companies.

Wynn and Jones (2022), in contrast, claimed that where firms are pursuing CE activities, the relationship with the adoption of digital technology is not obvious, despite the association with sustainability being made more generally. Greater efficiencies, improved workflows, and better data management brought about by digital technologies are supporting and enabling sustainability goals, but a more direct connection with the CE will require clearer-use cases of how particular digital technologies can advance the CE, both within organisations and across the SC. Improved information tools that make it easier to report on and compare the operational effectiveness of CE initiatives to predetermined goals will also be required. It will also be necessary to implement improved information systems that make it easier to report on and compare the operational performance of CE initiatives to predetermined goals.

Similarly, Demestichas and Daskalakis (2020) pointed out that there are indirect links as well as direct ones between the technologies used. The landscape of the globe has changed as a result of technology and digitisation. Since ICT developments started piling up a few decades ago, the structure of today's enterprises, manufacturing processes, healthcare, communication, education, mass media, and nearly every other element of human existence has undergone a drastic upheaval. It would be a mistake to undervalue any of these developments, especially those in seemingly unrelated fields.

In short, digital technologies can provide opportunities to mitigate the challenges of CE such as developing a global framework for CE, interconnect all the stakeholders, better organisation performance, and detecting the problems associated with internal and external of organisation.

4.2.3 Studies Focused on I4.0

I4.0 describes "smart" and interconnected production systems that are created to perceive, anticipate, and interact with the physical world in order to make decisions that support production in real-time. It can boost output, energy effectiveness, and sustainability in production. By decreasing downtime and maintenance expenses, it boosts productivity (Sirimanne, 2022). With more resource consumption that contributes to climate change and global warming, I4.0 has the potential to accelerate industrialisation but, on the other hand, upends the sustainability of current manufacturing SCs. The difficulties faced by manufacturing supply networks when they consider raising their sustainability levels and undergoing a digital transformation towards I4.0 must thus be thoroughly evaluated by researchers.

According to Ciliberto et al. (2021), I4.0 can incorporate the CE's guiding principles, resulting in a successful company built on the systematic use of technologies like digital (information technology), engineering (materials technology), and hybrids (a combination of those two). Long-term lean philosophy–based I4.0 uses smart sensors and metres, connected to the business' lean management system, combined with a database for environmental impact analysis (as instruments for lifecycle assessments), and supported by evaluations and feedback from the economic and social spheres. As a result, I4.0 tools can be used to implement sustainability, integrate CE principles, and take advantage of data collection and inventory information to do assessments of the consequences on the environment, economy, and society.

Hennemann Hilario da Silva and Sehnem (2022) stated that as cutting-edge digital technology supports sustainability activities, the I4.0 concept opens the path for the CE. The performance, flexibility, and interoperability of CE-oriented SCs have thereby improved because of I4.0. The IoT, BDA, and AM are the most extensively studied technologies in the nexus of CE and sustainable SC management, according to their analysis. Research disciplines for I4.0-driven sustainable operations and manufacturing are emerging, according to an analysis of intellectual, conceptual, and social frameworks.

Dongfang et al. (2022) showed that in post-COVID time, I4.0 has been identified as one of the key factors influencing the application's move towards more sustainable production through an economy that reuses, lowers, and recycles resources.

A study by Vacchi et al. (2021) explained that the digital technologies of the I4.0 environment can assist businesses in starting down a path towards circularity, both in terms of the increased operational efficiency that smart manufacturing implies as well as by encouraging a trajectory of organisational innovation. It is founded on the integration of two groups of production factors: tangible resources (materials and equipment) and intangible resources (data). The manufacturing company's capability to analyse the raw data intelligently collected by the equipment, i.e., to transform data from a simple accumulation of records (Big Data) into high-value assets (Smart Data), is therefore the enabling factor of circularity and, more generally, of sustainability. This manufacturing company must already be efficient from an operational point of view.

I4.0 can combine both tangible and intangible resources, can increase efficiency by implementing smart manufacturing, and can provide a more sustainable production process.

4.2.4   Studies Focused on SC

All manufacturing businesses must manage the movement of materials from suppliers through value-adding processes and distribution channels to customers. The SC is a networked set of activities that are concerned with organising, coordinating, and managing raw materials, spare parts, and finished items from the supplier to the client. In the past, only an operational level of the material flow has been considered. But now, it's impossible to overlook the advantages of SC integration. Companies that manage the SC as a single entity and ensure the proper use of tools and procedures to fulfil the needs of the market will not fall behind in the race for survival (Stevens, 1989).

De Giovanni (2022) proposed that by addressing issues like how consumers may ensure trust when purchasing a reconditioned good, contemporary business models can reduce some historical challenges that are related to CE outcomes. How can they confirm the recycled items' origins? How do they know that used goods have been put through all the necessary quality checks before being sold? As SC is a vital element to ensure a proper-running business system, which seen disruption during the period of COVID-19, many research articles are published after COVID-19 period. Liu et al. (2022) mentioned that CE framework could be effective in large organisations and relatively for leading organisations. But it is still difficult for SMEs. Without proper regulations by government, it is not possible to implement CE framework in less-developed countries like Bangladesh and India.

Del Giudice et al. (2020) suggested that the three investigated categories of CE practices—CE SC management design, CE SC relationship management, and CE human resource management—play a significant role in improving firm performance from a CE perspective. As a mediator of the relationship between CE HR management and company performance for a CE SC, big-data-driven SCs play a key role.

According to Rehman Khan et al. (2021), BT was discovered to have a beneficial function in the CE because of features like visibility, transparency, relationship management, and smart contracting. Environmental performance was also found to have a positive relationship with the firm's economic health, while green practices were found to have a positive relationship with both the environmental and economic paths to the firms' performance. It was also mentioned that improved economic and environmental performance contributed to an increase in organisational performance.

Lang and Mishra (2022) stated 24 challenges to implement the CE, which includes lack of government support and policies, lack of competency in adopting/applying new business models, lack of global standards and data-sharing protocols, lack of knowledge, lack of a digital culture, lack of information sharing, overconfidence in suppliers, low management support and dedication, lack of integration, financial constraints, poor agility and flexibility, poor research and development, unclear economic benefit of digital investments, and so on.

It is important to ensure a proper functioning of SC for a sustainable production process. After COVID pandemic, the use of technology to predict future trend for products and raw materials is increased as well as the research on this sector is also increased by a huge leap.

It is clear from all the discussion that in the last few years, researchers mainly focused on developing frameworks for a sustainable CE. Evidently, researchers point out mainly on areas such as big data, AI, I4.0, and BT, and they could be used to implement CE principles. But mostly these are still on theoretical phase, and in many cases, there are no clear evidence how these relationships of digital transformation and CE could ensure establishment of CE.

4.3   *Enablers of CE*

The transition to CE is not straightforward, rather this is a complex process. A wide range of enablers are driving and supporting this revolutionary approach to achieving economic and environmental sustainability. These enablers are essential in influencing the shift to a CE, encouraging innovation, and accelerating systemic change across various businesses and societies.

Big data is a vital element in today's world. Proper use of big data to decision-making can lead to a smooth-functioning business environment. Greater collaboration with different stakeholders and data sharing can provide an opportunity to include all the participants into the decision-making process. As CE is essential to ensure sustainability, big data can be used in all stages from planning to final production and to make a decision what to do with a commodity when no longer in use.

SC ensures proper functioning of market that involves collection of raw materials to final distribution. A data-driven SC could make it possible to reduce wastage and ensure efficient use of materials. Use of technologies like block chain, AI, and IoT makes it possible to forecast the demands and reduce wastages in fields such as food supply, agriculture, manufacturing, and so on. These ultimately lead to a sustainable CE.

New sustainable business models that were developed based on the concept of sustainability can be a driver for CE. Many scholars proposed different methods and models for sustainability and circularity. With careful consideration by implementing these, the target for a CE could be achieved.

In short, big data, block chain, and circular-based business models are the main enablers of CE that is directly related to digital transformation.

Besides these, organisations should have a proper understanding on how to accept digital technologies and digital transformation because they have to play a crucial role in transformation towards a CE. Starting with designing products and services with circularity in mind, organisations can move forward. This necessitates the creation of items that are recyclable, repairable, and long lasting. A product's whole lifecycle, from creation to disposal, must be taken into account. They could utilise techniques to cut waste by utilising fewer resources and, whenever possible, reusing materials and components. Having procedures in place to gather and process recyclable materials for subsequent usage in the production cycle should be a top focus. Proper use of big data, digital technologies, AI, and other elements of digital transformation could ensure to produce more sustainable products, and take data-driven decisions as well as a better forecast for upcoming future.

In the current world, CE is mainly practised in developed countries compared to less-developed ones. Governments can take policies to ensure sustainable business, and production process. Government should play an active role in educating and sharing knowledge on CE. To enable CE, government can use digital technologies to collect data, formulate policies, and involve all the relevant stakeholders for decision-making.

5   Discussion

Because it provides a means of addressing some of the most critical issues the world is currently facing, such as climate change, resource shortages, and pollution, the CE is significant. We must come up with new strategies to produce and use products and services in a more sustainable manner because the existing linear economic paradigm is unsustainable.

This study set out to explore two main issues—to explore the link between CE and digital transformation, and to find out the enablers of CE that relate with digital transformation. A SLR on the application of digital transformation in the CE is represented by this chapter. Forty-six articles from the WoS and ProQuest databases that address the issue have been used. The four study themes that have been used to group the shortlisted articles into categories are: (1) studies focused on big data, (2) studies focused on digital technologies, (3) studies focused on I4.0, and (4) studies focused on SC.

Findings from this study indicate that both digital transformation and CE are in the phase of development. Most of the businesses, organisations, and governments are still not aware of the process of CE and how digital transformation could be used to ensure sustainable environment.

By proper utilisation of big data technology, a transition towards CE is possible. As big data is regarded as a decision-making facilitator, it's functionalities can be used to generate insights for integrating operations and sharing resources in the context of CE. Areas such as waste management, product design, and value creation opportunities could be identified by using big data, which is a key driver for a sustainable CE. Big data and CE are complementary concepts that each assist and advance the other in the quest for sustainability and resource efficiency.

But to ensure this proper collaboration, data safety and knowledge on proper use of efficient technology is essential. The promotion and achievement of the objectives of the CE now depend heavily on digital technologies. Digital technologies improve the CE's guiding principles of minimising waste, maximising resource utilisation, and minimising environmental impact by enabling the effective sharing of information, monitoring of resource flows, and automation of activities. The design of products can be improved for repair ability and recycling due to AI and machine learning, which also enable smarter decision-making. Along with increasing product longevity and responsible use, these technologies also support cutting-edge business models like PaaS. In essence, digital technologies play a crucial role in transforming industries and SCs towards circularity, encouraging sustainability and building a more robust and ecologically sensitive global economy.

I4.0 uses all sorts of available technologies, but they are responsible for more consumption of resources. Thus, already-developed frameworks should be used to get the anticipated result from the desired industries. The IoT, AI, and automation, which are all components of I4.0, collide with the CE to form a mutually beneficial connection with broad ramifications. A more effective and sustainable approach to resource management is made possible by I4.0's data-driven, networked production processes, which are in line with the key tenets of the CE. I4.0 lowers waste, extends product lifecycles, and encourages resource optimisation through real-time monitoring, SC transparency, and predictive maintenance. Products that are made to be repairable and recyclable benefit from customisation and product lifecycle management solutions. The capabilities of I4.0 support CBMs like PaaS, while resource recovery and sustainable innovation are further advanced. By enabling industries to move towards circular practices, this convergence successfully conserves resources, reduces waste, and makes a positive impact on the environment.

BT and other existing technologies could be used to ensure a smooth-functioning SC for CE. But only adoption of block chain and other related technologies are not sufficient, it is necessary to involve the relevant parties and ensure a proper knowledge on adopting circularity and digital-technology-based SC. Technology-based SC can mitigate few circularity issues like origin of the refurbished product and ensure involvement of all the relevant parties. To make this change, SC management is essential for guaranteeing the smooth flow of products and materials while reducing waste at every turn. Transparency and traceability are made possible by technologies like block chain and IoT sensors, which enable efficient tracking and management of resources and goods throughout their lifecycles. Together, SC optimisation and the principles of the CE aim to lessen negative environmental effects, save resources, and build more resilient and sustainable economic systems. Businesses and industries may help create a future that is both environmentally responsible and commercially viable by reimagining SCs within a circular framework.

From all the discussion, it is evident that in recent years, researchers have mostly concentrated on creating frameworks for a sustainable CE. Evidently, academics focus mostly on fields like big data, AI, I4.0, and BT, all of which might be used to execute the ideas of the CE. However, most of these are still in the theoretical stage, and there is frequently no conclusive proof showing how these connections between the digital transformation and CE may guarantee the establishment of the latter.

There are clear limitations to this study. In this case, WoS and ProQuest databases were the only databases used as sources of information. However, this is a very minor issue given that both search engines are well regarded for their thorough coverage and high-quality content. But only the articles with open access were utilised, which might impact the outcome if other articles could be used. Although the chosen research underwent a thorough and rigorous peer-review procedure, additional potentially pertinent information sources, such as books, chapters, and conference papers, can be added in future studies to acquire further insights. If CE is to take hold, then it will be necessary to network the manufacturing industry, the waste-management industry, and businesses creating software and technology for the digital transition to construct a functional value creation network. Therefore, for the best financial outcomes, circularity options can be considered while this network is installed. The IoT, I4.0, and related advancements are already under progress. However, any postponed or later introduction would come at a large cost premium and necessitate pricey system modification. On the road to enabling the CE through digital transformation, it is crucial to understand that hurdles and complexities abound. Care must be taken when addressing worries about data privacy, digital inclusion, and the possibility for more electronic waste. Additionally, as the impact and usability of digital technologies differ among businesses and countries, a one-size-fits-all strategy is impractical.

6   Conclusion

Although the number of publications are increasing each year, researchers are focused either on pure technical concepts or from environmental and business perspective. Very few literatures were found that have prepared from multi-dimensional and disciplinary perspectives. For a future prospect, researcher could focus on cross-disciplinary collaboration such as business, environment, and technology.

This study has clarified the revolutionary potential of digital transformation in bringing about a CE, highlighting the significance of strategic planning, cross-sector collaboration, and accountable governance. While limitations still exist, the data in this study suggests that the advantages of this synergy outweigh them significantly. It is essential that we use the power of digital transformation as we advance to build a more sustainable and regenerative economy that benefits both the present and the next generation. Achieving an empowered CE through digital transformation is an ongoing process, and everyone involved, who is dedicated to a more sustainable and prosperous future, must work together to make it happen.

References

Agrawal, R., Wankhede, V. A., Kumar, A., Luthra, S., Majumdar, A. and Kazancoglu, Y. (2021). An Exploratory State-of-the-Art Review of Artificial Intelligence Applications in Circular Economy using Structural Topic Modeling. *Operations Management Research*, 15, pp. 609–626. https://doi.org/10.1007/s12063-021-00212-0

Alonso-Muñoz, S., González-Sánchez, R., Medina-Salgado, M.-S. and García-Muiña, F.-E. (2022). Technology Development as a Tool towards Circularity: A Research Agenda. *Economic Research-Ekonomska Istraživanja*, 36, pp. 1–21. https://doi.org/10.1080/1331677x.2022.2142636

Andriole, S. J. (2017). Five Myths about Digital Transformation. *MIT Sloan Management Review*, 58(3), pp. 20–22. Available at: https://sloanreview.mit.edu/article/five-myths-about-digital-transformation/?switch_view=PDF

Awan, U., Shamim, S., Khan, Z., Zia, N. U., Shariq, S. M. and Khan, M. N. (2021). Big Data Analytics Capability and Decision-making: The Role of Data-driven Insight on Circular Economy Performance. *Technological Forecasting and Social Change*, 168, p. 120766. https://doi.org/10.1016/j.techfore.2021.120766

Bag, S., Pretorius, J. H. C., Gupta, S. and Dwivedi, Y. K. (2020). Role of Institutional Pressures and Resources in the Adoption of Big Data Analytics Powered Artificial Intelligence, Sustainable Manufacturing Practices and Circular Economy Capabilities. *Technological Forecasting and Social Change*, 163, p. 120420. https://doi.org/10.1016/j.techfore.2020.120420

Bianchini, A., Rossi, J. and Pellegrini, M. (2019). Overcoming the Main Barriers of Circular Economy Implementation through a New Visualization Tool for Circular Business Models. *Sustainability*, 11(23), p. 6614. https://doi.org/10.3390/su11236614

Bloomberg, J. (2018). Digitization, Digitalization, and Digital Transformation: Confuse Them at Your Peril. *Forbes*. [online] Available at: https://moniquebabin.com/wp-content/uploads/articulate_uploads/Going-Digital4/story_content/external_files/Digitization%20Digitalization%20and%20Digital%20Tra nsformation%20Confusion.pdf

Bressanelli, G., Adrodegari, F., Perona, M. and Saccani, N. (2018). Exploring How Usage-Focused Business Models Enable Circular Economy through Digital Technologies. *Sustainability*, 10(3), p. 639. https://doi.org/10.3390/su10030639

Chari, A., Niedenzu, D., Despeisse, M., Machado, C. G., Azevedo, J. D., Boavida-Dias, R. and Johansson, B. (2022). Dynamic Capabilities for Circular Manufacturing Supply Chains—Exploring the Role of Industry 4.0 and Resilience. *Business Strategy and the Environment*, 31(5), pp. 2500–2517. https://doi.org/10.1002/bse.3040

Chaudhuri, A., Subramanian, N. and Dora, M. (2022). Circular Economy and Digital Capabilities of SMEs for Providing Value to Customers: Combined Resource-based View and Ambidexterity Perspective. *Journal of Business Research*, 142, pp. 32–44. https://doi.org/10.1016/j.jbusres.2021.12.039

Chidepatil, A., Bindra, P., Kulkarni, D., Qazi, M., Kshirsagar, M. and Sankaran, K. (2020). From Trash to Cash: How Blockchain and Multi-Sensor-Driven Artificial Intelligence Can Transform Circular Economy of Plastic Waste? *Administrative Sciences*, 10(2), p. 23. https://doi.org/10.3390/admsci10020023

Ciliberto, C., Szopik-Depczyńska, K., Tarczyńska-Łuniewska, M., Ruggieri, A. and Ioppolo, G. (2021). Enabling the Circular Economy Transition: A Sustainable Lean Manufacturing Recipe for Industry 4.0. *Business Strategy and the Environment*, 30(7). https://doi.org/10.1002/bse.2801

Coble, K. H., Mishra, A. K., Ferrell, S. and Griffin, T. (2018). Big Data in Agriculture: A Challenge for the Future. *Applied Economic Perspectives and Policy*, 40(1), pp. 79–96. https://doi.org/10.1093/aepp/ppx056

Ćwiklicki, M. and Wojnarowska, M. (2020). Circular Economy and Industry 4.0: One-Way or Two-way Relationships? *Engineering Economics*, 31(4), pp. 387–397. https://doi.org/10.5755/j01.ee.31.4.24565

da Silva, T. H. H. and Sehnem, S. (2022). The Circular Economy and Industry 4.0: Synergies and Challenges. *Revista de Gestão*, 29(3), pp. 300–313. https://doi.org/10.1108/rege-07-2021-0121

D'Amato, D., Droste, N., Allen, B., Kettunen, M., Lähtinen, K., Korhonen, J., Leskinen, P., Matthies, B. D. and Toppinen, A. (2017). Green, Circular, Bio Economy: A Comparative Analysis of Sustainability Avenues. *Journal of Cleaner Production*, 168, pp. 716–734. https://doi.org/10.1016/j.jclepro.2017.09.053

De Giovanni, P. (2022). Leveraging the Circular Economy with a Closed-loop Supply Chain and a Reverse Omnichannel Using Blockchain Technology and Incentives. *International Journal of Operations & Production Management*, 42(7). https://doi.org/10.1108/ijopm-07-2021-0445

Del Giudice, M., Chierici, R., Mazzucchelli, A. and Fiano, F. (2020). Supply Chain Management in the Era of Circular Economy: The Moderating Effect of Big Data. *The International Journal of Logistics Management*, 32(2), pp. 337–356. https://doi.org/10.1108/ijlm-03-2020-0119

Demestichas, K. and Daskalakis, E. (2020). Information and Communication Technology Solutions for the Circular Economy. *Sustainability*, 12(18), p. 7272. https://doi.org/10.3390/su12187272

Denyer, D. and Tranfield, D. (2009). Producing a Systematic Review. In D. Buchanan and A. Bryman (eds.). *The Sage Handbook of Organizational Research Methods* (pp. 671–689). SAGE Publications, Ltd.

Dongfang, W., Ponce, P., Yu, Z., Ponce, K. and Tanveer, M. (2022). The Future of Industry 4.0 and the Circular Economy in Chinese Supply Chain: In the Era of Post-COVID-19 Pandemic. *Operations Management Research*. https://doi.org/10.1007/s12063-021-00220-0

Dubey, R., Gunasekaran, A., Childe, S. J., Papadopoulos, T. and Helo, P. (2019). Supplier Relationship Management for Circular Economy. *Management Decision*, 57(4), pp. 767–790. https://doi.org/10.1108/md-04-2018-0396

Dwivedi, A., Moktadir, Md A., Chiappetta Jabbour, C. J. and de Carvalho, D. E. (2022). Integrating the Circular Economy and Industry 4.0 for Sustainable Development: Implications for Responsible Footwear Production in a Big data-driven World. *Technological Forecasting and Social Change*, 175, p. 121335. https://doi.org/10.1016/j.techfore.2021.121335

Ellen Macarthur Foundation (2023). The Circular Economy in Detail. [online] ellenmacarthur-foundation.org. Available at: https://ellenmacarthurfoundation.org/the-circular-economy-in-detail-deep-dive

European Parliament (2023). Circular Economy: Definition, Importance and Benefits | News |. European Parliament. [online] Available at: https://www.europarl.europa.eu/news/en/headlines/economy/20151201STO05603/circular -economy-definition-importance-and-benefits

Fallahi, S., Mellquist, A., Mogren, O., Listo Zec, E., Algurén, P. and Hallquist, L. (2022). Financing Solutions for Circular Business Models: Exploring the Role of Business Ecosystems and Artificial Intelligence. *Business Strategy and the Environment*. https://doi.org/10.1002/bse.3297

Fraga-Lamas, P., Lopes, S. I. and Fernández-Caramés, T. M. (2021). Green IoT and Edge AI as Key Technological Enablers for a Sustainable Digital Transition towards a Smart Circular Economy: An Industry 5.0 Use Case. *Sensors*, 21(17), p. 5745. https://doi.org/10.3390/s21175745

Frenken, K. and Schor, J. (2017). Putting the Sharing Economy into Perspective. *Environmental Innovation and Societal Transitions*, 23, pp. 3–10. https://doi.org/10.1016/j.eist.2017.01.003

Geissdoerfer, M., Pieroni, M. P. P., Pigosso, D. C. A. and Soufani, K. (2020). Circular Business Models: A Review. *Journal of Cleaner Production*, 277, p. 123741. https://doi.org/10.1016/j.jclepro.2020.123741

Gil Lamata, M. and Latorre Martínez, M. P. (2022). The Circular Economy and Sustainability: A Systematic Literature Review. *Cuadernos de Gestión*, 22(1), pp. 129–142. https://doi.org/10.5295/cdg.211492mg

Gong, Y., Wang, Y., Frei, R., Wang, B. and Zhao, C. (2022). Blockchain Application in Circular Marine Plastic Debris Management. *Industrial Marketing Management*, 102, pp. 164–176. https://doi.org/10.1016/j.indmarman.2022.01.010

Heim, H. and Hopper, C. (2022). Dress Code: The Digital Transformation of the Circular Fashion Supply Chain. *International Journal of Fashion Design, Technology and Education*, 15(2), pp. 233–244. https://doi.org/10.1080/17543266.2021.2013956

Hess, T., Matt, C., Benlian, A. and Wiesböck, F. (2016). Options for Formulating a Digital Transformation Strategy. ResearchGate. [online] Available at: https://www.researchgate.net/publication/291349362_Options_for_Formulating_a_Digital_ Transformation_Strategy

Hettiarachchi, B. D., Seuring, S. and Brandenburg, M. (2022). Industry 4.0-driven Operations and Supply Chains for the Circular Economy: A Bibliometric Analysis. *Operations Management Research*. https://doi.org/10.1007/s12063-022-00275-7

Huber, A. (2017). Theorising the Dynamics of Collaborative Consumption Practices: A Comparison of Peer-to-peer Accommodation and Cohousing. *Environmental Innovation and Societal Transitions*, 23, pp. 53–69. https://doi.org/10.1016/j.eist.2016.12.001

Ismail, M., Khater, M. and Zaki, M. (2017). Digital Business Transformation and Strategy: What Do We Know So Far? [online] Available at: https://cambridgeservicealliance.eng.cam.ac.uk/resources/Downloads/Monthly%20Papers/ 2017NovPaper_Mariam.pdf

Jeble, S., Dubey, R., Childe, S.J., Papadopoulos, T., Roubaud, D. and Prakash, A. (2018). Impact of Big Data and Predictive Analytics Capability on Supply Chain Sustainability. *The International Journal of Logistics Management*, 29(2), pp. 513–538. https://doi.org/10.1108/ijlm-05-2017-0134

Jinru, L., Changbiao, Z., Ahmad, B., Irfan, M. and Nazir, R. (2021). How Do Green Financing and Green Logistics Affect the Circular Economy in the Pandemic Situation: Key Mediating Role of Sustainable Production. *Economic Research-Ekonomska Istraživanja*, 35(1), pp. 1–21. https://doi.org/10.1080/1331677x.2021.2004437

Kazancoglu, Y., Ozbiltekin Pala, M., Deniz Sezer, M., Luthra, S. and Kumar, A. (2021). Drivers of Implementing Big Data Analytics in Food Supply Chains for Transition to a Circular Economy and Sustainable Operations Management. *Journal of Enterprise Information Management*. [online] Available at: https://repository.londonmet.ac.uk/id/eprint/6419

Khan, S. A. R., Piprani, A. Z. and Yu, Z. (2022). Digital Technology and Circular Economy Practices: Future of Supply Chains. *Operations Management Research*, 15, pp. 676–688. https://doi.org/10.1007/s12063-021-00247-3

Kirchherr, J., Reike, D. and Hekkert, M. (2017). Conceptualizing the Circular Economy: An Analysis of 114 Definitions. *Resources, Conservation and Recycling*, 127, pp. 221–232. https://doi.org/10.1016/j.resconrec.2017.09.005

Koech, M. K. and Munene, K. J. (2019). Circular Economy in Kenya. In S. Ghosh (ed.), *Circular Economy: Global Perspective* (pp. 223–239). Singapore: Springer. https://doi.org/10.1007/978-981-15-1052-6_12

Korhonen, J., Honkasalo, A. and Seppälä, J. (2018). Circular Economy: The Concept and Its Limitations. *Ecological Economics*, 143(1), pp. 37–46. https://doi.org/10.1016/j.ecolecon.2017.06.041

Kristoffersen, E., Blomsma, F., Mikalef, P. and Li, J. (2020). The Smart Circular Economy: A Digital-enabled Circular Strategies Framework for Manufacturing Companies. *Journal of Business Research*, 120, pp. 241–261. https://doi.org/10.1016/j.jbusres.2020.07.044

Kristoffersen, E., Mikalef, P., Blomsma, F. and Li, J. (2021). Towards a Business Analytics Capability for the Circular Economy. *Technological Forecasting and Social Change*, 171, p. 120957. https://doi.org/10.1016/j.techfore.2021.120957

Kurniawan, T. A., Liang, X., O'Callaghan, E., Goh, H., Othman, M. H. D., Avtar, R. and Kusworo, T. D. (2022). Transformation of Solid Waste Management in China: Moving towards Sustainability through Digitalization-Based Circular Economy. *Sustainability*, 14(4), p. 2374. https://doi.org/10.3390/su14042374

Liberati, A., Altman, G. A., Tetzlaff, J., Mulrow, C., Gøtzsche, P. C., P.A. Ioannidis, J. P. A., Clarke, M., Devereaux, P. J., Kleijnen, J., and Moher, D. The PRISMA Statement for Reporting Systematic Reviews and Meta-Analyses of Studies That Evaluate Health Care Interventions: Explanation and Elaboration. *Annals of Internal Medicine*, 151, 4.

Liu, J., Quddoos, M. U., Akhtar, M. H., Amin, M. S., Tariq, M. and Lamar, A. (2022). Digital Technologies and Circular Economy in Supply Chain Management: In the Era of COVID-19 Pandemic. *Operations Management Research*, 15, pp. 326–341. https://doi.org/10.1007/s12063-021-00227-7

Liu, P., Hendalianpour, A., Hamzehlou, M., Feylizadeh, M. R. and Razmi, J. (2021). Identify and Rank the Challenges of Implementing Sustainable Supply Chain Blockchain Technology Using the Bayesian Best Worst Method. *Technological and Economic Development of Economy*, 27(3), pp. 656–680. https://doi.org/10.3846/tede.2021.14421

Luoma, P., Penttinen, E., Tapio, P. and Toppinen, A. (2022). Future Images of Data in Circular Economy for Textiles. *Technological Forecasting and Social Change*, 182, p. 121859. https://doi.org/10.1016/j.techfore.2022.121859

Mamedov, O., Tumanyan, Y., Ishchenko-Padukova, O. and Movchan, I. (2018). Sustainable Economic Development and Post-economy of Artificial Intelligence. *Entrepreneurship and Sustainability Issues*, 6(2), pp. 1028–1040. [Online] Available at: https://econpapers.repec.org/RePEc:ssi:jouesi:v:6:y:2018:i:2:p:1028-1040

Merli, R., Preziosi, M. and Acampora, A. (2018). How Do Scholars Approach the Circular Economy? A Systematic Literature Review. *Journal of Cleaner Production*, 178, pp. 703–722. https://doi.org/10.1016/j.jclepro.2017.12.112

Murray, A., Skene, K. and Haynes, K. (2017). The Circular Economy: An Interdisciplinary Exploration of the Concept and Application in a Global Context. *Journal of Business Ethics*, 140(3), pp. 369–380. https://doi.org/10.1007/s10551-015-2693-2

Neligan, A., Baumgartner, R. J., Geissdoerfer, M. and Schöggl, J. (2022). Circular Disruption: Digitalisation as a Driver of Circular Economy Business Models. *Business Strategy and the Environment*. https://doi.org/10.1002/bse.3100

OECD Science, Technology and Industry Scoreboard 2017. (2017). *OECD Science, Technology and Industry Scoreboard*. OECD. https://doi.org/10.1787/9789264268821-en

PACE (2020). The Circularity Gap Report 2020. World Resources Institute. Available at: https://pacecircular.org/sites/default/files/2020-01/Circularity%20Gap%20Report%202020.pdf

Pagoropoulos, A., Pigosso, D. C. A. and McAloone, T. C. (2017). The Emergent Role of Digital Technologies in the Circular Economy: A Review. *Procedia CIRP*, 64, pp. 19–24. https://doi.org/10.1016/j.procir.2017.02.047

Pakseresht, A., Ahmadi Kaliji, S. and Xhakollari, V. (2022). How Blockchain Facilitates the Transition toward Circular Economy in the Food Chain? *Sustainability*, 14(18), p. 11754. https://doi.org/10.3390/su141811754

Pati, D. and Lorusso, L. N. (2017). How to Write a Systematic Review of the Literature. *HERD: Health Environments Research & Design Journal*, 11(1), pp. 15–30. https://doi.org/10.1177/1937586717747384

Patwa, N., Sivarajah, U., Seetharaman, A., Sarkar, S., Maiti, K. and Hingorani, K. (2020). Towards a Circular Economy: An Emerging Economies Context. *Journal of Business Research*, 122. https://doi.org/10.1016/j.jbusres.2020.05.015

Pearce, D. W., and Turner, R. K. (1990) Economics of Natural Resources and the Environment. In *International Monetary Fund Joint Library*, Baltimore: The John Hopkins University Press.

Piyathanavong, V., Huynh, V.-N., Karnjana, J. and Olapiriyakul, S. (2022). Role of Project Management on Sustainable Supply Chain Development through Industry 4.0 Technologies and Circular Economy during the COVID-19 Pandemic: A Multiple Case Study of Thai Metals Industry. *Operations Management Research*. https://doi.org/10.1007/s12063-022-00283-7

Rehman Khan, S. A., Yu, Z., Sarwat, S., Godil, D. I., Amin, S. and Shujaat, S. (2021). The Role of Block Chain Technology in Circular Economy Practices to Improve Organisational Performance. *International Journal of Logistics Research and Applications*, 25, pp. 1–18. https://doi.org/10.1080/13675567.2021.1872512

Riesener, M., Dölle, C., Mattern, C. and Kreß, J. (2019). *Circular Economy: Challenges and Potentials for the Manufacturing Industry by Digital Transformation*. IEEE Xplore, Hangzhou, China. [Online] https://doi.org/10.1109/TEMS-ISIE46312.2019.9074421

Rosa, P., Sassanelli, C., Urbinati, A., Chiaroni, D. and Terzi, S. (2019). Assessing Relations between Circular Economy and Industry 4.0: A Systematic Literature Review. *International Journal of Production Research*, 58(6), pp. 1662–1687. https://doi.org/10.1080/00207543.2019.1680896

Silva, T. H. H. and Sehnem, S. (2022). Industry 4.0 and the Circular Economy: Integration Opportunities Generated by Startups. *Logistics*, 6(1), p. 14. https://doi.org/10.3390/logistics6010014

Sirimanne, S. (2022). *What Is 'Industry 4.0' and What Will It Mean for Developing Countries?* World Economic Forum. [Online] Available at: https://www.weforum.org/agenda/2022/04/what-is-industry-4-0-and-could-developing-countries-get-left-behind/

Snyder, H. (2019). Literature Review as a Research methodology: An Overview and Guidelines. *Journal of Business Research*, 104(1), pp. 333–339. https://doi.org/10.1016/j.jbusres.2019.07.039

Spring, M. and Araujo, L. (2017). Product Biographies in Servitization and the Circular Economy. *Industrial Marketing Management*, 60, pp. 126–137. https://doi.org/10.1016/j.indmarman.2016.07.001

Stevens, G. C. (1989). Integrating the Supply Chain. *International Journal of Physical Distribution & Materials Management*, 19(8), pp. 3–8. https://doi.org/10.1108/eum0000000000329

Tavana, M., Shaabani, A., Raeesi Vanani, I. and Kumar Gangadhari, R. (2022). A Review of Digital Transformation on Supply Chain Process Management Using Text Mining. *Processes*, 10(5), p. 842. https://doi.org/10.3390/pr10050842

Tavera Romero, C. A., Castro, D. F., Ortiz, J. H., Khalaf, O. I. and Vargas, M. A. (2021). Synergy between Circular Economy and Industry 4.0: A Literature Review. *Sustainability*, 13(8), p. 4331. https://doi.org/10.3390/su13084331

Uçar, E., Dain, M. -A. L. and Joly, I. (2020). Digital Technologies in Circular Economy Transition: Evidence from Case Studies. *Procedia CIRP*, 90, pp. 133–136. https://doi.org/10.1016/j.procir.2020.01.058

Vacchi, M., Siligardi, C., Cedillo-González, E. I., Ferrari, A. M. and Settembre-Blundo, D. (2021). Industry 4.0 and Smart Data as Enablers of the Circular Economy in Manufacturing: Product Re-Engineering with Circular Eco-Design. *Sustainability*, 13(18), p. 10366. https://doi.org/10.3390/su131810366

Vijverman, N., Henkens, B. and Verleye, K. (2019). *Engagement and Technology as Key Enablers for a Circular Economy*. Edward Elgar Publishing eBooks. https://doi.org/10.4337/9781788114899.00011

Wilts, H. (2017). The Digital Circular Economy: Can the Digital Transformation Pave the Way for Resource-Efficient Materials Cycles? *International Journal of Environmental Sciences & Natural Resources*, 7(5). https://doi.org/10.19080/ijesnr.2017.07.555725

www.circularity-gap.world. (n.d.). CGR 2023. [online] Available at: https://www.circularity-gap.world/2023

Wynn, M. and Jones, P. (2022). Digital Technology Deployment and the Circular Economy. *Sustainability*, 14(15), p. 9077. https://doi.org/10.3390/su14159077Xin, L., Lang, S. and Mishra, A. R. (2022). Evaluate the Challenges of Sustainable Supply Chain 4.0 Implementation under the Circular Economy Concept Using New Decision Making Approach. *Operations Management Research*, 15, 773–792. https://doi.org/10.1007/s12063-021-00243-7

2

ARTIFICIAL INTELLIGENCE OF THINGS

Unlocking New Business Sustainability Possibilities or Opening Pandora's Box?

Luke Treves

1   Introduction

The integration of artificial intelligence (AI) technologies and the Internet of Things (IoT), colloquially known as the Artificial Intelligence of Things (AIoT), has garnered increased adoption among various entities such as companies and organizations, as it enables them to optimize their operations, augment human–machine interactions, and elevate the efficiency of data management and analytics. Consequently, AIoT is significantly transforming industries from banking to energy to agriculture and is vastly changing our personal lives (Bronner et al., 2021). AIoT, an emerging megatrend, plays a crucial role in accelerating ongoing technological transformation through its capacity to establish networks of intelligent devices and objects capable of effecting faster, more substantial, and more efficient impacts than ever before. Consequently, companies, organizations, and governments will gain the ability to shape domestic and international affairs in unparalleled ways, owing to a heightened awareness of the world, and access to intelligent tools that monitor and respond to changing circumstances without human intervention (EY, 2020). For instance, deep-learning capabilities of AI empower companies to effectively extract, process, and simulate business-relevant insights and actions from the colossal amounts of data generated by AIoT systems through sensors, software, and other embedded technologies. From a sustainability perspective, AIoT can and has been used as part of sustainability efforts and to manage environmental consequences and changes in a variety of economic contexts and settings. For example, AIoT enables safer supply chains, environmental control and regulation, and weather forecasting. Another area where AIoT is changing the game is agriculture where modern agribusinesses use AI to analyze their farms' data for crop yield predictions or climate control (Soon & Hui, 2022).

Additionally, societal impacts heavily influence acceptance and adoption of AIoT. People (the customer) increasingly expect a shift in value creation from pure economic benefits toward holistic sustainability, including social and environmental perspectives (Schulz & Flanigan, 2016). To manage these demands, it is imperative for companies, and economies more broadly, to transform to equally meet economic, environmental,

DOI: 10.4324/9781003433743-3

and social standards to ensure a comprehensive sustainable development, summarized in the approach of the "Triple Bottom Line (TBL)" (Norman & MacDonald, 2004; Elkington, 1994), which is, in turn, essential for effective adoption of technology like AIoT (Hahn et al., 2010; Khan et al., 2021).

Given the significant impact AIoT is having on our lives, it is imperative that business leaders consider, monitor, and react to sustainability implications of its use. These actions require them to closely observe their operations' social and environmental aspects, along with their traditional goal of generating sufficient profits to achieve enduring prosperity, create a sense of purpose among associates, and gain societal acceptance (Bronner et al., 2021). Despite the potential advantages of AIoT, the negative consequences are frequently disregarded in the quest for benefits, thereby undermining sustainability goals. The energy-intensive nature of AI systems, for instance, necessitates immediate attention from practitioners in the AI domain to confront the sizable ecological ramifications that may result. Additionally, while AIoT can simplify automation and produce new sources of value, it can also be a pathway to greater inequality in income wealth. Economists like Brynjolfsson (2022) observe that a focus on automation rather than augmentation "amplifies the market power of a few" who own the technologies, whilst driving down the real wages of the majority, and resulting in the loss of jobs, particularly amongst low-skill and low-educated members of the workforce. This situation is particularly biting in developing and poor countries where AIoT technologies risk widening the gap between rich and poor countries by shifting more investment to advanced economies where automation is already established. This scenario could in turn have negative consequences for jobs in developing countries by threatening to replace rather than complement their growing labor force, which has traditionally provided an advantage to less-developed economies (Alonso et al., 2020). There are also increasing ethical concerns regarding AIoT, including biased responses, the ability to spread misinformation, and impact on consumer privacy. Consequently, some of the biggest names in technology, including Tesla, SpaceX, and Twitter CEO Elon Musk and Apple co-founder Steve Wozniak, are calling for AI labs to stop training the most powerful AIoT systems for at least six months, citing "profound risks to society and humanity." It also said that independent experts should use the proposed pause to jointly develop and implement a set of shared protocols for AIoT tools that are safe "beyond a reasonable doubt" (Metz & Schmidt, 2023). These juxtapose scenarios raise the question:

"Will the unstoppable development of AIoT result in the unlocking of new and unthought of business and sustainability possibilities, or are we opening Pandora's box?"

To address this question, the TBL framework developed by John Elkington in the mid-1990s is used to consider whether AIoT supports business sustainability, based on an analysis of publicly available company information and peer-reviewed academic articles. The TBL framework is a suitable tool for this inquiry as it includes the interrelated dimensions of profits (economic), the planet (environment), and people (social responsibility) (Bronner et al., 2021; Elkington, 1994). Allowing us to understand whether the relentless advancement of AIoT will lead to the discovery of unimaginable business and sustainability opportunities or will it lead to more complicated problems. As part of this investigation, conceptual frameworks are proposed, which highlight the main positive and negative consequences of AIoT and possible mitigating factors that guide us toward a more sustainable future for business, society, and the environment.

2   Understanding the TBL Sustainability Framework and the Role of AIoT

2.1   *Explanation of the TBL Framework and Its Three Dimensions: Economic, Social, and Environmental*

During periods of significant technological change coupled by megatrends like population growth, resource scarcity, climate change, and social fragmentation of societies, business leaders and the companies they work for must demonstrate a heightened awareness of the social and environmental aspects, alongside generating sufficient profits, to attain enduring business success, foster employee purpose, and gain societal acceptance. These requirements necessitate companies to consistently align themselves with these drivers using modern reporting and accounting frameworks, which move beyond the traditional reporting of profits, return on investments, and shareholder value to include environmental and social dimensions (Bronner et al., 2021). These requirements have led to the development of several strategies to provide a comprehensive assessment of sustainability performance and impact, including the United Nations Sustainable Development Goals, the Integrated Reporting Framework developed by the International Integrated Reporting Council, and the Ellen MacArthur Foundations Circular Economy Framework.

A commonality among these frameworks is their complementary nature to the TBL, an accounting framework that contributes to a broader understanding of sustainability and helps companies and other types of organizations to plan, assess, and report their performance across three pillars: profits (economic), which aim to secure liquidity and ensure profit (Schulz & Flanigan, 2016); people (social), which contribute to the development of human and societal capital; and planet (environmental), i.e., the consumption and preservation of natural resources – also referred to as the three P's (3Ps) (Bronner et al., 2021; Elkington, 1994; Khan et al., 2021) (Figure 2.1).

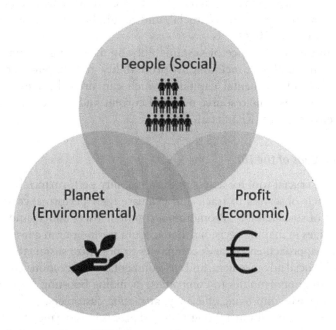

FIGURE 2.1   Triple Bottom Line (TBL) framework.

The main difference between TBL and other frameworks is its inclusion of ecological (or environmental) and social measures that can be difficult to assign appropriate measurement components. Despite their being no single set of measurement components, the following are commonly used:

- *People (Social)* – refers to a community's or region's social dimensions and may include measures of education, equity and access to social resources, health and well-being, quality of life, and social capital. Potential variables include unemployment rate, median household income, and health-adjusted life expectancy. These measures collect state, national, and local community-level data (Stedman & Gillis, 2023; Schulz & Flannigan, 2016).
- *Planet (Environmental)* – represents measurements of a company's or organization's environmental impact and their efforts to operate in sustainable ways. Variables should represent measurements of natural resources and reflect potential influences on their viability. Key metrics include reducing carbon footprints through cutting greenhouse gas emissions, ethical sourcing of materials, and reducing waste production (Stedman & Gillis, 2023).
- *Profits (Economic)* – are measurements that deal with the bottom line and flow of money, but in TBL the bottom line goes beyond simple profit measurements, and can look at income or expenditures, taxes, business climate factors, and business diversity factors. Examples include personal income, job growth, employment distribution by sector, and revenue by sector contributing to gross state product (Stedman & Gillis, 2023).

TBL is seen as an important tool in the sustainability efforts of companies and organizations as it prompts business leaders to look beyond standard measurements of profit and loss and to think more deeply about how their company or organization operates, particularly their impact on sustainability (Stedman & Gillis, 2023). Furthermore, considering all three dimensions in conjunction is crucial, and should be included in company strategies (Schulz & Flannigan, 2016).

The TBL "captures the essence of sustainability by measuring the impact of a company's activities on the planet, including its profitability and shareholder values and its social, human and environmental capital", which can drive business transformation within companies to meet the resource needs of current and future generations without hampering the environment (Khan et al., 2021).

2.2 Pros and Cons of the TBL

TBL has become a crucial tool for assessing sustainability performance because it enables companies and their observers to track and evaluate their performance across the three main dimensions of sustainability. Promoting a comprehensive understanding of sustainability aids companies in making decisions that account for long-term consequences of their actions. The TBL approach encourages companies to prioritize sustainability and balance economic growth, social advancement, and environmental conservation. This strategy offers various benefits and opportunities to companies, including boosting long-term profitability by minimizing waste, improving efficiency, attracting customers, and enhancing brand value. It introduces avenues for increasing sales and profits by appealing to environmentally conscious clients. This approach also promotes a healthier work environment by advocating for fair compensation, employee well-being, engagement, diversity, and safety. Companies can enhance their reputation in local communities through community development, job creation, transparency, and environmental stewardship. Innovation and competitiveness thrive as companies creatively tackle sustainability challenges for market differentiation. Operational efficiencies and reduced expenses follow, along with improved brand image and customer loyalty. TBL aids in mitigating social and environmental risks, while fostering innovation and financial success (Khan et al., 2021; Kolkowska, 2023).

However, TBL is not without its detractors who highlight concerns including: (1) There are no precise guidelines for measuring TBL. (2) Balancing social and environmental aspects with financial profits can be challenging. (3) Absence of measurement standards allows businesses to claim adherence without significant effort. (4) Initial operational cost increases can arise from necessary investments in new technologies. Moreover, engaging stakeholders and their preferences is crucial but complex due to potential conflicts arising from diverse interests. (5) If companies raise prices to offset higher costs, then customers might have to pay more for products and services.

In summary, the TBL framework can enhance the evaluation of company's sustainability performance, allowing them to assess their impact across people, planet, and profit, and environmental dimensions and aid long-term decision-making. It encourages prioritizing sustainability, fostering innovation, enhancing brand reputation, reducing emissions, and improving operational efficiency. Nevertheless, challenges include a lack of precise measurement guidelines, difficulty in balancing profit with social and environmental impacts, potential minimal effort claims, initial cost increases for technology adoption, stakeholder conflicts, and the possibility of higher product prices for customers.

3   Sustainable Synergy: Unveiling AIoT's Impact via the TBL Framework

AIoT has the capacity to reconfigure sectors, amplify procedural effectiveness, and fundamentally transform the dynamics of societal engagement within its surroundings. This potential has complex and diverse ramifications for sustainability spanning the dimensions of TBL. The systematic examination of these ramifications assumes paramount significance in understanding the propulsive mechanisms through which AIoT can facilitate constructive changes, concurrently shedding light on latent challenges that warrant consideration. The positive and negative consequences of AIoT on sustainability applying the TBL framework are examined in the following sections.

3.1   Positive Consequences of AIoT on Sustainability

In addition to the intricate global socio-economic and environmental challenges, the international community is confronted with profound issues arising from the rapid advancements in technology, digitalization, and automation. These progressions, commonly referred to as Industry 4.0 (I4.0), encompass a wide array of state-of-the-art technologies, such as AIoT, and create a foundation to face challenges arising from intense competition, fluctuating market demands, customizations, and the short span of the product life cycle (Telukdarie et al., 2018), while contributing significantly to the sustainable development of society (Jayashree et al., 2021). Assimilation of AIoT capabilities into the pursuit of sustainability, as viewed through the prism of the TBL framework, lays the groundwork for developing data-driven business models that prioritize sustainability objectives (Bronner et al., 2021) through seamlessly connecting humans and machines, resources, products, and services in the real world (Khan et al., 2021), creating lasting and lasting value for all stakeholder groups (e.g., company, customer, local, and national governments). Whilst, reducing wastage, inefficiencies, and extraneous activities do not contribute to sustainable value creation.

Specifically, these technological advancements enable companies and organizations to augment their *business capabilities* – collective skills, knowledge, resources, and processes that enable an organization to effectively and efficiently – and *operational capabilities* – capabilities and processes required to execute day-to-day operations and deliver products or services to customers (Teece, 2010; Amit & Zott, 2001). These capabilities include application provision, data management and storage, monitoring and adjustment of manufacturing process, operation management, evaluation and optimization of resource flows, utilization, circularity, and consequences, and decision-making (Karttunen et al., 2021; Ghoreishi et al., 2022; Birkel et al., 2021). Thereby, presenting a significant opportunity for sustainable industrial value creation across the three dimensions of the TBL (Khan et al., 2021; Birkel et al., 2021).

Previous research emphasizes that AIoT presents substantial positive consequences for organizational and social sustainable development under the TBL framework, including the fostering of resource efficiency, enhancing overall organizational structures, improving decision-making processes, bolster skills, promoting employee well-being, elevating business value, equitable cost distribution, and enabling environmentally conscious design practices (Ghobakhloo et al., 2021; Khan et al., 2021) (Figure 2.2).

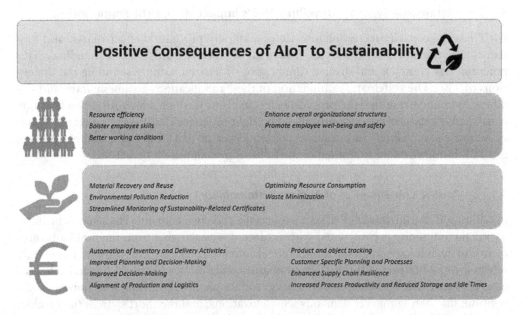

FIGURE 2.2 Artificial Intelligence of Things (AIoT)'s positive contributions to sustainability applying the TBL framework.

From a *people perspective*, AIoT can impact various stakeholders, including employees, customers, and the local community. For example, AIoT can enhance social well-being by improving the quality of life for individuals. For example, in healthcare, AIoT applications can monitor patients remotely, provide personalized treatment recommendations, and assist in early diagnosis. Improving access to healthcare services reduces hospital visits and enhances patient care. Additionally, AIoT can contribute to smart cities by optimizing transportation systems, reducing traffic congestion, and improving public safety, benefiting the community.

From a *planet perspective*, AIoT can facilitate more sustainable practices and help address environmental challenges by helping to optimize energy consumption (Khan et al., 2021), minimize waste production, increase energy savings, and encourage reuse and recycling (Yadav et al., 2020; Zhu et al., 2008). Data gathered and analyzed by AIoT can enable the development of machine learning algorithms that enable the optimization and reduction of resource consumption using the amount of data available in companies. For instance, natural resources forecasting tools have gained significant value in recent decades, notably in the supply chain management domain, where the whole logistical process remains expensive due to their storage. Discrepancies between the quantified volume of resources procured and their subsequent actual consumption engender substantial fiscal detriments to enterprises. Consequently, the integration of machine learning methodologies holds the potential to bolster these operational undertakings using predictive modeling.

From a *profit perspective*, AIoT can drive economic growth and competitiveness. AIoT technologies empower companies to extract invaluable insights from large data sets they collect to refine operational efficacy, elevate product excellence, and streamline supply chain processes. This integration further precipitates reductions in setup periods, labor expenditures, and lead times, fostering augmented organizational profitability and performance (Frank et al., 2019; Haseeb et al., 2019). Furthermore, AIoT is a conduit to novel business prospects and revenue streams, opening avenues for novel product and service innovations. A case in point is the application of predictive maintenance to industrial machinery where the amalgamated synthesis of machinery performance and maintenance data expedites adaptive responsiveness of machine learning paradigms even to the minutest deviations. This augmentation, in turn, can extend the operational lifespan of the machinery, thereby fostering an enhanced domain of control encompassing both the machinery itself and its attendant ecosystem.

Furthermore, by leveraging capabilities afforded by AIoT, companies and other organizations can achieve positive holistic sustainability objectives through heightened efficiencies in resource utilization, reduction of wastage, augmentation of accessibility, inclusivity, safety enhancements, and bolstered economic advancement and competitiveness (Khan et al., 2021). Incorporation of AIoT technology into both value chains and corporate entities facilitates continuous oversight of machinery, production workflows, operational processes, the movement of constituent elements, and the gathering and active dissemination of data (Beier et al., 2017). The capability for such vigilant monitoring empowers stakeholders to engender sustainable determinations concerning the recuperation of post-consumption products, facilitating a departure from the conventional linear "acquire, fabricate, employ, discard" mindset, thus yielding favorable outcomes within the TBL paradigm (Geissdoerfer et al., 2017; Khan et al., 2021).

3.2 Negative Consequences of AIoT on Sustainability

As has been shown, the potential of AIoT holds great promise in facilitating sustainable industrial value creation within the dimensions of the TBL. However, while AIoT has the potential to create positive consequences, it also carries negative connotations (Figure 2.3), including job displacement, privacy concerns, increased energy consumption, cost barriers, concentration of power in the hands of a handful of dominant companies, and economic inequalities. These connotations are given in Figure 2.3.

Primary apprehensions and potential *negative societal (people)* consequences of AIoT are its ability to amplify job displacement, unemployment, or underemployment. Across historical epochs, the development of technology has played a pivotal role in instigating transformative paradigm shifts of this nature. Modern predictions indicate that by 2030, approximately 40% of professions characterized by low-to-moderate skill levels may be susceptible to automation through AIoT deployment, resulting in a diminished necessity for direct human involvement (Arogyaswamy, 2020). Nevertheless, certain commentators have also posited that while nascent technological innovations frequently engender obsolescence of specific occupational classifications, they concurrently facilitate the emergence of new ones (White, 2011; Gordon, 2016). Nonetheless, an extensive body of empirical evidence posits that employment opportunities caused by the paradigmatic transition within the realms of robotics, automation, and AIoT are inclined to encompass roles demanding diminished skill thresholds, characterized by inadequate remuneration, culminating in a state of pervasive underemployment. Furthermore, predictions suggest that AIoT is poised to influence forthcoming roles that conventionally hinge upon human interaction (Arogyaswamy, 2020). Proactive measures such as governmental initiatives aimed at job retraining, the cultivation of entrepreneurial endeavors, and the augmentation of a pool of proficient workers could potentially address these negative impacts on

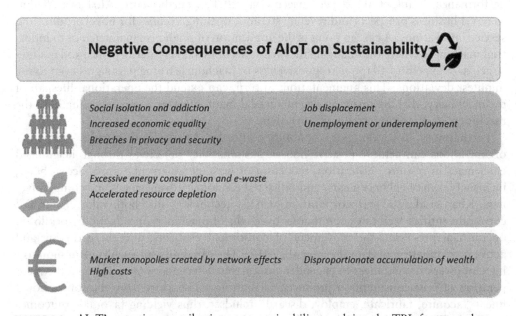

FIGURE 2.3 AIoT's negative contributions to sustainability applying the TBL framework.

employment. However, commentators also assert that these measures would potentially only yield limited effects (Arogyaswamy & Hunter, 2019).

Another potential significant negative consequence of AIoT is its potential to heighten social isolation and promote addictive behaviors, raising concerns about its impact on human interactions and psychological well-being. For example, virtual assistants and smart home systems could diminish face-to-face interactions, steering individuals toward greater reliance on technology for daily tasks and information (Anderson & Perrin, 2017). Furthermore, integration of AIoT into entertainment and communication platforms can foster addictive tendencies. For example, personalized, engaging content delivery facilitated by AIoT-driven platforms can result in excessive usage patterns (Billieux et al., 2015). Additionally, notifications, recommendations, and constant connectivity through AIoT devices create an environment conducive to compulsive use, escalating the risk of addiction (Elhai et al., 2017).

Commentators have also highlighted potential threats of AIoT to fundamental rights and democracy. The impact of AIoT is contingent upon its design and the data it employs, both of which can harbor intentional or inadvertent biases. Algorithmic design might omit crucial facets or perpetuate structural biases. While deployment of quantified representations for intricate societal realities can create an illusion of accuracy, a phenomenon known as "mathwashing." If not appropriately executed, then AI has the potential to influence decisions rooted in factors like ethnicity, gender, and age during processes such as hiring, firing, loan provision, and legal proceedings. AIoT's implications also extend to privacy and data protection, as it can be harnessed in facial recognition systems, online tracking, and individual profiling. Through amalgamating disclosed personal information, AIoT might yield unexpected outcomes. Furthermore, AIoT poses a threat to democratic processes, fostering online echo chambers that reinforce individuals' preexisting viewpoints rather than nurturing a diverse and inclusive public discourse. AIoT's capacity to produce convincing deepfake content – spanning video, audio, and imagery – carries financial risks, reputational harm, and decision-making challenges. This collective effect could exacerbate societal divisions, manipulate electoral outcomes, and undermine freedom of assembly by tracking and profiling individuals with beliefs or actions.

Finally, the escalating proliferation of AIoT has engendered a series of apprehensions concerning individual liberties and entitlements, communal unity, workforce dynamics, economic prosperity, and integrity of democratic systems. The prospect of concentrated authority and deficiency of clarity within mechanisms of decision formulation have elicited moral dilemmas. These dilemmas encompass hazards that impact personal freedoms and privileges, social cohesiveness, economic affluence, and the confidence vested in democratic frameworks. For example, AIoT introduces concerns associated with consolidating hegemonic influence, coupled with the plausible establishment of extensive surveillance measures and connected erosion of private spheres. Maturation of AIoT and associated machine learning algorithms also engenders reservations regarding the effectiveness, dependability, and transparency of decision-making procedures at all levels of society.

From a *planet perspective*, AIoT has been cited as a potential tool for tackling sustainability-related issues. However, AIoT and the broader realm of the internet and communications have faced increasing criticism for their substantial energy consumption. AIoT extensively depends on machine learning algorithms tasked with the rapid processing of substantial volumes of data. This processing necessitates a considerable computational capacity, resulting in huge energy demands. AIoT data centers resort to using fossil fuels for energy generation, a practice entailing the emission of carbon-based pollutants into the atmosphere (IT World Canada Staff, 2023). For example, advanced AI algorithms for data processing run on supercomputers, drawing power from public electricity grids, and rely on backup generators fueled by diesel. The process of training a single AI system alone can result in the release of over 250,000 pounds of carbon dioxide into the environment. Remarkably, utilizing AIoT across various sectors yields carbon dioxide emissions on par with the aviation industry. These additional emissions disproportionately impact historically marginalized communities, often residing in areas of high pollution, thereby facing heightened health risks associated with pollution exposure (Jones & Easterday, 2022).

Paradoxically, a notable ecological detriment emerging from AIoT is rooted in its ability to accelerate production processes, a facet commonly regarded as a positive consequence. The rapidity introduced by robotics within production inherently amplifies the consumption of commodities among the populace. Over an extended temporal scope, heightened consumption engenders the practice of planned obsolescence and contributes to the gradual exhaustion of finite environmental resources. Planned obsolescence encompasses the conception of commodities designed to become quickly outdated, necessitating their replacement. This practice not only expedites the utilization and depletion of resources but also culminates in the consistent accumulation of additional waste by-products (European Parliament, 2023; Joshi, 2021).

From a *profit perspective*, AIoT platform competition can create the risk of market monopolies wherein one company owns all the market share and can control prices and output (Banton, 2021). These monopolies result from network effects, which are a business principle built upon the idea that the value of a product or service increases as more people use it. The network effect holds substantial significance within the context of AIoT platforms. Projections indicate a growing trend where enterprises will progressively engage in professional activities, foster deeper interpersonal relationships, and facilitate research endeavors and diverse functionalities through these platforms, akin to the transformative influence observed during the proliferation of the internet. This phenomenon is notably conspicuous in online platforms that actively encourage users to expand their connections within the platform's network. Social media platforms like Facebook and Instagram exemplify instances of the network effect in action. In these examples, the increase of users within an individual's network correlates with an increased likelihood of an individual's engagement with the platform (Wharton Online, 2023).

Given the profound significance of network effects in shaping company's performance within the domain of AIoT, it is reasonable to anticipate that corporations will seek to benefit from these effects. This strategic utilization can be a potent tool for enhancing competitiveness, thereby serving as a mechanism to restrain potential competitors. However, this strategic posture may engender adverse economic repercussions across broader segments of society, encompassing consumers and other businesses. Under strong network effects, monopolies may emerge resulting in a winner-takes-all situation (Economides & Katsamakas, 2006).

The interconnected nature of devices and systems in the context of AIoT increases the potential of network effects. According to Manyika et al. (2015), the value proposition of AIoT platforms is connected to the scale of adoption, with more participants resulting in increased data flow, improved insights, and superior ecosystem synergies. As a result, corporations operating in the AIoT landscape are incentivized to strategically use network effects to amass a critical mass of users, amplifying the positive feedback loop. Eisenmann et al. (2006) delineates that the emergence of monopoly power within platform ecosystems hinges upon the convergence of three pivotal conditions: notably elevated multihoming costs experienced by entities situated on both facets of the platform, pronounced favorable indirect network effects, and a subdued demand for distinctive attributes. A perspective espoused by Sun and Tse (2007) illuminates that the existence of multiple platforms are sustainable if users possess the capacity for multihoming, thus fostering coexistence. Moreover, the scholarly discourse articulated by Belleflamme and Peitz (2019) underscores that the ability to engage in multihoming on a solitary side of a platform engenders potential benefits for stakeholders on both sides, transcending the advantage limited to a single facet (Basaure et al., 2020).

However, when companies employ network-effect-driven strategies and dominant platforms emerge, it can result in high market concentration and monopoly power. These conditions can be a concern because a dominant platform may compete aggressively to acquire the most price-sensitive users and erect high barriers to market entry, which can limit competition and harm consumer welfare through monopolistic tendencies. Such market dynamics may restrict consumer choice, inhibit innovation, undermine economic welfare, and distort fair competition (Basaure et al., 2020). There are also concerns that societal inequalities will worsen due to wealth accumulation becoming disproportionately skewed toward the custodians of technological enterprises (Arogyaswamy, 2020). AIoT platform Application Programming Interface (APIs), data schemas, and device communication technologies should be standardized concurrently to mitigate these consequences and facilitate competitive markets.

4   Discussion and Conclusion

AIoT presents a fascinating juxtaposition of potential positive impacts and inherent challenges within the sustainability landscape. The intricate interplay between AIoT's technological prowess and the guiding principles of the TBL framework underscores the potential for transformative changes across different sectors of national and international economies and society. The integration of AIoT capabilities has the capacity to unlock new dimensions of business value creation while simultaneously addressing pressing sustainability concerns. However, this surge of innovation also brings about apprehensions regarding societal, economic, and environmental repercussions. In this chapter, we examine and describe the prevalent positive impacts and inherent challenges.

4.1   Positive Impacts

Integrating AIoT into the TBL framework reveals its potential to revolutionize people, the planet, and profit. As AIoT encompasses a multitude of dimensions, the positive impacts on sustainability are significant. A *people (societal)* perspective points to AIoT as a tool for improving human well-being and social connectivity. Applications in healthcare and smart cities illustrate how AIoT can enhance public safety and access to medical services. As a result, technology contributes to improving the quality of life across society.

In terms of the *planet (environment)*, AIoT has the potential to optimize energy consumption, reduce waste, and enhance resource efficiency. Combining AI's analytical capabilities with the connectivity provided by IoT provides a powerful tool for data-driven decision-making that fosters sustainable practices. Combining these approaches could result in more accurate forecasting, simplified supply chain management, and environmentally conscious design practices, making our planet greener.

From a *profit (economic)* perspective, AIoT improves operational and business performance, which leads to greater efficiency, agility, and innovation capabilities for organizations. These capabilities contribute to economic growth and profitability by improving competitiveness, optimizing resources, and simplifying value chains. AIoT-driven predictive maintenance and resource utilization optimization can also result in substantial economic benefits.

4.2   Negative Impacts

Nonetheless, it is important to balance the enthusiasm for AIoT by recognizing its possible adverse outcomes. From a *people's (societal)* perspective, our research reveals apprehensions regarding the displacement of jobs due to automation, especially in fields that demand lesser skill levels. Although past patterns suggest that fresh employment opportunities will emerge alongside technological shifts, there exists a potential for the upcoming job market to be primarily characterized by roles with lower skills and compensation. There are also concerns over the potential threats to privacy and democracy stemming from AIoT's capacity for extensive data collection and analysis, which could infringe upon individual rights. AI's potential to perpetuate biases in decision-making, coupled with its role in fostering echo chambers and deepfake content, amplifies the threat to democratic processes, diversity, and public discourse.

From a *planet (environmental)* perspective, the energy consumption associated with AIoT's computational demands is a significant environmental concern. Expansion of data centers and AIoT computational requirements may result in increased carbon emissions, potentially undermining progress toward sustainability goals. The paradox of accelerated production processes resulting from AIoT efficiency improvements raises concerns about overconsumption and planned obsolescence, putting additional strain on finite environmental resources.

Regarding *profit (economic)* gains, AIoT's tendency to promote monopolies through network effects raises economic and competitive sustainability concerns. The concentration of power within a handful of dominant corporations can result in price manipulation, limited consumer options, and suppressed innovation. These market dynamics will potentially worsen economic disparities and erode the fundamental principles of fair competition.

Finally, revisiting our research question:

Will the unstoppable development of AIoT result in the unlocking of new and unthought of business and sustainability possibilities, or are we opening Pandora's box?

Like any emerging technology, AIoT offers both opportunities and challenges. Much depends on how well it is managed and incorporated into various economic and social sectors to determine whether it unlocks new business and sustainability possibilities. It is up to society and industry how to navigate these challenges and leverage the opportunities presented by AIoT to determine whether it leads to new and transformative possibilities or becomes Pandora's box. Developing AIoT responsibly, utilizing ethical considerations, ensuring the security measures are robust, and appropriate regulation are all necessary to maximize its benefits and minimize its downsides. As an integral component of systematically elucidating these intricate reverberations, a thorough empirical examination of AIoT's relevancy within TBL frameworks, supported by tangible illustrative examples, plays a crucial role.

5   Conclusion

The integration of AIoT into the fabric of business and society has the potential to be a double-edged sword. On one hand, it brings about a transformative paradigm shift with positive impacts that span economic growth, social well-being, and environmental sustainability. AIoT's ability to optimize processes, conserve resources, and drive innovation is poised to create a substantial positive influence within the TBL framework. On the other hand, the challenges and concerns associated with AIoT's deployment demand serious attention. The potential for job displacement, erosion of privacy, heightened energy consumption, and the creation of monopolistic market conditions warrant initiative-taking strategies for mitigation. Striking a balance between harnessing the benefits of AIoT and mitigating its adverse effects requires a collaborative effort among governments, industries, and academia.

In conclusion, the unstoppable growth of AIoT holds enormous potential for unlocking new dimensions of business and sustainability possibilities, as well as the potential to open Pandora's box of challenges. It will be critical to navigate this landscape cautiously, ensuring the maximization of its positive effects while proactively addressing negative consequences. A future shaped by the ethical and responsible integration of AIoT technologies can foster long-term growth, equitable progress, and a harmonious relationship among humans, technology, and the environment.

References

Alonso, C., Kothari, S. and Rehman, S. (2020). How Artificial Intelligence Could Widen the Gap between Rich and Poor Nations. Retrieved May 3, 2023, from https://www.imf.org/en/Blogs/Articles/2020/12/02/blog-how-artificial-intelligence-could-widen-the-gap-between-rich-and-poor-nations

Amit, R. and Zott, C. (2001). Value Creation in e-business. *Strategic Management Journal*, 22(6–7), 493–520. https://doi.org/10.1002/smj.187

Anderson, M. and Perrin, A. (2017). Tech Adoption Climbs among Older Adults. Pew Research Center. Retrieved August 15, 2023, from https://www.pewresearch.org/internet/2017/05/17/tech-adoption-climbs-among-older-adults/

Arogyaswamy, B. (2020). Big Tech and Societal Sustainability: An Ethical Framework. *AI and Society*, 35(4), 829–840. https://doi.org/10.1007/s00146-020-00956-6

Arogyaswamy, B. and Hunter, J. (2019). The Impact of Technology and Globalization on Employment and Equity: An Organizing Framework for Action. *International Journal of Global Sustainability*, 3(1), 55–57.

Banton, C. (2021). Monopolistic Markets: Characteristics, History, and Effects. *Investopedia*. Retrieved August 15, 2023, from https://www.investopedia.com/terms/m/monopolymarket.asp

Basaure, A., Vesselkov, A. and Töyli, J. (2020). Internet of Things (IoT) Platform Competition: Consumer Switching versus Provider Multihoming. *Technovation*, 90–91, 102101. https://doi. org/10.1016/j.technovation.2019.102101

Beier, G., Niehoff, S., Ziems, T. and Xue, B. (2017). Sustainability Aspects of a Digitalized Industry – A Comparative Study from China and Germany. *International Journal of Precision Engineering and Manufacturing Green Technology*, 4, 227–234. https://doi.org/10.1007/s40684-017-0028-8

Belleflamme, P. and Peitz, M. (2019). Platform Competition: Who Benefits from Multihoming? *International Journal of Industrial Organization*, 64, 1–26.

Billieux, J., Maurage, P., Lopez-Fernandez, O., Kuss, D. J. and Griffiths, M. D. (2015). Can Disordered Mobile Phone Use Be Considered a Behavioral Addiction? An Update on Current Evidence and a Comprehensive Model for Future Research. *Current Addiction Reports*, 2(2), 154–162. https://doi.org/10.1007/s40429-015-0054-y

Bronner, W., Gebauer, H. and Lamprecht, C. (2021). *Connected Business: Create Value in a Networked Economy*. Springer. https://doi.org/10.1007/978-3-030-76897-3

Brynjolfsson, E. (2022). The Turing Trap: The Promise & Peril of Human-Like Artificial Intelligence. *Daedalus*, 151(2), 272–287. https://doi.org/10.1162/DAED_a_01915

Economides, N. and Katsamakas, E. (2006). Two-sided Competition of Proprietary vs. Open-source Technology Platforms and the Implications for the Software Industry. *Management Science*, 52(7), 1057–1071. https://doi.org/10.1287/mnsc.1060.0549

Eisenmann, T., Parker, G. and Van Alstyne, M. W. (2006). Strategies for Two-sided Markets. *Harvard Business Review*, 84(10), 92.

Elhai, J. D., Dvorak, R. D., Levine, J. C. and Hall, B. J. (2017). Problematic Smartphone Use: A Conceptual Overview and Systematic Review of Relations with Anxiety and Depression Psychopathology. *Journal of Affective Disorders*, 207, 251–259. https://doi.org/10.1016/j.jad.2016.08.030

Elkington, J. (1994). Towards the Sustainable Corporation: Win-Win-Win Business Strategies for Sustainable Development. *California Management Review*, 36(2), 90–100. https://doi.org/10.2307/41165746

European Parliament (2023). Artificial Intelligence: Threats and Opportunities. *European Parliament Website*. Retrieved August 15, 2023, from https://www.europarl.europa.eu/news/en/headlines/society/20200918STO87404/artificial-intelligence-threats-and-opportunities?&at_campaign=20234-Digital&at_medium=Google_Ads&at_platform=Search&at_creation=RSA&at_goal=TR_G&at_audience=artificial%20intelligence&at_topic=Artificial_intelligence&at_location=FI&gclid=CjwKCAjwxOymBhAFEiwAnodBLGGiZwOS7n15HAEBUvuqEYu0vHQ8QUiL0ywyMEOhryLtJ20tB9yj4BoCRWgQAvD_BwE

EY. (2020). Are Your Reframing Your Future or Is the Future Reframing You? Understanding Megatrends Will Help You See Opportunities Where Others Don't—Megatrends 2020 and beyond. Retrieved May 3, 2023, from https://assets.ey.com/content/dam/ey-sites/ey-com/en_gl/topics/megatrends/ey-megatrends-2020-report.pdf

Frank, A. G., Dalenogare, L. S. and Ayala, N. F. (2019). Industry 4.0 Technologies: Implementation Patterns in Manufacturing Companies. *International Journal of Production Economics*, 210, 15–26. https://doi.org/10.1016/j.ijpe.2019.01.004

Geissdoerfer, M., Savaget, P., Bocken, N. M. P. and Hultink, E. J. (2017). The Circular Economy – A New Sustainability Paradigm? *Journal of Cleaner Production*, 143, 757–768. https://doi.org/10.1016/j.jclepro.2016.12.048

Ghobakhloo, M., Iranmanesh, M., Grybauskas, A., Vilkas, M. and Petraitė, M. (2021). Industry 4.0, Innovation, and Sustainable Development: A Systematic Review and a Roadmap to Sustainable Innovation. *Business Strategy and the Environment*, 30(8), 4237–4257. https://doi.org/10.1002/bse.2867

Ghoreishi, M., Treves, L. and Kuivalainen, O. (2022). Artificial Intelligence of Things as an Accelerator of Circular Economy in International Business. In S. Batas, O. Kuivalainen and R. R.

Sinkovics (eds.), *Megatrends in International Business. The Academy of International Business.* Cham: Palgrave Macmillan, pp. 83–104.

Gordon, R. (2016). *The Rise and Fall of American Growth.* Princeton: Princeton University Press.

Hahn, T., Figge, F., Pinkse, J. and Preuss, L. (2010). Trade-offs in Corporate Sustainability: You Can't Have Your Cake and Eat It. *Business Strategy and the Environment*, 19(4), 217–229. https://doi.org/10.1002/bse.674

Haseeb, M., Hussain, H. I., Ślusarczyk, B. and Jermsittiparsert, K. (2019). Industry 4.0: A Solution towards Technology Challenges of Sustainable Business Performance. *Social Sciences*, 8(5). https://doi.org/10.3390/socsci8050154

IT World Canada Staff. (2023). The Impact of Artificial Intelligence on the Environment. *IT World Canada.* Retrieved August 15, 2023, from https://www.itworldcanada.com/post/the-impact-of-artificial-intelligence-on-the-environment

Jayashree, S., Reza, M. N. H., Malarvizhi, C. A. N. and Mohiuddin, M. (2021). Industry 4.0 Implementation and Triple Bottom Line Sustainability: An Empirical Study on Small and Medium Manufacturing Firms. *Heliyon*, 7(8). https://doi.org/10.1016/j.heliyon.2021.e07753

Jones, E. and Easterday, B. (2022). Artificial Intelligence's Environmental Costs and Promises. *Council on Foreign Relations.* Retrieved August 15, 2023, from https://www.cfr.org/blog/artificial-intelligences-environmental-costs-and-promise

Joshi, N. (2021). The Negative Environmental Impact of Robotics. *Allerin.* Retrieved August 15, 2023, from https://www.allerin.com/blog/the-negative-environmental-impact-of-robotics

Karttunen, E., Pynnönen, M., Treves, L. and Hallikas, J. (2021), Capabilities for the Internet of Things Enabled Product-service System Business Models. *Technology Analysis & Strategic Management*, 35(12), pp. 1–17. https://doi.org/10.1080/09537325.2021.2012143

Khan, I. S., Ahmad, M. O. and Majava, J. (2021). Industry 4.0 and Sustainable Development: A Systematic Mapping of Triple Bottom Line, Circular Economy, and Sustainable Business Models Perspectives. *Journal of Cleaner Production*, 297, 126655. https://doi.org/10.1016/j.jclepro.2021.126655.

Kolkowska, N. (2023). Triple Bottom Line for Business. *Sustainable Review.* Retrieved August 15, 2023, from https://sustainablereview.com/triple-bottom-line-for-businesses/

Manyika, J., Chui, M., Bisson, P., Woetzel, J., Dobbs, R., Bughin, J. and Aharon, D. (2015). Unlocking the Potential of the Internet of Things. *McKinsey Global Institute.* Retrieved August 15, 2023, from https://www.mckinsey.com/capabilities/mckinsey-digital/our-insights/the-internet-of-things-the-value-of-digitizing-the-physical-world

Metz, C., Mac, R. and Conger, K. (2023). Elon Musk Ramps Up A.I. Efforts, Even as He Warns of Dangers. Retrieved May 3, 2023, from https://www.nytimes.com/2023/04/27/technology/elon-musk-ai-openai.html

Norman, W. and MacDonald, C. (2004). Getting to the Bottom of "Triple Bottom Line". *Business Ethics Quarterly*, 14, 243–262. https://doi.org/10.5840/beq200414211

Schulz, S. A. and Flanigan, R. L. (2016). Developing Competitive Advantage Using the Triple Bottom Line: A Conceptual Framework. *Journal of Business & Industrial Marketing*, 31(4), 449–458. https://doi.org/10.1108/JBIM-08-2014-0150

Soon, O. Y. and Hui, L. H. (2022). Sustainability Applications for Artificial Intelligence. Retrieved May 3, 2023, from https://sustainabilitymag.com/sustainability/sustainability-applications-for-artificial-intelligence

Stedman, C. and Gillis, A. S. (2023). Triple Bottom Line (TBL). *TechTarget.* Retrieved August 15, 2023, from https://www.techtarget.com/whatis/definition/triple-bottom-line-3BL

Sun, M. and Tse, E. (2007). When Does the Winner Take All in Two-Sided Markets? *Review of Network Economics*, 6, 25. https://doi.org/10.2202/1446-9022.1108

Teece, D. J. (2010). Business Models, Business Strategy and Innovation. *Long Range Planning*, 43(2–3), pp. 172–194. https://doi.org/10.1016/j.lrp.2009.07.003

Telukdarie, A., Buhulaiga, E., Bag, S., Gupta, S. and Luo, Z. (2018). Industry 4.0 Implementation for Multinationals. *Process Safety and Environmental Protection*, 118, 316–329. https://doi.org/10.1016/j.psep.2018.06.030

Wharton Online. (2023). What Is the Network Effect? *Wharton University of Pennsylvania*. Retrieved August 15, 2023, from https://online.wharton.upenn.edu/blog/what-is-the-network-effect/

White, R. (2011). *Railroaded: The Transcontinental and the Making of Modern America*. New York: Norton.

Yadav, G., Kumar, A., Luthra, S., Garza-Reyes, J.A., Kumar, V. and Batista, L. (2020). A Framework to Achieve Sustainability in Manufacturing Organisations of Developing Economies using Industry 4.0 Technologies' Enablers. *Computers in Industry*, 122, 103280. https://doi.org/10.1016/j.compind.2020.103280

Zhu, Q., Sarkis, J. and Lai, K.-H. (2008). Confirmation of a Measurement Model for Green Supply Chain Management Practices Implementation. *International Journal of Production Economics*, 111(2), 261–273. https://doi.org/10.1016/j.ijpe.2006.11.029

3

ADAPTATION OF ARTIFICIAL INTELLIGENCE BY START-UPS FOR A DATA-DRIVEN CIRCULAR ECONOMY

Evidence from Multiple Case Study in Finland

Malahat Ghoreishi, Iben Bolund Nielsen and Mikko Pynnönen

1   Introduction

The goal of a circular economy (CE) is to preserve the utility and value of products, components, and materials for as long as possible by "slowing, closing, and narrowing" production loops (Bocken et al., 2016). Transitioning to a CE involves a systemic shift aimed at mitigating the effects of the linear economy, building long-term resilience, creating economic and business opportunities, and delivering environmental and social benefits (Ellen MacArthur Foundation, 2015). In other words, it requires a radical change in business model (BM). Current research on circular business models (CBMs) is mostly centered around well-established companies and large corporations with only few studies focused on circular start-ups (Henry et al., 2020). The CBMs of incumbent firms and start-ups differ; incumbents can shape the ecosystem they are part of but may lack the flexibility of entrepreneurial start-ups in seizing opportunities and fostering groundbreaking innovations (Suchek et al., 2022). Entrepreneurs spot and exploit new opportunities by orchestrating novel combinations, leading to new products, production methods, raw material sources, markets, and organizational structures.

Circular entrepreneurship is described as the act of discovering and capitalizing on opportunities in the CE sector (Zucchella and Urban, 2019). As CE is seen as a strategy for achieving specific sustainability goals (Geissdoerfer et al., 2020), circular entrepreneurship can be embodied by "born-circular" companies. These are young enterprises specifically established to offer circular value propositions and explore opportunities in the CE sector (Zucchella and Urban, 2019). New circular businesses help address environmental issues by introducing new eco-friendly products, services, and institutions, actions that may pose greater risks to established companies (York and Venkataraman, 2010). However, research into the role of entrepreneurship in the transition towards a CE is still in its early stages and is a recent development (Heshmati, 2015).

At the same time, the fast and recent advancements in digital technologies (DTs) have elevated the importance of data and analytics in corporate strategies, leading to the assertion that "data is the new oil" that can be refined to unlock unparalleled value (Manyika

DOI: 10.4324/9781003433743-4

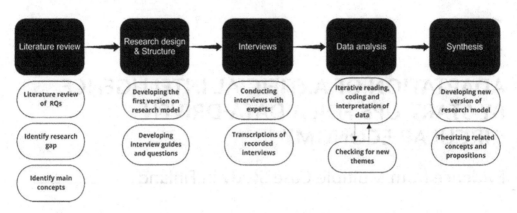

FIGURE 3.1   Research steps of the study.

et al., 2011; Mcafee and Brynjolfsson, 2012). As a result, researchers contend that the key to a CE transformation is closely tied to a digital transformation (Ingemarsdotter et al., 2020). This includes the effective use of DTs such as big data, artificial intelligence (AI), blockchain, the Internet of Things, and cloud computing, collectively known as Industry 4.0 technologies. Therefore, scholars concur that the adoption of CE is intimately connected with digitalization, as it can enable predictive analytics, tracking, and monitoring throughout an organization's product lifecycle (Bhatt et al., 2019; Ghoreishi and Happonen, 2020a).

Furthermore, recent advancements in AI are empowering machines to process vast unstructured data sets using complicated and adaptive algorithms to execute tasks that typically require human intelligence (Stone et al., 2018). AI and machine learning offer numerous benefits for the CE, including resource efficiency, ecosystem collaboration, recycling and resource recovery, reverse logistics, and closing the loops (Ghoreishi and Happonen, 2020a; Rajput and Singh, 2019; Sundui et al., 2021). This has prompted some to contemplate the generativity of AI, suggesting that the technology may not only provide a means of achieving cost and productivity benefits, but also represent a fundamental innovation to the tools we use to innovate.. However, these innovations also have broader potential negative impacts that start-ups must adapt to. Despite the growing prevalence of both mechanical and cognitive automation, there is limited literature on the intersection of start-ups and AI in CE, particularly on how start-ups utilize AI and machine learning technologies to accelerate CE. To bridge this gap, this study aims to answer the following question:

QR: What is the current implementation of AI in data-driven CBMs by start-ups?

To answer this question, this study employs thematic analysis of a series of semi-structured interviews to identify the key AI technologies implemented by start-ups in data-driven BMs and to explore how these BMs help born-circular start-ups to accelerate CE solutions. The rest of this work is as follows: first, the authors provide the background on the relationship between AI technologies and CE, followed by the theory of entrepreneurship in CE and capabilities of AI in BM innovations. Next, Section 3 describes the research methodology including the analysis of five semi-structured interviews with experts. Finally, the results and final discussions of the study are presented in Section 4.

2 Background

2.1 *AI as an Enabler of CE*

Digital tools can assist businesses in monitoring material movement, assessing circularity and its effects, identifying and seizing new commercial prospects, optimizing resource consumption, and depending on precise and reliable data exchange. Therefore, readily available data is the cornerstone of CE, enhancing internal procedures and profitability. Some companies have also introduced supplementary digital services to help their customers better manage or utilize their CE solution (Ahola and Tolonen, 2021). In the data value creation process, data is initially transformed into information, which is then merged with other sources and interpreted by humans to generate knowledge. This knowledge is further enriched with collective interpretation and experience to create wisdom (Luoma et al., 2021). Designing for circularity using data-driven insights can enhance the economic and environmental sustainability of products through efficient resource use. Such products, their components, and related processes can be designed and optimized using CE principles by applying predictive and prescriptive machine learning insights (Bressanelli et al., 2018). Historical and real-time data can forecast demand and manage inventory, reducing waste and promoting sustainable operations. AI is defined as a system's capability to act intelligently and expand its scope, accurately interpreting external data and using these lessons to achieve specific goals and activities through flexible adaptation (Kaplan, 2016). AI and machine learning can be used in various ways to offer and manage smart products, services, and experiences by sharing information for collaboration or creating optimal and sustainable value (Brynjolfsson and Mcafee, 2017). The primary advantage of AI techniques for CE is their ability to gather, process, and analyze large amounts of data quickly and in real-time from various sources (Mühlroth and Grottke, 2020). AI techniques can support the circularity of the entire value chain by predicting consumption and demand, enabling smart product design, and enhancing remanufacturing processes through remote monitoring (Ghoreishi and Happonen, 2020b). AI techniques can facilitate CE opportunities by promoting circular product design and development, optimizing infrastructure to ensure product flows, and implementing CBMs (Ellen MacArthur Foundation and Google, 2019). Table 3.1 presents how data creates value in CE and how AI techniques utilize data to boost circularity.

2.2 *Role of Entrepreneurship in CE*

The interplay between an individual and the contextual forces that hinder or enable an entrepreneurial individual has been difficult to translate to theoretical development in the field, as have the opportunities an entrepreneurial individual responds to. Venkataraman (York and Venkataraman, 2010) defines the field of entrepreneurship as "how opportunities to bring into existence 'future' goods and services are discovered, created, and exploited, by whom, and with what consequence". Even though two decades have passed since Shane and Venkataraman's (2000) article on establishing entrepreneurship as a separate research field, the topic of entrepreneurial opportunity is as relevant as ever, also in the emerging CE.

The construct of entrepreneurial opportunity has been manifested in research, arguing that entrepreneurship cannot occur without an accompanying opportunity no matter

TABLE 3.1 The type and value of data in CE, CBMs, and utilization of AI

Data value	Type of data	Data-driven business models enabled by AI	Role of AI techniques	Reference
Data for prolonging products' life	Data on customer's needs and demands enables optimization of product's design. Data on product condition and waste stream helps companies to provide services to support longer lifetime (e.g., maintenance service, reuse, refurbish, remanufacturing services).	Product-service systems	Cloud computing technologies enable digital platforms that can manage operational activities and services. Cloud technologies utilizing AI and machine learning can integrate and show data to the company for better decision-making on products/services.	(Ranta et al., 2021)
Data for operation optimization	Data transparency on each stage of product lifecycle increases efficiency in supply change management and optimization as well as better product quality. System operation and performance data, data from value chains.	Cloud-based enabled supply chain	AI and data analytics techniques enable visibility and outsourcing in price and revenue decisions through predictive capabilities. Digital platforms transfer real-time data that enables transparency throughout the entire supply chain.	(Ivanov et al., 2022)
Data for resource efficiency	Data on consumer's behavior and use of products increases resource optimization through collaborative consumption (sharing, exchanging, renting). Sharing data on shared assets and resources improves resource efficiency by reducing ownership of assets and products.	Sharing economy	AI enables predictive maintenance through analysis of real-time data transferred by Internet of Things–embedded sensors on products and assets. Digital platforms enable transferring of data between companies and various consumers, and enable tracking of consumer behavior in using products and assets.	(Centobelli et al., 2020)
Data for inventory management	Data on conditions of different parts of products improves quality of remanufacturing. Historical data on a product design, use, and return enhances product development, process development, and after-sales services. Data on material flow and returns improves response time to drive changes.	Digital remanufacturing business model	Cloud-based services support the development of distribution process planning in decentralized dynamic remanufacturing environment through machine learning algorithms. Smart robots enable intelligent sensing remanufacturing through real-time data adaptation.	

Abbreviations: AI, artificial intelligence; CBMs, circular business models; CE, circular economy.

how much motivation or expertise the entrepreneur possesses. This research adopts this view and assumes an individual–opportunity nexus approach as the basis for research within the field of entrepreneurship as detailed by Eckhardt and Shane (2003).

Entrepreneurial opportunities exist when new goods, services, raw materials, and organizing methods can be utilized and sold for more than the cost of production and are discovered when someone realizes that the resource in question is not put to its "best use". The entrepreneurial opportunity construct concerns the existence, discovery, and exploitation of opportunities (Eckhardt and Shane, 2003). The quality and value of such opportunities vary greatly and thus understanding them is imperative to explaining entrepreneurship.

Scientific research on CE has previously been centered around engineering, natural science, and technical solutions, while research on CBMs, circular business strategies, and management supporting CE has been diminutive (de Sousa Jabbour et al., 2018; Stall et al., 2018). Further research on CE is needed to convince businesses and governments that CE is a feasible alternative to the current predominantly linear economy.

Both internal and external factors that are pushing the CE agenda include stricter regulations, changes in consumer behavior, and new technologies available in the market. Also, renewed commitment from consumers to consume more responsibly is a global trend that shows through a willingness to pay more for eco-friendly and recyclable products, and a desire for plastic-free purchases. These examples pose significant changes to the business environment and are therefore considered external enablers (Davidsson et al., 2020), pushing the CE of which we focus on the new aspects of aspect in the form of AI. Internal motivations to redesign a firm's BMs are to boost resource efficiency, and close the loops of energy and material flow (Geissdoerfer et al., 2020) as cost-reduction measures. The CE is quickly gaining traction as a method for enhancing and reimagining economies. It addresses increasing resource-related issues, creates employment opportunities, stimulates innovation, and yields significant environmental benefits (European Commission, 2020). This approach not only promotes sustainability but also has the potential to drive economic growth. It's a win–win situation for both the environment and the economy.

Recent studies identifies that "entrepreneurship, innovation, and socio-economic development" increases circularity significantly. (Kostakis and Tsagarakis, 2022). Kostakis and Tsagarakis (2022), realize that the above elements have positive impacts on circularity. According to their findings, 1% increase in entrepreneurship in Europe increases circularity rate by 0.19% whereas 1% increase of research and development which leads to innovative solutions enhances circularity rate by 0.65% on average. On the other hand, 1% increase of economic growth increases circularity rate annually by 0.73%. Therefore, by providing more opportunities for entrepreneurship in Europe, innovation level will rise and leads to an advancement in socio-economic matters which all in return leads to faster progress in circularity. However, there is limited literature on how entrepreneurs adapt DTs such as AI to provide innovative solutions for circularity. Therefore, this study aims to fill this gap by analyzing cases that implement innovative circular solutions and examining their current situation in adaptation of AI. (Kostakis and Tsagarakis, 2022). Entrepreneurially inclined individuals drive collaborations by sharing a vision, enthusiasm, and importantly, a convincing proposition for a CE. Moreover, collaboration is pursued at an early stage to co-develop the problem and solution space and to integrate diverse knowledge from across the value network, thereby mitigating increased complexity (Brown et al., 2019). Additionally, sustainable entrepreneurship can advocate for changes in institutional structures, enabling the exploitation of sustainable opportunities, enhancing the competitiveness of sustainable behaviors, and fostering new entrepreneurial mindsets. This approach not only promotes sustainability but also encourages innovation and entrepreneurial spirit.

3 Research Methodology

3.1 Research Design

A multiple case study analysis was conducted of Finnish small companies and start-ups specifically providing CE solutions. Due to the nascent stage of research on the topic of CE, a case study approach is a suitable methodology for empirical investigation to understand the phenomenon as well as to help build theory at such an early stage.

Case studies seek to understand the dynamics of a single setting (Eisenhardt, 1989) or to investigate a contemporary phenomenon (Yin, 2014); therefore, a qualitative multiple case study research strategy is the methodological framework best suited for this exploratory research into the novel and innovative business ecosystems of digital start-ups enhancing or accelerating a CE. The case study research strategy, furthermore, has distinct advantages when researching how a contemporary set of events take form, particularly when the researchers have no control over the events. External validity is sought through the use of replication logic in the research design and to choose which companies to include in the research.

3.2 Data Collection

Each of the five case companies were carefully chosen according to our three core criteria for inclusion: (1) start-up or small size of company, (2) specifically providing solutions for the transition to a CE, and (3) availability of CEO or founder for online interviews due to COVID-19 restrictions on travel and physical meetings. The interviews were conducted during February, March, and April 2021. The data is centered around in-depth semi-structured interviews with either founders or CEOs of each of the case companies, although several types of data are being collected to strengthen the construct validity. Therefore, the data includes interviews, press releases and other online news, and each company's website, although the documents available differ between the case companies due to their small size and relatively young age in many cases. The interviews were conducted online via videocalls and were all recorded and immediately transcribed to ensure accuracy during the data analysis phase. The majority of the case companies were identified through an industry expert after which three additional companies were added after a comprehensive internet search. The cases are carefully chosen within this single digital CE ecosystem setting. The selection criteria for inclusion in the research were (1) explicit purpose to create a CE-enhancing solution, (2) inability to have created the same CE business solution without the use of DTs, (3) from Finland, and (4) categorized as a "small" business, rather than medium or large.

TABLE 3.2 Case company details including circular objectives and BMs

Company name	Year established	Business area	CE objectives	Circular business model
Biocode	2017	The most reliable tool for climate smart food that helps conscious companies to identify tangible ways to decarbonize food production.	Reducing carbon footprints of food products Reducing the climate impact of the food products to different stakeholders Reducing food waste within different phases of value chain	Online services Software-as-a-service Climate smart product tags Online product profiles
Emmy	2015	An online Nordic marketplace for pre-owned premium clothing.	Reducing emissions in textile and fashion industry Reducing waste Support the European Commission's Zero Carbon Emission strategy Reducing the raw material extraction	Resell clothes Resale as a service platform
Kauppaval mennus	2014	A company that studies and trains processes and software in retail according to lean management principles.	Reducing food waste Increasing efficiency of food shortages and excess storage	Software-as-a-service
Biocode	2017	The most reliable tool for climate smart food that helps conscious companies to identify tangible ways to decarbonize food production.	Reducing carbon footprints of food products Reducing the climate impact of the food products to different stakeholders Reducing food waste within different phases of value chain	Online services Software-as-a-service Climate smart product tags Online product profiles
Emmy	2015	An online Nordic marketplace for pre-owned premium clothing.	Reducing emissions in textile and fashion industry Reducing waste Support the European Commission's Zero Carbon Emission strategy Reducing the raw material extraction	Resell clothes Resale as a service platform

(Continued)

TABLE 3.2 (Continued)

Company name	Year established	Business area	CE objectives	Circular business model
Kauppaval mennus	2014	A company that studies and trains processes and software in retail according to lean management principles.	Reducing food waste Increasing efficiency of food shortages and excess storage	Software-as-a-service
RePack	2011	A packaging service that enables the return and reuse of delivery packaging for online retailers and their users.	Reducing the waste from packaging Reducing raw material extraction	Package reuse model
Yield Systems	2018	An AI company with science background that develops machine learning solutions for agri-food value chain enhancement and video intelligence.	Reducing CO_2 emission	Data collection and analytic services

Abbreviation: BMs, business models.

All interviews were conducted in English and data reliability has been addressed through the use of a simple case study protocol and a common database of case material accessible to all authors.

3.3   Data Analysis

The data analysis will follow an abductively developed model currently being developed. The model is developed specifically for this research based on the data gathered and theoretical components from relevant literature. For the data analysis, the Nvivo12 software was used as a tool to code, analyze, and compare the data. To address internal validity, two authors independently of each other will code all interviews and then compare and discuss where dissimilarities are found until agreement is reached. The analysis is planned to occur in two phases due to the two levels of analysis. A within-case analysis (Eisenhardt, 1989) of the unit of analysis is the first stage in which each company will be analyzed separately. The second stage of analysis will be a cross-case analysis to compare and contrast the findings to bring the level of analysis up the meso-level where patterns and trends can be identified. Therefore, the unit of analysis is the DTs that the start-up companies utilize in accelerating a CE and the level of analysis is the digital circular start-up ecosystem.

4   Results and Discussions

In CE, entrepreneurship is viewed as the inventive process of discovering and capitalizing on new business opportunities to boost circularity (Veleva and Bodkin, 2018). By creating innovative BMs, entrepreneurs can contribute to circular solutions through new products and services, which pose more challenges and risks to established firms (York and Venkataraman, 2010). Meanwhile, the shift towards CE is rapidly progressing with

TABLE 3.3 DTs and CE strategies of case companies

DTs utilized	CE solutions
Cloud-based, APIs, user-interfaces, databases, database integrations.	Lifecycle assessment of food products to reduce the carbon footprint and developing more value to the value chain of the food products.
Big data, software development (coding)	Reducing food waste by forecasting the precise amount of food shops need to order and preventing extra storage and food waste.
Digital platform	Reducing waste in packaging by durable and reusable packages. Reduce natural resource usage by using recycled polypropylene as raw material and will be upcycled in case the package breaks.
APIs, headless architecture, opensource website.	Connecting individuals to designers and organizations in local areas to share upcycled/recycled/sustainably produced products and services.
Algorithms, cloud infrastructure, AI, machine learning.	Reducing CO_2 by accelerating the field and breeding better plants that absorb CO_2.

Abbreviations: APIs, application programming interfaces; DTs, digital technologies; RFID, radio frequency identification.

TABLE 3.4 Type of data, DTs, and utilization of AI in circular solutions of cases

Type of data	DTs	Utilization of AI technologies
Data on different parts of food products' lifecycle Data on individual land-based farming such as data on the type of soil, nutrients, fertilizers, and fuel	Azure cloud-based technology Modern interface coding Conventional software development technologies Database integrations between different operators and APIs	Not yet Huge potential for machine learning algorithms and AI in company's product roadmap Requires having bigger data pools
Data on lifecycle and durability of textile products Data on resale price Data on quality of the product Data on material Process data	Digital platform Machine learning for databases AI for pricing automation AI for matching products Google analytics Cloud-based platforms RFID tags for products and packs	Yes
Data on lifecycle of products Data on waste Data on sales	Big data Conventional software development technologies	Not yet High potential for AI Potential of QR codes that hold expiry dates
Data on lifecycle of packages Data on logistic processes	Digital platforms In-house-developed system Conventional software	No Potential of automated inspection by machine vision Potential of utilizing sensors to track real-time data on logistics
Digital phenotypical data on plants in various plots Data on conditions, disease symptoms, and number of grains in plots Data on agri-food value chain	AI-based analytics Mobile apps Algorithms	Yes AI Machine vision Deep learning

the expansion of the DT field and its capabilities related to circularity. However, research in the area of CE and entrepreneurship remains abstract, with only a few studies focusing on the applications of DTs in circular entrepreneurship (Suchek et al., 2022).

The findings of this study revealed that all start-ups highlighted the essential role of data in their solutions, and that data utilization enables their products and services to align with CE objectives. Despite the use of DTs in all their solutions, only two companies utilize AI technologies, such as machine learning and analytics. The other three cases mentioned that they still use traditional software solutions but recognize the potential of AI in many solutions. This is attributed to a shortage of skills and the high cost of modern technologies for young ventures with low revenue. This highlights the need for more accessible and affordable AI solutions to further drive innovation in the CE space.

As presented in Table 3.4, data plays essential role in tracking lifecycle of the products. Moreover, the interviewees described the enablers of their business factors such as global megatrend of climate change, the pressure towards producers for their impacts of activities for supplying raw materials on climate and increasing consumer awareness about climate change. For example, the enabler of the Emmy start-up has been the global warming and high emission of fashion industry, challenges and complexity in recycling of textiles, difficulty to access flea markets, and the need for a safe, risk-free seller–customer marketplace in which products are curated. Hence, digital platforms can be considered as a suitable and practical solution in enabling CE and AI can play crucial role in this case. The value of digitalization of the processes is evident for all the companies especially since the conventional data collection is costly, not efficient, and not accurate. There is still a lack of direct integration of data to the systems while data is exchanged mostly through google sheet. On the other hand, EU regulations are forcing companies to look for more innovative environmental solutions that are linked to data and require utilization of DTs. In this regard, digitalization and automation of supply chain can help in accessibility of data through the entire value chain, which is currently lacking.

TABLE 3.5 Entrepreneurial ecosystem actors of circular start-ups studied in this chapter

Policies	Paris Climate Agreement
	EU's climate goals
	National climate goals
	EU's policies on environment
Competitors	Consultancies and research institutes
	Public assistance
	Traditional farming system
Finance	Spin-off by two established companies
	Innovation funding agencies
	Growth funding sources from Finland or the EU
	Private equity markets
	100% financed by the owner
	Venture capital funding
	Public funding (business Finland)
	Horizon2020 funding
Culture	Mission-driven organization
	Lean community, especially Lean-yhdistys
	Progressive culture due to the growth of company
	Data sharing culture from plant breeders
Support	Collaboration with marketing agencies in terms of branding, marketing, and communication activities
	Collaboration with research organizations
	Partnering with VTT, LUKE, and Finnish metrological institute
	Stores as customers
	IT infrastructures
	Non-governmental institutions like the Ellen MacArthur Foundation
	Different kinds of competitions
	NGOs that are organized around the circular economy
	Research institutes
	Governmental research institutes like Sitra
	Cloud infrastructure
	Policy agencies
Crowdsourcing	Lot of potentials but not yet fully utilized

(Continued)

TABLE 3.5 (Continued)

Human Capital	The core of the company is a skilled and knowledgeable team
	Collaboration with educational institutes, universities, Aalto University, and Haga Helia
	Software developers
	IT experts are the core
	Industrial design
	Logistics
	Graduate students from education institution
Market	Valio Carbo® Farm calculator for the carbon footprint assessment of raw milk
	HKScan a tool to assess the carbon footprints of beef, pork, and poultry
	Assessed carbon footprint of Finnish bakery Vaasan's selected bread brands
	Assessed carbon footprint of oat flakes for Kinnusen Mylly
	Assessed carbon footprint of fava bean brand Härkis and Beanit for Verso Foods
	Misunderstanding of the offered service is the biggest challenge
	Early customers, Finalyson, New fashion webshops focused on sustainability brands
	Early customers, media like Seed World group, testing institute such as LUKE in Finland, industrial dynamics
Partnerships	Partnership with digital marketing company
	Partners in logistics
	Partnership with Shopify for customer interface

Furthermore, companies explained the role of different actors in their ecosystems and how the entire entrepreneurial ecosystem enables them to achieve their CE goals. For example, environmental policy regulations play significant roles in the birth and survival of the business. Ecosystems were considered important factors for the circularity of the company since the assessment of product circularity and sustainability in the entire value chain is essential. Table 3.5 presents different actors of the case companies' ecosystem in Finland within this study.

References

Ahola, N. and Tolonen, E. (2021), *The Winning Recipe for a Circular Economy-What Can Inspiring Examples Show Us?*, available at: https://www.sitra.fi/en/publications/the- winning-recipe-for-a-circular-economy/.

Bhatt, B.V., Garg, L. and Chauhan, K.A. (2019), Smarter Economic Opportunities for Surat Metropolitan Region. In *Advances in 21st Century Human Settlements*, available at: https://doi.org/10.1007/978-981-10-8588-8_11.

Bocken, N.M.P., de Pauw, I., Bakker, C. and van der Grinten, B. (2016), "Product Design and Business Model Strategies for a Circular Economy", *Journal of Industrial and Production Engineering*, Vol. 33, No. 5, pp. 308–320.

Bressanelli, G., Adrodegari, F., Perona, M. and Saccani, N. (2018), "The Role of Digital Technologies to Overcome Circular Economy Challenges in PSS Business Models: An Exploratory Case Study", *Procedia CIRP*, Vol. 73, pp. 216–221.

Brown, P., Bocken, N. and Balkenende, R. (2019), "Why Do Companies Pursue Collaborative Circular Oriented Innovation?", *Sustainability (Switzerland)*, Vol. 11 No. 3, pp. 1–23.

Brynjolfsson, E. and Mcafee, A. (2017), "The Business of Artificial Intelligence: How AI Fits into Your Data Science Team", *Harvard Business Review*, July 2017, pp. 1–20.

Centobelli, P., Cerchione, R., Chiaroni, D., Del Vecchio, P. and Urbinati, A. (2020), "Designing Business Models in Circular Economy: A Systematic Literature Review and Research Agenda", *Business Strategy and the Environment*, Vol. 29, No. 4, pp. 1734–1749.

Davidsson, P., Recker, J. and von Briel, F. (2020), "External Enablement of New Venture Creation: A Framework", *Academy of Management Perspectives*, Vol. 34, No. 3, pp. 311–332.

de Sousa Jabbour, A.B.L., Jabbour, C.J.C., Godinho Filho, M. and Roubaud, D. (2018), "Industry 4.0 and the Circular Economy: A Proposed Research Agenda and Original Roadmap for Sustainable Operations", *Annals of Operations Research*, Vol. 270, No. 1, pp. 273–286.

Eckhardt, J.T. and Shane, S.A. (2003), "Opportunities and Entrepreneurship", *Journal of Management*, Vol. 29, No. 3, pp. 333–349.

Eisenhardt, K.M. (1989), "Building Theories from Case Study Research", *Academy of Management Review*, Vol. 14, pp. 532–550.

Ellen MacArthur Foundation. (2015), *Towards a Circular Economy: Business Rationale for an Accelerated Transition*, available at: https://ellenmacarthurfoundation.org/towards-a-circular-economy-business-rationale-for-an-accelerated-transition.

Ellen MacArthur Foundation and Google. (2019), *Artificial Intelligence and the Circular Economy - AI as a Tool to Accelerate the Transition*, available at: https://www.ellenmacarthurfoundation.org/publications.

European Commission. (2020), *A New Circular Economy Action Plan For a Cleaner and More Competitive Europe*, available at: https://eur-lex.europa.eu/legal-content/EN/TXT/?qid=1583933814386&uri=COM:2020:98:FIN.

Geissdoerfer, M., Pieroni, M.P.P., Pigosso, D.C.A. and Soufani, K. (2020), "Circular Business Models: A Review", *Journal of Cleaner Production*, Vol. 277, available at: https://doi.org/10.1016/j.jclepro.2020.123741.

Ghoreishi, M. and Happonen, A. (2020a), "Key Enablers for Deploying Artificial Intelligence for Circular Economy Embracing Sustainable Product Design: Three Case Studies", *AIP Conference Proceedings*, Vol. 2233, American Institute of Physics Inc., p. 050008.

Ghoreishi, M. and Happonen, A. (2020b), "New Promises AI Brings into Circular Economy Accelerated Product Design: A Review on Supporting Literature", *E3S Web of Conferences*, Vol. 158, available at: https://doi.org/10.1051/e3sconf/202015806002.

Henry, M., Bauwens, T., Hekkert, M. and Kirchherr, J. (2020), "A Typology of Circular Start-Ups: Analysis of 128 Circular Business Models", *Journal of Cleaner Production*, Vol. 245, available at: https://doi.org/10.1016/j.jclepro.2019.118528.

Heshmati, A. (2015), "A Review of the Circular Economy and its Implementation by Almas Heshmati::SSRN", *SSR*, available at: https://papers.ssrn.com/sol3/papers.cfm?abstract_id=2713032 (accessed 21 March 2021).

Ingemarsdotter, E., Jamsin, E. and Balkenende, R. (2020), "Opportunities and Challenges in IoT-Enabled Circular Business Model Implementation – A Case Study", *Resources, Conservation and Recycling*, Vol. 162, No. November, p. 105047.

Ivanov, D., Dolgui, A. and Sokolov, B. (2022), "Cloud Supply Chain: Integrating Industry 4.0 and Digital Platforms in the 'Supply Chain-as-a-Service'", *Transportation Research Part E: Logistics and Transportation Review*, Vol. 160, No. February, p. 102676.

Kaplan, J. (2016), *Artificial Intelligence: What Everyone Needs to Know*, Oxford Press, New York.

Kostakis, I. and Tsagarakis, K.P. (2022), "The Role of Entrepreneurship, Innovation and Socio-economic Development on Circularity Rate: Empirical Evidence from Selected European Countries", *Journal of Cleaner Production*, Vol. 348 No. February, p. 131267.

Luoma, P., Toppinen, A. and Penttinen, E. (2021), "The Role and Value of Data in Realising Circular Business Models -A Systematic Literature Review", *Journal of Business Models*, Vol. 9 No. 2, pp. 44–71.

Manyika, J., Chui, M., Brown, B., Bughin, J., Dobbs, R., Roxburgh, C. and Hung Byers, A. (2011), "Big Data: The Next Frontier for Innovation, Competition and Productivity", *McKinsey Global Institute*, No. June, p. 156.

Mcafee, A. and Brynjolfsson, E. (2012), "Big Data: The Management Revolution", *Harvard Business Review*, available at: https://hbr.org/2012/10/big-data-the-management-revolution (accessed 18 April 2021).

Mühlroth, C. and Grottke, M. (2020), "Artificial Intelligence in Innovation: How to Spot Emerging Trends and Technologies", *IEEE Transactions on Engineering Management*, pp. 1–18.

Rajput, S. and Singh, S.P. (2019), "Connecting Circular Economy and Industry 4.0", *International Journal of Information Management*, Vol. 49, No. March, pp. 98–113.

Ranta, V., Aarikka-Stenroos, L. and Väisänen, J.M. (2021), "Digital Technologies Catalyzing Business Model Innovation for Circular Economy—Multiple Case Study", *Resources, Conservation and Recycling*, Vol. 164, No. August 2020, p. 105155.

Stall, S., Yarmey, L., Boehm, R., Cousijn, H., Cruse, P., Cutcher-Gershenfeld, J., Dasler, R., et al. (2018), "Advancing FAIR Data in Earth, Space, and Environmental Science", *Eos*, American Geophysical Union (AGU), Vol. 99, available at: https://doi.org/10.1029/2018eo109301.

Stone, M., Knapper, J., Evans, G. and Aravopoulou, E. (2018), "Information Management in the Smart City", *Bottom Line*, Vol. 31, No. 3–4, pp. 234–249.

Suchek, N., Ferreira, J.J. and Fernandes, P.O. (2022), "A Review of Entrepreneurship and Circular Economy Research: State of the Art and Future Directions", *Business Strategy and the Environment*, Vol. 31, No. 5, pp. 2256–2283.

Sundui, B., Ramirez Calderon, O.A., Abdeldayem, O.M., Lázaro-Gil, J., Rene, E.R. and Sambuu, U. (2021), "Applications of Machine Learning Algorithms for Biological Wastewater Treatment: Updates and Perspectives", *Clean Technologies and Environmental Policy*, Vol. 23, No. 1, pp. 127–143.

Veleva, V. and Bodkin, G. (2018), "Corporate-entrepreneur Collaborations to Advance a Circular Economy", *Journal of Cleaner Production*, Vol. 188, pp. 20–37.

Yin, R.K. (2014), *Case Study Research*, edited by Dickman, Leonard and Rog, D. J., 3rd ed., Sage Publications.

York, J.G. and Venkataraman, S. (2010), "The Entrepreneur–Environment Nexus: Uncertainty, Innovation, and Allocation", *Journal of Business Venturing*, Vol. 25, No. 5, pp. 449–463.

Zucchella, A. and Urban, S. (2019), *Circular Entrepreneurship*, available at: https://doi.org/10.1007/978-3-030-18999-0.

SUSTAINABLE HORIZONS

The authors would like to express their gratitude for the financial support for research and publication of this chapter to Sustainable Horizons funding grant (GA 101071300) from the Horizons Europe Program.

4

ORGANIZATIONAL READINESS OF A MANUFACTURING FIRM FOR SUSTAINABLE BUSINESS GROWTH WITH DIGITAL INITIATIVES

The Role of Sales and Sustainability

Titta Pitman and Jenni Sipilä

1   Introduction

Managers embracing sustainable business growth should consider the economically sustainable growth of a company, that is, business practices that are beneficial to firm's growth. Furthermore, stakeholders increasingly expect companies to assess their performance on environmental factors and society at large in their growth endeavors (Silva et al., 2019). Accordingly, in manufacturing industries, such as paper and steel industries, companies have invested in sustainability issues, such as improving waste management and sourcing more environmentally friendly raw materials. The adoption of new technologies can promote sustainability with integral societal and environmental benefits, particularly through the integration of sustainability into a company's strategy (Saunila et al., 2019). Digital transformation, or Industry 4.0, plays a crucial role in enabling businesses to achieve sustainability goals by leveraging the power of digital technologies and data.

Recently, manufacturing companies have been pressured to adopt the Industry 4.0 paradigm, also known as smart manufacturing, to remain relevant and competitive in the global market (Schumacher et al., 2016). The term "Industry 4.0" was introduced to explain the next industrial revolution (Lasi et al., 2014), which revolutionizes how firms produce, develop, and distribute their products or services using new technologies, such as cloud computing, data analytics, the Internet of Things, and artificial intelligence (AI). The core of the revolution is digital transformation, which is not only a technological change but also a strategic one (Loonam et al., 2018; Matt et al., 2015). Digitalization is an ongoing process (Wengler et al., 2021) that involves all organizational layers of a firm. One major benefit of digitalization is that manufacturing firms can automate their production and thus improve product quality, production efficiency, and machine uptime (McKinsey, 2023). In some industries, the adoption of automation can increase productivity by 20%–30% (Thomas, 2023).

However, the adoption of automation has challenges, such as a lack of strategy for automation, managerial or adoption issues, and gaps in readiness or organizational structure

DOI: 10.4324/9781003433743-5

(Gardner, 2019). Furthermore, due to its complexity, firms often use digitalization to enhance efficiency instead of growing the company (Björkdahl, 2020). Consequently, manufacturing firms experience unique challenges in adopting digital technologies. Manufacturing companies aim to produce items as efficiently and cost effectively as possible without compromising the quality or reliability of production or machines (Bjökdahl, 2020). The increased availability of data enables closer observation of costs and the flow of products, which requires appropriate software to capture the data and skills to code the machines and analyze the captured data.

Furthermore, growth-oriented firms do not expand solely through investments in production technology. They must also effectively market and sell their products and expertise. Just as digitalization has revolutionized industrial manufacturing, it has also profoundly affected the sales industry (Singh et al., 2019). Sales transformation influences all layers of the firm and is necessary in supporting the sales team's success (Lauzi et al., 2023). The sales department is responsible for identifying potential customers, maintaining relationships, and positioning the firms' products or services as valuable solutions. In growth-oriented manufacturing firms, the sales team plays a vital role in driving revenue and business growth. Digital tools and automation can streamline the sales process, enabling sales teams to work more efficiently (Guenzi & Habel, 2020). These tools can automate manual tasks, freeing up time for sales representatives to focus on high-value activities, such as building relationships and closing deals (Lin & Lin, 2023). Digital transformation also facilitates the collection and analysis of vast amounts of data, which can be used to generate accurate sales forecasts and provide valuable insights for sales decision-making (Syam & Sharma, 2018).

Against this background, this study aims to identify the organizational readiness of a growth-oriented small- and medium-sized enterprise (SME) in manufacturing, with digital initiatives, to achieve sustainable growth. Furthermore, we discuss the role of sales and sustainability in sustainable business growth. We approach this objective by addressing the following research questions: How is a growth-oriented manufacturing firm digitalizing and why? What constitutes sustainable business growth, and how can it be achieved? What are the roles of sales and sustainability in a manufacturing firm in the digital era in supporting a company's sustainable growth?

2 Background

2.1 Digitalization in Manufacturing: Industry 4.0

Industry 4.0 is described as "a multidimensional system of value creation that includes... organizational and business-related variables ...technological and manufacturing-related variable... and several interdependencies that co-occur between them" with the purpose of "optimization of production cost while leveraging the trend of mass customization resulting from individual changes in customer needs" (Nosalska et al., 2020, pp. 348, 837).

The core components of Industry 4.0 encompass the interconnection of machines, devices, and people; information transparency, which means that information systems can form digital twins of the physical world; decentralized decision-making, which focuses on autonomous and independent decision-making; and technical assistance, in which the work previously done by humans is transferred to machines (Hermann et al., 2016).

Many manufacturing firms use digitalization to achieve greater efficiency instead of utilizing it for company's growth, possibly due to its simplicity, as well-established and benchmarked procedures have been set for efficiency improvements (Björkdahl, 2020). Simultaneously, firms may not invest in digitalization for innovation and growth due to its unpredictability and complexity (Björkdahl, 2020). Furthermore, some attempts to apply digitalization for profitable growth have failed (Davenport & Spanyi, 2019).

3   Organizational Readiness for Digital Transformation

Digitalization is defined as "a process that aims to improve an entity by triggering significant changes to its properties through combinations of information, computing, communication, and connective technologies" (Vial, 2021, p. 118). Furthermore, digital transformation refers to "a change in how a firm employs digital technologies to develop a new digital business model that helps to create and appropriate more value for the firm" (Verhoef et al., 2021, p. 889). Digitalization serves as a driving force for change, disrupting the entire organization. Major system changes or upgrading to new technology involves several steps that should be organized both inside and outside the organization. Weiner (2009, pp. 1, 6) described organizational readiness for change as an organizational-level construct, a "team property," in which "organizational members' shared resolve to implement a change (change commitment) and shared belief in their collective capability to do so (change efficacy)." Therefore, the team where the change is implemented should be committed to change and have the capability to implement and push through the different phases of the project. According to Hizam-Hanafiah et al. (2020), the company should focus on technology, people, strategy, leadership, process, and innovation to better prepare for digital transformation.

In addition to organizational readiness, to succeed in digitalization initiatives, the organization should align its goals with digital technologies and have top management support for identifying organizational possibilities for using Industry 4.0 technology (De Sousa Jabbour et al., 2018). Firms should also consider whether to maintain all the necessary skills within the organization or have specialized partners to handle major technological changes and IT challenges (Ghobakhloo, 2018) and invest in training and infrastructure to enable cross-functional integration (Pirola et al., 2019).

In SMEs, technological changes should be aligned with the company's business strategy (Gerow et al., 2014; Renaud et al., 2016; Yeow et al., 2018), and middle managers and workers should be closely involved in the process (Machado et al., 2021). In digital initiatives, addressing the technology acceptance or resistance of the staff is crucial. As digital strategy challenges companies due to its dynamism, the alignment of the digital strategy is an ongoing process. According to Bharadwaj et al. (2013), digital strategy is, by nature, multifunctional, and achieving alignment necessitates the concurrent creation and reconfiguration of IT and business resources across organizational activities.

4   Sustainable Business Growth

To ensure a sustainable digital transformation, businesses must consider and assess the environmental, social, and economic impacts of their actions. However, companies can be categorized into different levels of maturity regarding sustainability issues (Vásquez et al., 2021). At a low level of maturity, companies perceive sustainability as isolated from their core business, addressing sustainability issues superficially or not at all. In contrast, at a high level of maturity, companies closely integrate sustainability into their strategies and operations (Vásquez et al., 2021). To integrate sustainability into their strategies and operations, companies are advised to identify sustainability issues relevant to both society and business performance (Porter et al., 2019).

Digitalization plays an important role in developing sustainable strategies and operations. For instance, smart technologies can support the development of highly efficient and sustainable operations, as well as introduce new ways of communicating and collaborating, ultimately contributing to the overall sustainability of the company (Saunila et al., 2019). However, digitalization also poses new challenges, such as issues related to privacy, the use of AI, and surveillance, necessitating the development of digital responsibility programs (Grigore et al., 2017; Lobschat et al., 2021). Ultimately, the benefits of digitalization depend on the responsible application of new technologies (Grigore et al., 2017).

Furthermore, companies exhibit varying motives for engaging in sustainability and for using technology in the context of sustainability (Grigore et al., 2017). On the one hand, companies may engage in sustainability mainly for instrumental and self-serving reasons, such as managing their reputations (Grigore et al., 2017) or enhancing their economic performance (Rasche et al., 2017). On the other hand, companies may have a more altruistic motivation to engage in sustainability, stemming from a perceived duty to serve society (Foreh & Grier, 2003). In general, stakeholders perceive a company's self-serving sustainability motives more negatively than altruistic ones, especially when they perceive that a company is trying to hide its self-serving motives through misleading communication (Foreh & Grier, 2003).

In summary, digitalization plays a crucial role in enabling businesses to achieve sustainability goals when implemented strategically and responsibly. Nevertheless, the varying levels of maturity among companies regarding their sustainability engagement, coupled with instances where sustainability is pursued mainly for reputational reasons without broader societal concerns, present challenges for both research and practical implementation at the intersection of sustainability and digitalization within the business context.

5   Digital Transformation in B2B Sales

As in any business operation, the pursuit of greater efficiency and effectiveness is a priority in B2B sales. Digitalization affects professional salespeople and the sales profession (Guenzi & Nijssen, 2023; Zoltners et al., 2021). The various phases of the sales process can now be analyzed through collected data (Guenzi & Habel, 2020), and digitalization offers new possibilities for value (co-)creation (Guenzi & Nijssen, 2023), such as servitization (Linde et al., 2021). Social media and social selling also provide novel avenues to maintain customer connections (Sombultawee & Wattanatorn, 2022) and aid salespeople in improving performance (Franck & Damperat, 2023; Terho et al., 2022). However, not all aspects of digitalization are positive, as salespeople may experience stress due to technological changes (Guenzi & Nijssen, 2021; Kramer & Krafft, 2023). In addition, acquiring new skills is essential for effectively utilizing emerging sales tools and tactics (Choudhury & Harrigan, 2014; Mattila et al., 2021).

6 Role of Sales in Manufacturing in the Digital Age

By integrating sales strategies with digital transformation initiatives, manufacturing firms can establish a powerful competitive advantage (Zoltners et al., 2021) and gain several benefits. *First*, sales efficiency may be increased, as digital tools and automation can streamline the sales process (Syam & Sharma, 2018). *Second*, digital tools offer data and analytics that provide enhanced customer insights. These insights empower sales teams to tailor their approach, offer personalized solutions, and anticipate customer needs, leading to higher conversion rates and customer satisfaction (Lin & Lin, 2023). *Third*, digital tools provide real-time access to information, enabling rapid responses to customer inquiries, access to product specifications and availability, and accurate quotes and proposals. This approach can help sales representatives be more proactive and responsive, leading to increased productivity and faster sales cycles (Franck & Damperat, 2023; Zoltners et al., 2021). *Fourth*, digital transformation enables sales teams to tap into new markets and customers by leveraging online platforms, social media, and digital marketing strategies (Lamrhari et al., 2022). *Fifth*, digital transformation facilitates the collection and analysis of vast amounts of data, generating accurate sales forecasts and providing valuable insights for sales decision-making. This allows manufacturing firms to make data-driven decisions, allocate resources effectively, identify market trends, and optimize sales strategies for maximum effectiveness and profitability (Syam & Sharma, 2018; Zoltners et al., 2021).

Businesses are increasingly adopting sales enablements to support their sales teams in aligning fragmented firm resources, improving client contacts, and streamlining disorganized sales support operations that impede revenue growth (as seen in Peterson et al., 2021; Gartner, 2019). Conceptualizing sales enablement as a company-wide strategic program that combines the "People, Process, and Performance" (3Ps) benefits both seller

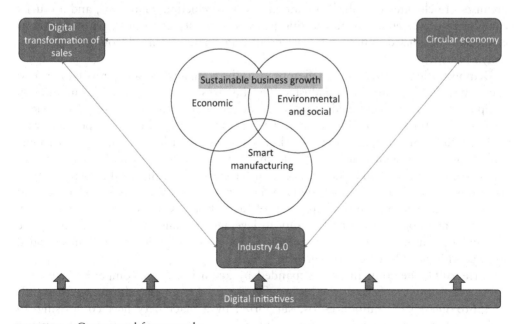

FIGURE 4.1   Conceptual framework.

firms and buyers (Rangarajan et al., 2020). This approach entails close collaboration between the sales team, production, marketing, and other departments to share data and analytics, enhancing performance and customer care.

We summarize our conceptual framework in Figure 4.1, illustrating the interrelations between Industry 4.0, the digital transformation of sales, and cleaner production to result in sustainable business growth.

7   Methodology

The research design is structured around a single case study, examining the readiness for digital transformation in a growth-oriented SME manufacturing firm and exploring the roles of sales and sustainability efforts in achieving sustainable business growth. We employed a qualitative research method to collect and analyze data through face-to-face interviews with the company's executive board. Semi-structured interviews were conducted in June 2023. In addition, data were collected from the company's website, executive meeting presentations, and other materials obtained from the firm. The interview questions were adapted from Machado et al. (2021).

8   Case Company

The company, founded in 1980, operates across three locations and employs approximately 90 individuals. The company offers "technically demanding, high-quality machined products as well as sub-assemblies for machine and equipment manufacturers." The company invested in cutting-edge technology and contemporary industrial automation to ensure cost-effective manufacturing and swift delivery. By utilizing robotics, the company can produce flexibly tailored products, even in small quantities. The premises are climate controlled to maintain ideal production conditions, and a crucial component of the entire manufacturing process is quality controlled, with operations continually optimized to meet customer needs (information sourced from the case company's website).

Demonstrating a growth-oriented approach, the company's strategy revolves around becoming a leading force in the industry. This involves investing in reliable and modern equipment, a commitment evident since the acquisition of the first computer numeric control (CNC) machine in 1999, when the company employed only ten people. From 2005 to 2006, the company moved to larger premises and introduced the first robots and automation systems, such as the flexible manufacturing system. The decisions to automate and expand production capacity in the early 2000s shifted the customer base toward machine and equipment manufacturers. The shift in the business model occurred simultaneously with the strong expansion of the industry. Consequently, the company management recognized the opportunity to leverage machines and robotics to replace human labor for more efficient and profitable serial product production and thus decided to align with the industry's strong growth.

Since 2009, the company has expanded by acquiring other companies, with the latest acquisitions occurring in the last five years. At present, the turnover stands at approximately 20 million euros, supported by a machinery fleet comprising 40 CNC machines and 15 robots, showcasing a high level of automation. The growth

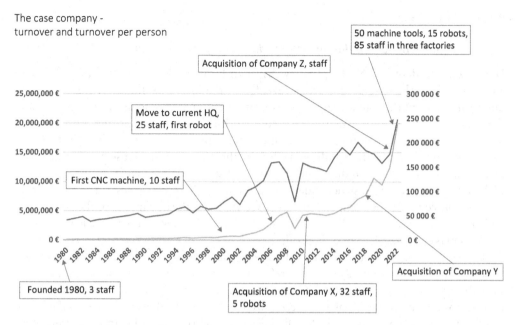

The case company - turnover and turnover per person

FIGURE 4.2   Case company turnover development.

TABLE 4.1 Interviewees

Referred to as	Title/role	Location	Education	Interview duration
Owner A	Owner, Chairman of the Board	HQ, Factory 1	Vocational	3 hours
Owner B	Owner, CFO	HQ, Factory 1	University	1.5 hours
CEO	CEO	HQ, Factory 1	University	1.5 hours
Business Director	Business Director	HQ, Factory 1	Applied science university	1 hour
Sales Manager	Sales Manager	HQ, Factory 1	University	1.5 hours
Production Director	Production Director	HQ, Factory 1	University	1 hour
FM2	Factory Manager	Factory 2	Vocational	1 hour
FM3	Factory Manager	Factory 3	University	

orientation and advanced automation capabilities make this company an ideal case study. The competitive strategy of the company is encapsulated by the term "operational excellence," and the company's turnover development is visually represented in Figure 4.2.

The interviews were conducted face-to-face at the company's premises and lasted for one to three hours (Table 4.1). Utilizing a semi-structured format, the interviewees did not receive the questions in advance. Each interview was recorded and transcribed. Coding was performed in MS Word by selecting entire sentences and associating them with themes and topics discussed. The findings were then synthesized under each theme and topic, and the results are presented in the following chapter.

9 Findings

9.1 *Organizational Conditions and Readiness for Digitalization*

Digitalization, identified as the primary driver in Industry 4.0 (Lasi et al., 2014), plays a crucial role in the case company, as revealed in the interview findings. It serves as an important concept that facilitates the utilization of automated machines and robotics and the collection of key data essential for making critical business decisions. Furthermore, digitalization has enabled more efficient and reliable production. According to the CEO, the paramount benefit of digitalization lies in the elimination of useless routines and mistakes, "We are able to reduce unnecessary and stupid routine work.... when the new ERP is working, we are less dependent on humans in these processes." The production manager agreed, "As the company grows... We want to take advantage of these solutions which lessen human work... We can then control things better and with the least possible work to make the biggest possible profit."

Based on the role and age of the board member, the discussion and focus on digitalization varies. However, the company's history reflects the continuous use of digital technologies since the introduction of the first CNC machine in 1999. Digitalization is not a recent development for the company; it has been recognized as a megatrend, as indicated in the board meeting materials from 2021 to 2023. Digitalization is also discussed within the framework of Industry 4.0–5.0, in which digitalization, software robotics, and factory monitoring and leading through information and knowledge are integral elements of factory systems.

According to Thomas (2023), automation can increase firm's productivity by 20% to 30%. This productivity surge is also mirrored in the case company's growth figures (Figure 4.2). The data collected from various sources, including production machines, human work, customer interactions through sales efforts, and invoicing activities, play a key role in the company's success, profitability, and enhanced work efficiency. Business intelligence (BI) software is employed to analyze this data. The company owner (A) is unequivocal about the reasons for investing in digital initiatives, "Why do anything if it does not improve the performance?"

As the machines are automated, manpower has primarily been tasked with ensuring quality and changing parts. Thus, digitalization has made work easier for employees. This shift also necessitated a change in the skills required by the staff. Real-time alarms and adaptable systems are easily tailored to acceptable data. Keeping up with the changes, for example, in the development of BI software and AI, is challenging, according to the CEO,

Two years ago, I felt I was on top of the BI, now the change is so fast that there is no time to keep up with what is going on in digitalization and development of, for example, BI... Also, AI is developing constantly and somehow, we must find a way to use it in the future.

The manufacturing business is customer oriented. In digital initiatives, customer needs come first. For orders, client portals where information is obtained are available. The integration and access levels of the client portal are customer specific. To respond to changing customer needs, the case company must also evolve. As Owner A stated, "The industry is customer oriented: The customer informs us that they have deployed a new system or platform. Owner B studies the system and introduces it to others in the company."

Every aspect of the company is affected by digitalization: management, infrastructure within the premises (e.g., climate control), production workers, and the entire production process, including CNC machine control, factory automation systems, and information transfer. Digitalization influences the entire value chain, horizontally and vertically. The transition to new enterprise resource planning (ERP) is a major digitalization leap, and management has been entirely focused on this project throughout the current year.

9.2   *Digitalization Strategy and Projects*

Ghobakhloo and Iranmanesh (2021, p. 1540) recommended the "Manufacturing Digitalization Strategic Roadmapping to manage the complexities of digital transformation". This approach includes mapping the current digital stage of the company and outlining action steps for future digital initiatives (Colli et al., 2019). However, the case company does not currently have a digitalization plan or strategy. Digitalization is not solely employed to increase the degree of digitalization but also to enable more efficient production and improve analytics for evaluating both production and business development. The aim is to be at the forefront of the industry, prompting investments in automation and digitalization. The competitive strategy is operational excellence. As Owner B stated, "In our business, we detach chips from steel in a machine, and that is the main thing. Everything else is supporting that and making it possible."

The company purchased its first CNC machine in 1999, marking the beginning of their machine automation. In 2007, the company further invested in robotics. Between 2000 and 2008, the turnover grew from 500,000€ to 5,000,000€. The firm has steadily invested in one to two new machines each year since the early 2000s. ERP investment in 2005 and software investment to improve production flow in 2008 were important steps in digitalization and automation. These steps play a crucial role in integrating the value chain into the same system. Consequently, the time used for production and the actual costs can be calculated, enabling a more accurate offer calculation, and ensuring expected profit. Some machines have digital twins, making it possible to digitally monitor production and receive alerts in case of anomalies. In 2018, a BI system was integrated to create and present data visualizations compiled from various data sources. This strategy was considered as the most important digitalization leap in the company in years. As a production manager stated,

> ...the implementation of Power BI by our CEO has been a huge development. ... different reports, which makes the work at the office easier. [This has resulted in] a focus on utilizing the data better because it is more visible there, and we can go deeper in the wanted details.

The company's digital strategy is to apply digital tools, machines, and software that improve manufacturing efficiency and productivity. No investments are made in haste, and the company sees no benefit in testing or piloting programs or tools. New systems must improve access to and analysis of the desired data. As Owner A said, "It is easier to buy technology that has been tested already."

This year, the company transitioned to a new modern ERP, which is a complicated but necessary change as the old ERP is nearing the end of its lifespan. The new ERP allows the digitalization of work orders; however, the firm management has raised concerns about losing its efficiency. The most important challenges are transferring the data from the old ERP to the new one and making the new ERP work seamlessly. According to Owner B, "When we push 'play' in the new system, we must be certain that it works."

As a benefit of the changeover, the company's three factories will have the same system. The new ERP encompasses the entire production, from raw material sourcing to production, work queues, and billing. This allows for the collection of more data from the machines. The different phases of the process become more visible, and the steerability of machines and processes improves.

9.3   Evaluation of Resources and Investments for Digitalization

Smaller firms often have fewer financial resources, are less resilient to risk, and have less negotiating power with suppliers of technologies (Masood & Sonntag, 2020). To succeed in digital transformation, the management team must have a clear strategic vision and goals to implement the necessary digital initiatives and must have the ability to properly allocate resources in moving the company forward (Moeuf et al., 2020). The company's strategy is to grow, and it can be done by growing the capacity, which means investments in premises, machines, and people or buying existing business or customers' production. As the production manager stated, "We make investments continuously... We have increased demand. Also, in the old ones, the repair cost increases, so we have replaced some machines with new ones. ...and technology is upgraded, too."

Investment in the new ERP is the largest immaterial investment in a long time. During the COVID-19 pandemic, the company also invested in green studio technology to enable virtual factory tours. Quality controls are conducted by internal and external audits, but digital investments are not similarly evaluated. Investments are made only in tested and proven technology. According to the CEO, "We are a high-quality company that has very high delivery reliability... the customers give us good feedback, and we are an award-winning partner. We offer world-class products and services. I am proud to work in this company."

The success of digitalization is measured by its results. For instance, product quality is measured, and machines that do not produce high-quality products are sold. Thus far, no investments have failed. Furthermore, when a company grows, the risks involved in a single decision are reduced. The chairman of the board (Owner A) evaluates the success, stating, "It is measured by the results. Everything in the big picture is transformed into euros. Either by the growth of the turnover or profit."

9.4   Data, Data Analytics, and Key Performance Indicators

Data are collected in each production process, as the production manager explained,

> I would like to say we collect data in each step [of the production]. The work is divided into different phases, and we measure time in each step... The workers feed the information ... the software has the clock running to see how long each step takes. ... we compare the cost to the time used and how many items we have produced... Some machines have their own software to count the utilization degree of the machine... we can see how many hours per day the machine is used.

The company measures lead times, quality, sales, efficiency, productivity, and performance (by products and by customers). The data are used to analyze production efficiency and to make business decisions regarding improvements and investments. The management considers the data and analytics to be extremely important in making justified business decisions. Power BI is linked with many data sources where it collects the data, "We need to produce high quality sellable products. With the time that is efficiently used" (Owner B).

In a broader context, the company must be profitable. Profitability can be damaged by incorrect pricing or if the products are not moved as planned. Due to the business model, some products should be stocked, and the stock flow must be monitored. The business is based on selling time, directly affecting the bottom line by several euros the company makes per hour.

The key performance indicators (KPIs) used in the case company include the following:

- Profit earning capacity or productivity
- Profitability (product or customer)
- Product lead time
- Accrual (the balance of the planned hours compared to actual hours in producing an item)
- Capacity to produce high-quality products
- Delivery reliability

10   Digital Capabilities

To succeed in digital transformation and keep the production facilities modern and competitive, management should have sufficient digital capabilities (Pessot et al., 2022) regarding the firm's processes, skills, structures, knowledge, and technology (Hirvonen & Majuri, 2021). The members of the executive board believe that the case company's management has sufficient digital capabilities. Many members mentioned how important the application of BI analytics has been in obtaining better data for analysis for the board. If the people at the top have no interest or experience in applying new technologies, then the company can fall behind from the development and lose its competitive advantage. In several interviews, the CEO was mentioned as a key person in smart manufacturing. However, given the speed of change, even the CEO thinks that he is falling off the digital wagon. As Owner A stated, "We try to stay onboard."

However, management capabilities related to digitalization have not been measured. At the executive board level, each member is responsible for developing their own digital capabilities. Nevertheless, this does not apply to newly purchased software or machinery, as everybody, including factory production workers, is trained to use the new software and machinery. The training happens based on needs. If knowledge or skill gaps exist, then the person will be trained accordingly. As a production manager said,

We discuss those projects that are part of digitalization, but we do not discuss that our aim is to increase our digitalization degree or maturity. Digitalization is a no-brainer, I think, and we apply it everywhere where it makes sense, but it is not an end in itself.

10.1   Challenges after the Application of Digital Technologies and Automation

As the machines and the programs to run them are complex, workers need new skills to use them. However, monitoring production becomes easier as the machines work. According to Ghobakhloo et al. (2022), employees may find it challenging to adjust to new technologies. Accordingly, the interviewees think that resistance to change is the most important challenge at every level in the case company. As the sales manager stated, "The resistance to change [to new technology] is always there."

However, usually after the initial stiffness, everything works quite well when the first stage of resistance is overcome. Other challenges involve taking full advantage of digital technologies and having the time to keep up with the race.

11   Digital Transformation of B2B Sales

The digital transformation of B2B sales forces organizations to consider new sales practices; old business practices should be unlearned to incorporate new routines that include digital technologies (Mattila et al., 2021). To successfully transform the sales function, organizations should understand that digitalization is an ongoing and evolving process that requires full management support (Wengler et al., 2021). Depending on organizational structure and quantity of business transactions and clients, companies integrate new digital sales tools into their customer relationship management (CRM) systems, such as AI (Chatterjee et al., 2021) or social media applications (Choudhury & Harrigan, 2014; Lamrhari et al., 2022). As in most digital initiatives, the transformation aims to gain efficiency and improve sales results. However, in many companies, digital transformation fails (Davenport & Westerman, 2018).

In the case company, the sales manager discussed digitalization from the digital marketing perspective, which they outsourced to a marketing agency. Today, Facebook and LinkedIn visibility are considered very important. Because of the COVID-19 pandemic, the company invested in the green studio concept, where they can host virtual factory tours. A sales manager said,

> Good example [about digital marketing] is our virtual factory tours ... We can showcase our world-class production machines. Our customers have been very grateful because they save time... if they are located five-hour drive away and all they need is a Teams connection... We can actually show more in our virtual factory tour than in actual factory tour.

Digitalization affects sales in the case company's industry. A substantial change is the customer–supplier interface. Previously, selling required more active manual labor, thus limiting the number of suppliers. With current customer portals, a large network of suppliers can be easily managed. A lot of information is stored in the portal, so salespeople can save time and focus on different things than before. According to a business director,

> Sales is more automatic nowadays... There is a lot of information available, and you can easily see who has the lowest price. Pricing is nowadays way more—not aggressive, but lose. Nobody is negotiating the prices as the purchasing is automatic.

Customers can utilize the portals for bidding competitions. However, this has not changed the business model, mainly because the portal is a different way of receiving customer orders. However, it has changed sales as a profession, as the business director explained,

> It is easier for me to go online and make an order. This is digitalization. If I call some-one and they take my order and write it on the paper, the potential to make a mistake is huge... This all has changed so that we are pushed to online [to do our business]... More incompetent staff is hired on the customer interface... You only meet once or twice a year asking "how are you doing and bring a box of chocolate?"... The human contact has lost its meaning... Sales as we have known it before does not exist any-more. There is no sales as a profession anymore... It is all fake. If you only meet once or twice a year, how do you get to know anyone?

Sales data are collected and analyzed by comparing the offers and actual deals. The key KPIs in sales are supply security, customer profitability, product profitability, and cus-tomer's gross profit accrual.

When asked what digital sales tools were used in the company, the business direc-tor responded "none." He said that CRM is not used because the potential cus-tomer register can be maintained in Excel. The existing customer base is established on long-standing B2B relationships, and the products are highly specialized, cus-tomer-optimized products. The competitive strategy is operational excellence rather than based on low prices and mass production (Treacy & Wiersema, 1993). Sales planning has development potential, as they have aimed to grow by one million euros per year. However, no investment plans have been considered for modern sales tech-nology. AI is considered as a future potential. The management has high hopes for the capabilities of new ERP, as it aids with offer calculations and raw-material-availability estimations.

Social media plays a major role in digital marketing, and the company uses Facebook and LinkedIn. Digital marketing is done with a partner because they have expertise in the area. The CEO stated,

> We use social media for brand image marketing... It [social media] has a big role in employee acquisition and to build our company image... We use Facebook, LinkedIn, our website, and newsletter... The purpose is to raise awareness [of our company]... when we contact new potential customers, we hope they have heard about us... that they would have a positive image about us. We have seen good results [in our HQ employee acquisition] through social media... we got good job applications [to open positions].

The management team believes that sales support is sufficient, as the hierarchy is consid-erably low, and individuals in the company are easy to reach. A sales manager stated that a sense of ongoing support among the staff is being provided, "We get lots of support if needed. Support can come from the owners or the production manager. We have very good cooperation here with everyone."

12   Supporting Company's Growth with Digitalization

Björkdahl (2020) concluded that manufacturing firms maximize the advantage of digital initiatives and utilize them to improve efficiency. However, the interviews revealed that the case company has identified several ways to improve competitiveness with automation and digitalization, which include the following:

1 Improved effectiveness. Fewer people are needed to do the same work. Shifts with no human labor can be applied to some production processes.
2 Less mistakes can result in more stable production.
3 Improved quality. Machines can produce better and more-precise-quality products compared to human labor. Machines do not tire with time and consistently produce the same quality.
4 Improved flow. Better production planning and effective use of machines, which improves effectiveness.
5 Less unproductive work. Machines replace human work.
6 Predict customer needs and then match them.
7 Added value to the customers, such as attaching RFID chips to their products so they can automatically acknowledge the delivery.

Due to digitalization, the company has not changed its business model, as stated by the CEO,

> The customers are forcing us to use their portals, which means it makes no sense for us to start developing a world where they would assumingly enter... The challenge is that customers' needs and systems are so different [from one another] that it would be very difficult to integrate them all somehow into the same system.

In the case company's industry, creating new business models is challenging. Platform-based businesses have been tested by another company, but the model would not complement the case company, as their products are highly customized.

However, customer needs and products have changed. Quality control has improved as machines can do continuous measurements and adjust production to meet the required quality. This measurement service has added a new line of business to the case company, which, however, is not yet very large. As Owner A stated,

> The design and planning for products and machines have changed a lot... As we have purchased more capable machines, we can offer more demanding products to our customers... The customers' changing needs could not be fulfilled with old machinery or production methods. Or it would be so expensive that nobody would pay such prices... The measuring equipment has evolved so that already during the production the machine measures the products' dimensions and makes the required changes [to meet the customer requirements].

13   Sustainability

Sustainable business growth involves generating long-term value for the firm, its stakeholders, and society while minimizing the negative environmental and social impacts of its operations. In this regard, the case company's maturity level is currently relatively low, as exemplified by the low level of sustainability considerations in the core strategy and internal activities of the company (Vásquez et al., 2021). Furthermore, the focus of sustainability engagement is to respond to customers' expectations. The interviews revealed that the company aims to collect expectations and tips from customers regarding what is important for them. However, the company does not currently engage in systematic materiality analysis, which reveals sustainability issues with the greatest impact on a broader set of stakeholders and businesses (Whitehead, 2017). To illustrate this concept, the CEO explained how sustainability is discussed with customers, "What they intend, like, during the next five years to do about this, what it means for, like, the suppliers, and so on, so that we would understand that."

The main motivation behind the company's sustainability engagement is extrinsic (Grimstad et al., 2020), which is reflected in the company's hopes that sustainability engagement will provide a competitive advantage and can be used to improve the company's marketing image. Thus, sustainability is seen from an instrumental perspective (Rasche et al., 2017), which implies that sustainability engagement is expected to advance the economic performance of the company. As the CEO stated,

> They [the customers] do ask about these. Tons [of CO_2] and, and other things, but, like, as a starting point if we then brand ourselves, like this, that. We always offer the lowest carbon option.
>
> Within a two to three-year time window, this could be, like, a significant competitive advantage.

The company mainly approaches sustainability through the environmental dimension and, more specifically, CO_2 emissions, potentially because this is an issue requested by customers. Despite acknowledging the importance of CO_2 emission reduction, the company does not currently perceive itself as having considerable control over its CO_2 emissions and does not have accurate data or calculations to support the development of its activities in this regard. Nevertheless, the company has identified some opportunities to reduce its CO_2 emissions, such as short transportation distances. The CEO explained,

> …this green transition carbon footprint issue, so, so we cannot much. Influence that. In steel, the tons [of CO_2] are what they are.
>
> …for carbon footprint calculation, so we do not have the numbers now. We should be able to tell that. This is 20%. For example. [interviewer: "yep"] 20% lower carbon footprint. This channel of ours.

The company is also considering megatrends, particularly from the customer needs point of view, and focusing on climate change, which affects businesses as they are required to reduce their carbon emissions. The future with renewable hydrogen interests the company, and it is involved in working committees in which a more sustainable future in manufacturing is discussed.

In addition, social sustainability is mentioned from the perspective of threats to mental health and the increasing level of surveillance, which are the negative societal impacts of digitalization. Interestingly, however, these issues are considered as external threats rather than issues that the company could influence, such as through a more systematic corporate digital responsibility engagement. As a business director stated, "But somehow the. Orwellian worldview, like, puzzles me a bit. Because we are pretty close already, after all, like, people are apathetic."

Another demonstration of the company's narrow conception of sustainability issues is that they do not currently acknowledge the sustainability implications of their current operations. For instance, the company already prioritizes high-quality products, which can potentially be more durable and therefore sustainable than their lower-quality counterparts; however, this is not viewed as a sustainability topic. The same applies to efficiency. The company acknowledges that digitalization allows for efficiency but does not consider this as a sustainability topic. In addition, the virtual factory tours and remote working environments mentioned earlier can have sustainability benefits; however, the interviewees still do not view them from this perspective. These observations may serve as a starting point as the company develops its sustainability engagement in the future.

14   Future: Feelings and Thoughts about Digitalization

The feelings and thoughts regarding the future and the impact of digitalization varied from positive to negative. As FM2 stated, "I feel a bit conflicted about digitalization. I am fearfully waiting for my retirement. Maybe I should just go to the cave and find some reindeer fur and live there."

Mental health was also raised, as digitalization may have negative side effects and cause technostress or anxiety. Furthermore, cybersecurity is a concern, as the company identifies threats to privacy, as well as company data. As Owner B considered, "When will Elon Musk have some chips implanted on our heads, and as soon there is an email, you will have to rush to read it?"

The potential of AI and machine learning has also been recognized. However, the company does not yet have enough skills or resources to explore that avenue. Especially in production, AI can assist in coding and organizing work queues in the future. However, undoubtedly, humans will remain necessary in conducting final check-ups and ensuring that the machines function properly.

Digitalization should make lives easier and is considered as an enabler, especially in the company's current business model. Unnecessary routines can be eliminated, and resources can be allocated to more productive work. One problem is finding people who have the skills to tap to all the potential. In summary, several possibilities exist, and to utilize their advantages properly, the executive board must make the right and smart decisions.

15   Discussion

15.1   Reflection on the Findings and Theoretical Contributions

Industry 4.0, also called smart manufacturing, has transformed the manufacturing industry (Schumacher et al., 2016). Digitalization affects technology, the people who use it, and the business processes involved (Nosalska et al., 2020). Digitalization enables companies to automate their production and manufacture products faster and more cost efficiently, serving as the foundation for a company's growth. However, Björkdahl (2020) suggested that firms use digitalization to achieve greater efficiency instead of growth, potentially because digitalization is complex, and rapid change causes management to struggle to grow their businesses. With this background, we use a qualitative research method to study a growth-oriented case company and investigate how the company utilizes digital initiatives to grow sustainably.

In this study, we found that the manufacturing firm was digitalizing its production facility, manufacturing processes, and systems to enhance its data flow, efficiency, profitability, quality, and customer satisfaction, thus enabling business growth. Furthermore, while sustainable business growth encompasses economic, environmental, and social sustainability, that is, the triple bottom line (Norman & MacDonald, 2004), the latter two are not yet at the core of this manufacturing firm. In addition, sales played a crucial role in the manufacturing firm by facilitating the adoption of digital solutions, building trust and loyalty with customers, and creating new market opportunities. However, the company has not yet taken advantage of digital sales tools, and the digital transformation of sales is not at the core of the company's development initiatives.

These findings contribute to the emerging field of research at the intersection of digitalization and sustainable business by revealing their interconnections, as well as the related challenges of a manufacturing SME. Given that prior research has studied these concepts mostly in isolation (Isensee et al., 2020), our study synthesizes prior research on sustainability and digitalization in the context of SMEs, therefore serving as an inspiration for a broader research agenda for this important topic. Consistent with prior research on Industry 4.0 (Ghobakhloo, 2020), this study confirms that a manufacturing firm primarily focuses on digitalizing its production to gain efficiency and profitability. However, contrary to Björkdahl's (2020) suggestion that manufacturing firms do not use digitalization to expand the company, we conclude that, besides gaining efficiency, growth may be one of the main reasons for a manufacturing firm to digitalize and automate production.

Furthermore, our study aligns with previous research (see, e.g., De Sousa Jabbour et al., 2018), suggesting that top management team's support is crucial for successful digital initiatives. In our study, the management team had a shared goal, which was clear to all members, aiding the organization in adopting new technologies despite the encountered resistance. Our study also showed that in an SME, the recruitment of key managers is an important decision, as they bring with them digital capabilities and skills that will either benefit or hinder the firm's digital transformation.

The economic component of sustainability was successfully pursued by the case company, such as by investing in modern manufacturing technology. However, the company is less mature regarding environmental and social sustainability engagements. Among these, environmental sustainability is addressed to a greater extent, whereas social sustainability is the most challenging sustainability dimension for the case company, which aligns with prior research on manufacturing firms' sustainability engagement (Eslami et al., 2019). Given the widespread acknowledgment of the positive impacts of Industry 4.0 on economic and environmental sustainability and the lack of consensus about its influence on social sustainability in academic research (Sartal et al., 2020), our study confirmed the acute need to understand social sustainability in the context of Industry 4.0 among academics and practitioners.

We also investigated the role of sales in sustainable business growth and found that the studied manufacturing industry is customer oriented, with highly customized and high-quality products. This often results in long-standing B2B relationships. However, the company aims to grow and is thus keen on developing new partnerships. Prior research suggests that digital transformation challenges the salesforce to unlearn old routines and identify new selling methods using digital technologies (Mattila et al., 2021). Our findings show that the digital transformation of sales is not at the top of digitalization priorities in a SME manufacturing firm. The low adoption of digital technologies can be due to the missing skills or understanding of the available digital solutions or can be the result of resistance to adopting them in a customer-driven environment (Giovannetti et al., 2022). Prior research suggests that salespeople may employ new sales technology if they can gain productivity or efficiency with it, and the most important obstacles are the lack of technical assistance and management, with training proving to be the most successful strategy for boosting adoption (Buehrer et al., 2005). Our findings suggest that salespeople do not see the benefits of adopting digital technologies for their sales practices. Sales management benefits from the digitalization of production and processes, as they obtain accurate data and analysis to sell profitably. However, digital transformation, which refers to the modification of business processes and models in B2B sales (Guenzi & Habel, 2020), remains in an early phase.

We also found that customer experience is influenced by digital initiatives, often because customers request change (Giovannetti et al., 2022). Sales as a profession is greatly affected by digital transformation, which was also evident in the case company. In this industry, "old-fashioned" sales work is dead, as buyers and sellers often meet only once or twice a year, and customer representatives are hired to handle basic tasks. Relationship building requires new ways of using digital channels, and relationship building no longer seems valuable. Business is done increasingly online, and even more work tasks will be handled by AI in the near future. As suggested in a prior study (Ghobakloo, 2018), the case company uses a partner—a marketing agency—to manage their digital marketing, including social media.

16   Managerial Implications

In practice, the EU is pushing companies toward sustainability, as it requires large companies and listed SMEs to report their impact on the environment, human rights, social standards, and work ethics, which are based on common standards, for the first time in the 2024 fiscal year (European Parliament, 2022). This initiative is part of the European green deal (European Commission, n.d.), aiming to help company's stakeholders in examining the sustainability performance of firms. This also affects non-listed SMEs, as they are often part of large companies' value chains. The case company participated for the first time in the EcoVadis sustainability rating, as suggested by one of their major partners. Thus, other partners have not required any kind of sustainability rating. However, EcoVadis is used globally by over 100,000 companies across multiple industries and in more than 175 countries (EcoVadis, n.d.). Focusing on sustainability efforts beforehand to match the requirements is beneficial for companies. This strategy may provide a clear competitive advantage, especially in the near future.

From the perspective of sustainability, our analysis of the empirical case reveals several development opportunities for the company and potentially more broadly for the manufacturing industry. First, we recommend employing a strategic approach to sustainability, such that sustainability is not viewed as a "mandatory add-on to business as usual" but rather as an opportunity to add long-term value to the company, its stakeholders, and the society at large (Polman & Winston, 2021). In this context, the first points of departure can be the training of key management and, subsequently, the entire organization in sustainable business, the identification of key stakeholders' interests, the establishment of regular stakeholder dialog, and the identification and management of sustainability risks (Crane & Matten, 2010). Furthermore, articulating a clear sustainability ambition, identifying material sustainability issues, embedding sustainability in the entire organization, producing business model innovations, and collaborating with various stakeholders can likely support the development of a company's sustainability activities (Kiron et al., 2017). Analyzing the company's contribution to the United Nations Sustainable Development Goals (United Nations, n.d.) can serve as a fruitful starting point for the future development of the company's sustainability engagement.

Managers can benefit from sustainable business growth in several ways. Sustainable business practices can help companies establish a positive reputation and differentiate themselves from competitors. By becoming more efficient in their processes and manufacturing, companies can reduce costs and increase profits. Increased social responsibility can attract and retain employees, which can increase workforce engagement. Furthermore, sustainable business practices can mitigate risks by proactively addressing environmental and social issues. All these steps can help managers create long-term value for the company while contributing to a more sustainable future.

Based on our analysis of the case company, we see development potential from a sales perspective. Sales management can benefit from exploring modern sales technology, specifically from more detailed customer analytics. Business may be lost if customer needs in quantity cannot be met. Some sort of sensing system should be obtained to recognize whether a customer is doing something that possibly means that they have an opportunity to sell more. There is a skills and knowledge gap in the use of generative AI, which can be filled either by recruiting technologically capable staff or outsourcing it to a partner (Ghobakhloo, 2018). We suggest that when recruiting new staff, companies should also pay attention to the required digital skills and capabilities of the particular role. Contemporary digital marketing and sales tools can improve customer engagement, enhance and boost the skills and performance of salespeople, and create new ways to support a customer-focused business model. Is the company failing at digital transformation if it does not modify its business model? Or is it industry-specific to require a business model change to succeed? (see Ibarra et al., 2018; Kastalli & Van Looy, 2013).

17   Limitations and Opportunities

This study has several limitations. This is a single case study, and the findings vary depending on the industry or the exact size of the company. We did not study sustainable growth from an acquisition perspective. The case company has also grown by acquiring companies. Seemingly, sustainability has not been one of the measures considered when purchasing another firm. However, companies should focus on sustainability and the sustainable growth potential of the companies acquired in the future as the EU is advocating for more sustainable value chains.

References

Bharadwaj, A., Sawy, O. A., Pavlou, P. A., & Venkatraman, N. (2013). Digital business strategy: Toward a next generation of insights. *MIS Quarterly, 37*(2), 471–482.

Björkdahl, J. (2020). Strategies for digitalization in manufacturing firms. *California Management Review, 62*(4), 17–36. https://doi.org/10.1177/0008125620920349

Buehrer, R. E., Senecal, S., & Pullins, E. B. (2005). Sales force technology usage—reasons, barriers, and support: An exploratory investigation. *Industrial Marketing Management, 34*(4), 389–398.

Chatterjee, S., Chaudhuri, R., Vrontis, D., Thrassou, A., & Ghosh, S. K. (2021). Adoption of artificial intelligence-integrated CRM systems in agile organizations in India. *Technological Forecasting and Social Change, 168*.

Choudhury, M. M., & Harrigan, P. (2014). CRM to social CRM: The integration of new technologies into customer relationship management. *Journal of Strategic Marketing, 22*(2), 149–176.

Colli, M., Berger, U., Bockholt, M., Madsen, O., Møller, C., & Wæhrens, B. V. (2019). A maturity assessment approach for conceiving context-specific roadmaps in the Industry 4.0 era. *Annual Reviews in Control, 48*, 165–177.

Crane, A., & Matten, D. (2010). *Business ethics: Managing corporate citizenship and sustainability in the age of globalization*. Oxford University Press.

Davenport, T. H., & Spanyi, A. (2019). Digital transformation should start with customers. *MIT Sloan Management Review*. https://sloanreview.mit.edu/ article/digital-transformation-should-start-with-customers/

Davenport, T. H., & Westerman, G. (2018). Why so many high-profile digital transformations fail. *Harvard Business Review, 9*(4), 15.

De Sousa Jabbour, A. B. L., Jabbour, C. J. C., Foropon, C., & Godinho Filho, M. (2018). When titans meet—can Industry 4.0 revolutionise the environmentally-sustainable manufacturing wave? The role of critical success factors. *Technological Forecasting and Social Change, 132*, 18–25.

EcoVadis. (n.d.). Sustainability ratings for global supply chains. https://ecovadis.com/solutions/ratings/

Eslami, Y., Dassisti, M., Lezoche, M., & Panetto, H. (2019). A survey on sustainability in manufacturing organisations: Dimensions and future insights. *International Journal of Production Research, 57*(15–16), 5194–5214.

European Commission. (n.d.) The European green deal: Striving to be the first climate-neutral continent. https://commission.europa.eu/strategy-and-policy/priorities-2019-2024/european-green-deal_en

European Parliament. (2022). New social and environmental reporting rules for large companies. European Parliament News Online. https://www.europarl.europa.eu/news/en/press-room/20220620IPR33413/new-social-and-environmental-reporting-rules-for-large-companies

Foreh, M. R., & Grier, S. (2003). When is honesty the best policy? The effect of stated company intent on consumer skepticism. *Journal of Consumer Psychology, 13*(3), 349–356.

Franck, R., & Damperat, M. (2023). How social media use enhances salesperson performance. *Journal of Business & Industrial Marketing, 38* (8), 1720–1737. https://doi.org/10.1108/JBIM-02-2022-0082

Gardner, C. (2019). Predictions 2020: Automation strike teams and services rise to fend off a paradox. Forrester Online Blog. https://www.forrester.com/blogs/predictions-2020-automation/

Gartner. (2019). Optimizing sales enablement to accelerate and win more deals. https://www.gartner.com/en/marketing/ research/optimizing-sales-enablement-to-accelerate-and-win]

Gerow, J. E., Grover, V., Thatcher, J., & Roth, P. L. (2014). Looking toward the future of IT-business strategic alignment through the past: A meta-analysis. *MIS Quarterly, 38*(4), 1159–1186.

Ghobakhloo, M. (2018). The future of manufacturing industry: A strategic roadmap toward Industry 4.0. *Journal of Manufacturing Technology Management, 29*(6), 910–936.

Ghobakhloo, M. (2020). Industry 4.0, digitization, and opportunities for sustainability. *Journal of Cleaner Production, 252*.

Ghobakhloo, M., & Iranmanesh, M. (2021). Digital transformation success under Industry 4.0: A strategic guideline for manufacturing SMEs. *Journal of Manufacturing Technology Management, 32*(8), 1533–1556.

Ghobakhloo, M., Iranmanesh, M., Vilkas, M., Grybauskas, A., & Amran, A. (2022). Drivers and barriers of Industry 4.0 technology adoption among manufacturing SMEs: A systematic review and transformation roadmap. *Journal of Manufacturing Technology Management, 33*(6), 1029–1058. https://doi.org/10.1108/JMTM-12-2021-0505.

Giovannetti, M., Sharma, A., Cardinali, S., Cedrola, E., & Rangarajan, D. (2022). Understanding salespeople's resistance to, and acceptance and leadership of customer-driven change. *Industrial Marketing Management, 107,* 433–449.

Grigore, G., Molesworth, M., & Watkins, R. (2017). New corporate responsibilities in the digital economy. In Theofilou, A., Grigore, G., Stancu, A. (eds)., *Corporate social responsibility in the post-financial crisis era: CSR conceptualisations and international practices in times of uncertainty.* Palgrave Studies in Governance, Leadership and Responsibility, Palgrave Macmillan, Cham, pp. 41–62. https://doi.org/10.1007/978-3-319-40096-9_3.

Grimstad, S. M. F., Glavee-Geo, R., & Fjørtoft, B. E. (2020). SMEs motivations for CSR: An exploratory study. *European Business Review, 32*(4), 553–572.

Guenzi, P., & Habel, J. (2020). Mastering the digital transformation of sales. *California Management Review, 62*(4), 57–85.

Guenzi, P., & Nijssen, E. J. (2021). The impact of digital transformation on salespeople: An empirical investigation using the JD-R model. *Journal of Personal Selling & Sales Management, 41*(2), 130–149.

Guenzi, P., & Nijssen, E. J. (2023). The relationship between digital solution selling and value-based selling: A motivation-opportunity-ability (MOA) perspective. *European Journal of Marketing, 57*(3), 745–770.

Hermann, M., Pentek, T., & Otto, B. (2016). Design principles for Industrie 4.0 scenarios. *49th Hawaii International Conference,* pp. 3928–3937.

Hirvonen, J., & Majuri, M. (2020). Digital capabilities in manufacturing SMEs. *Procedia Manufacturing, 51,* 1283–1289.

Hizam-Hanafiah, M., Soomro, M., & Abdullah, N. (2020). Industry 4.0 readiness models: A systematic literature review of model dimensions. *Information, 11*(7), 364. https://doi.org/10.3390/info11070364

Ibarra, D., Ganzarain, J., & Igartua, J. I. (2018). Business model innovation through Industry 4.0: A review. *Procedia Manufacturing, 22,* 4–10.

Isensee, C., Teuteberg, F., Griese, K. M., & Topi, C. (2020). The relationship between organizational culture, sustainability, and digitalization in SMEs: A systematic review. *Journal of Cleaner Production, 275.*

Kastalli, I. V., & Van Looy, B. (2013). Servitization: Disentangling the impact of service business model innovation on manufacturing firm performance. *Journal of Operations Management, 31*(4), 169–180.

Kiron, D., Unruh, G., Reeves, M., Kruschwitz, N., Rubel, H., & ZumFelde, A. M. (2017). Corporate sustainability at a crossroads. *MIT Sloan Management Review, 58*(4).

Kramer, V., & Krafft, M. (2023). When and how information and communication technology orientation affects salespeople's role stress: The interplay of salesperson characteristics and environmental complexity. *European Journal of Marketing, 57*(3), 659–682.

Lamrhari, S., El Ghazi, H., Oubrich, M., & El Faker, A. (2022). A social CRM analytic framework for improving customer retention, acquisition, and conversion. *Technological Forecasting and Social Change, 174.*

Lasi, H., Fettke, P., Kemper, H. G., Feld, T., & Hoffmann, M. (2014). Industry 4.0. *Business & Information Systems Engineering, 6,* 239–242.

Lauzi, F., Westphal, J., Rangarajan, D., Schaefers, T., Parra-Merono, M. C., & De-Juan-Vigaray, M. D. (2023). Understanding sales enablement in complex B2B companies: Uncovering similarities and differences in a cross-functional and multi-level case study. *Industrial Marketing Management, 108*, 47–64.

Lin, S., & Lin, J. (2023). How organizations leverage digital technology to develop customization and enhance customer relationship performance: An empirical investigation. *Technological Forecasting and Social Change, 188*.

Linde, L., Frishammar, J., & Parida, V. (2021). Revenue models for digital servitization: A value capture framework for designing, developing, and scaling digital services. *IEEE Transactions on Engineering Management, 70*(1), 82–97.

Lobschat, L., Mueller, B., Eggers, F., Brandimarte, L., Diefenbach, S., Kroschke, M., & Wirtz, J. (2021). Corporate digital responsibility. *Journal of Business Research, 122*, 875–888.

Loonam, J., Eaves, S., Kumar, V., & Parry, G. (2018). Towards digital transformation: Lessons learned from traditional organizations. *Strategic Change, 27*(2), 101–109.

Machado, C. G., Winroth, M., Almström, P., Ericson Öberg, A., Kurdve, M., & AlMashalah, S. (2021). Digital organisational readiness: Experiences from manufacturing companies. *Journal of Manufacturing Technology Management, 32*(9), 167–182.

Masood, T., & Sonntag, P. (2020). Industry 4.0: Adoption challenges and benefits for SMEs. *Computers in Industry, 121*.

Matt, C., Hess, T., & Benlian, A. (2015). Digital transformation strategies. *Business & Information Systems Engineering, 57*, 339–343.

Mattila, M., Yrjölä, M., & Hautamäki, P. (2021). Digital transformation of business-to-business sales: What needs to be unlearned? *Journal of Personal Selling & Sales Management, 41*(2), 113–129.

McKinsey. (2023). Unlocking the industrial potential of robotics and automation. Online article. https://www.mckinsey.com/industries/industrials-and-electronics/our-insights/unlocking-the-industrial-potential-of-robotics-and-automation

Moeuf, A., Lamouri, S., Pellerin, R., Tamayo-Giraldo, S., Tobon-Valencia, E., & Eburdy, R. (2020). Identification of critical success factors, risks and opportunities of Industry 4.0 in SMEs. *International Journal of Production Research, 58*(5), 1384–1400.

Norman, W., & MacDonald, C. (2004). Getting to the bottom of "triple bottom line." *Business Ethics Quarterly, 14*(2), 243–262.

Nosalska, K., Piątek, Z. M., Mazurek, G., & Rządca, R. (2020). Industry 4.0: Coherent definition framework with technological and organisational interdependencies. *Journal of Manufacturing Technology Management, 31*(5), 837–862. https://doi.org/10.1108/JMTM-08-2018-0238

Pessot, Z. A., Battistella, C., Rocchi, V., Sala, A., & Sacco, M. (2021). What matters in implementing the factory of the future: Insights from a survey in European manufacturing regions. *Journal of Manufacturing Technology Management, 32*(3), 795–819. https://doi.org/10.1108/JMTM-05-2019-0169

Peterson, R. M., Malshe, A., Friend, S. B., & Dover, H. (2021). Sales enablement: Conceptualizing and developing a dynamic capability. *Journal of the Academy of Marketing Science, 49*, 542–565.

Pirola, F., Cimini, C., & Pinto, R. (2019). Digital readiness assessment of Italian SMEs: A case-study research. *Journal of Manufacturing Technology Management, 31*(5), 1045–1083. https://doi.org/10.1108/JMTM-09-2018-0305

Polman, P., & Winston, A. (2021). The net positive manifesto. *Harvard Business Review, 99*(5), 124.

Porter, M., Serafeim, G., & Kramer, M. (2019). Where ESG fails. *Institutional Investor, 16*(2).

Rangarajan, D., Dugan, R., Rouziou, M., & Kunkle, M. (2020). People, process, and performance: Setting an agenda for sales enablement research. *Journal of Personal Selling & Sales Management, 40*(3), 213–220.

Rasche, A., Morsing, M., & Moon, J. (2017). The Changing Role of Business in Global Society: CSR and Beyond. In A. Rasche, M. Morsing, & J. Moon (Eds.), *Corporate Social Responsibility: Strategy, Communication, Governance* (pp. 1–30). Cambridge University Press.

Renaud, A., Walsh, I., & Kalika, M. (2016). Is SAM still alive? A bibliometric and interpretive mapping of the strategic alignment research field. *The Journal of Strategic Information Systems*, *25*(2), 75–103.

Sartal, A., Bellas, R., Mejías, A. M., & García-Collado, A. (2020). The sustainable manufacturing concept, evolution and opportunities within Industry 4.0: A literature review. *Advances in Mechanical Engineering*, *12*(5).

Saunila, M., Nasiri, M., Ukko, J., & Rantala, T. (2019). Smart technologies and corporate sustainability: The mediation effect of corporate sustainability strategy. *Computers in Industry*, *108*, 178–185.

Schumacher, A., Sihn, W., & Erol, S. (2016). Automation, digitization and digitalization and their implications for manufacturing processes. In *Innovation and Sustainability Conference Bukarest* (pp. 1–5). Elsevier.

Silva, S., Nuzum, A. K., & Schaltegger, S. (2019). Stakeholder expectations on sustainability performance measurement and assessment: A systematic literature review. *Journal of Cleaner Production*, *217*, 204–215.

Singh, J., Flaherty, K., Sohi, R. S., Deeter-Schmelz, D., Habel, J., Le Meunier-FitzHugh, K., ... & Onyemah, V. (2019). Sales profession and professionals in the age of digitization and artificial intelligence technologies: concepts, priorities, and questions. *Journal of Personal Selling & Sales Management*, *39*(1), 2–22.

Sombultawee, K., & Wattanatorn, W. (2022). The impact of trust on purchase intention through omnichannel retailing. *Journal of Advances in Management Research*, *19*(4), 513–532.

Syam, N., & Sharma, A. (2018). Waiting for a sales renaissance in the fourth industrial revolution: Machine learning and artificial intelligence in sales research and practice. *Industrial Marketing Management*, *69*, 135–146.

Terho, H., Mero, J., Siutla, L., & Jaakkola, E. (2022). Digital content marketing in business markets: Activities, consequences, and contingencies along the customer journey. *Industrial Marketing Management*, *105*, 294–310.

Thomas, S. (2023). 100+ significant automation statistics in 2023. MarketSplash Online Business article. https://marketsplash.com/automation-statistics/#link2

Treacy, M., & Wiersema, F. (1993). Customer intimacy and other value disciplines. *Harvard Business Review*, *71*(1), 84–93.

United Nations. (n.d.). THE 17 GOALS. https://sdgs.un.org/goals

Vásquez, J., Aguirre, S., Puertas, E., Bruno, G., Priarone, P. C., & Settineri, L. (2021). A sustainability maturity model for micro, small and medium-sized enterprises (MSMEs) based on a data analytics evaluation approach. *Journal of Cleaner Production*, *311*.

Verhoef, P. C., Broekhuizen, T., Bart, Y., Bhattacharya, A., Dong, J. Q., Fabian, N., & Haenlein, M. (2021). Digital transformation: A multidisciplinary reflection and research agenda. *Journal of Business Research*, *122*, 889–901.

Vial, G. (2021). Understanding digital transformation: A review and a research agenda. *Managing Digital Transformation*, *28*(2), 13–66.

Weiner, B. J. (2009). A theory of organisational readiness for change. *Implementation Science*, *4*(67). https://doi.org/10.1186/1748-5908-4-67

Wengler, S., Hildmann, G., & Vossebein, U. (2021). Digital transformation in sales as an evolving process. *Journal of Business & Industrial Marketing*, *36*(4), 599–614.

Whitehead, J. (2017). Prioritizing sustainability indicators: Using materiality analysis to guide sustainability assessment and strategy. *Business Strategy and the Environment*, *26*(3), 399–412.

Yeow, A., Soh, C., & Hansen, R. (2018). Aligning with new digital strategy: A dynamic capabilities approach. *The Journal of Strategic Information Systems*, *27*(1), 43–58.

Zoltners, A. A., Sinha, P., Sahay, D., Shastri, A., & Lorimer, S. E. (2021). Practical insights for sales force digitalization success. *Journal of Personal Selling & Sales Management*, *41*(2), 87–102.

5

INTERACTION BETWEEN TECHNOLOGICAL, ECONOMIC, AND SOCIAL CHANGES

Hiranmoy Roy, Parveen Kumar Sharma and Hari P. Sharma

1   Introduction

The most significant and least known factor influencing the cost of future climate change mitigation is technological progress. According to scientific studies, there is a need to modify government strategies to specific energy technologies because long-term trends in the innovation process and focus, also known as "technology life cycles," vary across these sectors. The investigators, experts, and policymakers from all over the globe are becoming interested in the social innovation (SI) paradigm, which is remarkableIt is still understudied in the humanities and social sciences and has grown into a "buzzword" as well as a "container notion". Social transformation and conflict are two factors that interact. Social change is fueled by conflict, but social change also fuels conflict. These ailments can appear in both huge and tiny proportions. A constant process of change occurs in every civilization.

Numerous avenues exist for distinct cultures to evolve, and some civilizations change more quickly than others. These changes may be substantial or little, and their processes may be lengthy or swift. Social values, conventions, organizational behavior, institutions, strata, power, authority, and interpersonal relationships may all change in a society. If a new study addresses one of these two qualities—urgent or interesting—then it will be worthwhile. The phrase "sustainability transitions" refers to significant social adjustments required to address important societal problems. Existing systems are disrupted by these transitions, such as the energy transition. They are propelled by social movements, outsiders, and prevailing actors. Research on sustainability transitions tries to comprehend these changes' dynamics and causes, provide analytical tools, and create governance methods to avoid lock-in. Environment, water, assets, food, mobility, medical care, educational opportunities, and transforming regions, cities, and populations towards sustainability are just a few of the several industries and fields it encompasses. Conflict is necessary for both complete social transformation and sweeping social change. It will be worthwhile if new research addresses at least one of the two qualities—urgent and interesting. Global enterprises and society have been impacted by the major

DOI: 10.4324/9781003433743-6

technical, economic, and sociological advancements brought forth by COVID-19. The interaction between socioeconomic circumstances, welfare regimes, and economic results is the main emphasis of the current investigation's examination of SI ecosystems utilizing the idea of SI regimes.

2 Review of Literature

Siregar, in 2022, employed discourse relation analysis to examine the associations between various variables while delineating each context-dependent element.

The analysis's conclusions bolstered the significance and sensitivity of the argumentative perspective in uncovering and explaining the connection underlying disagreement and societal change. The research study aimed to gather contrasting viewpoints on the correlation between dispute and social transformation. The findings of the study held considerable implications for the forecasting and portrayal of the social circumstances that prevailed prior to and following conflicts or other social transformations.

Sun et al. (2021) revealed a favorable encouraging and significant correlation between knowledge transfer and a nation's performance in energy efficiency. The regional innovation potential had been crucial for reducing energy consumption and carbon emissions without impeding the growth of the global economy. The examination revealed a significant and satisfactory correlation between the expansion of knowledge and the attainment of local green energy objectives from 1994 to 2013. The study analyzed data from the Triadic Patents Persons database of the Organizational for Economic Development, encompassing 24 innovative nations. The study assessed the effectiveness of each nation's innovation endeavors in relation to the energy efficiency initiatives undertaken by neighboring countries. The USA, France, the UK, the Netherlands, and the Swiss nation were regarded as some of the most economically efficient countries, even though all nations exhibited a consistent upward trend in efficiency. These findings emphasized the importance of fostering domestic renewable energy development, which carries policy implications for promoting environmentally friendly energy consumption and safeguarding the natural surroundings.

Terstriep et al. (2020) conducted a study on the favorable SI ecosystems. According to Murray et al. (2010), Rettel and Webber (1973), and Weber and Khademian (2008), for example, wicked problems were identified as those that presented challenges or were impractical to solve due to their involvement with numerous variables, contradictory or incomplete knowledge, and a significant financial burden. These issues were also emphasized in the research. The study relied on data provided by both European investigation initiatives, Boosting the Impact of Social Innovation in Europe through Economic Underpinnings (SIMPACT) and Social Innovation – Driving Force of Social Change (SI-DRIVE). As an analytical strategy, the study employed regional innovation to reflect on the SI ecosystem. The findings of the study revealed that research on regional innovation systems required the integration of various complementary disciplines of expertise to facilitate opportunities for education and cross-sector innovation. Additionally, the study uncovered a connection between rural self-organization strategies and autonomous collectives, which fostered SI. Another aspect of the research focused on identifying suitable business models.

Pan et al. (2019) investigated the internal dynamic connection between environmental government oversight, scientific advancement, and power efficiency. The researchers utilized Vector Autoregression (VAR) and directed acyclic graph approaches to examine the data. The findings from the evaluation of the directed acyclic graph indicated the presence of various behavioral channels through which market incentives accelerated technological progress and exerted a direct influence on energy efficiency. The Structural Vector Autoregression (SVAR)-model-based decomposition of predicted error variance validated the notion that, in the short term, no noticeable distinction existed between environmental policies that provided market incentives for energy efficiency and those that were command based. Moreover, throughout both the immediate and distant future, advancements in technology played a pivotal role in facilitating the advancement of energy conservation.

Wittmayer et al. (2019) examined the descriptions of transformation that four socially innovative initiatives provided, presenting potential alternatives to the then-prevailing neoliberal capitalist system. Furthermore, the study highlighted the significant role played by narratives of change (NoC) in developing social and individual identities, as well as the efforts undertaken to establish widely embraced worldviews. The study concluded that NoC tested the model of change advocated by socially innovative initiatives by exposing flaws within the existing systems and suggesting a possible improvement.

Li (2018) examined the nation's "Industry 4.0" strategy in conjunction with the country's "Made-in-China 2025" plan to ascertain China's position within the plan. Based on the data, China was not the country with the lowest labor costs or the most dominant high-tech industry. Nonetheless, the evidence indicated an increasing trend in investment in human capital, dedication to scientific and technological advancements, and the ability to develop production capacity. This study contributed to our understanding of the link between technological innovation and socioeconomic changes in developing nations.

Loorbach et al. (2017) carried out a study on sustainability transitions, which emerged as an independent field of research focused on the nonlinear dynamics of social change. This research has had significant implications for policies and societies in response to pressing societal concerns. Referred to increasingly as transformational science, the study of transitions underwent multidisciplinary development alongside societal changes and public discourse. It fostered a unique culture of interdisciplinarity, with active research groups operating at the intersection of science and society. The field has played a pivotal role in promoting the growth of interdisciplinary and transdisciplinary approaches in academia, shaping what is now commonly known as "complex persistent problems" knowledge in policy and society.

Hobson and Lynch (2016) investigated a strategy for economic expansion and a sustainable future, the circular economy, which gained traction in the European Union. Forms of participation through technical means were overvalued, and the role of the consumer was depoliticized. The sharing economy was addressed to demonstrate how consumer habits lead to discrepancies between anticipated advantages and socio-environmental effects. Alternative socioeconomic plans for a more radical CE were explored, including degrowth and "the diverse economy." However, CE proponents asserted that their agenda was "radical," despite its incapacity to address numerous deeply ingrained consumer and consumption-related concerns and its echoes of problematic agendas for environmentally friendly consumption and lifestyles. The CE needed to be open to more "radical" criticism and reassessment if it was to bring about the substantial reforms that its proponents asserted were within everyone's reach.

Huenteler et al. (2016) examined the technological life cycles of wind and solar electricity from 1963 to 2009. Wind power accompanied the developmental stages of advanced objects and systems, but solar photovoltaics (PVs) sustained a continuous life cycle sequence of producing vast amounts of goods and commodities. The findings indicated that although the construction of wind turbines approximated the overall lifespan of complex items and systems, solar PV technologies followed the trend of goods that were mass-produced. These results highlighted the need to adapt technology policy to reflect the characteristics of emerging technologies as well as the various creative and educational processes in the field of energy innovations. They also assisted in conceptualizing earlier contradictory data regarding the historical effects of advancements in technology initiatives.

Cajaba-Santana (2014) conducted a study on technological forecasting and social change. The research discovered that realm of SI propelled society forward. Methods for social creativity were previously categorized into structuralist and agentic approaches. The study's main goal was to explore innovative thinking as a catalyst for societal transformation. Additionally, it emphasized the indispensability of SI as a framework for subsequent studies that relied on institutional and structural theories. The study primarily focused on SI that was developed through legislative social actions.

Edwards-Schachter et al. (2012) examined the primary concerns explored in previously published research regarding the concept of SI, its objectives, and unique characteristics associated with identifying individuals' needs, citizen participation, and improving quality of life. They proposed the utilization of a living-lab approach for collaborative place-based innovation, placing particular emphasis on the disparities observed between the requirements of senior citizens and the emergence of commercial prospects. The investigation delved into several definitions of diverse types of innovation presented by scholars such as Edwards-Schachter et al. (2012). The adoption of a socio-technological innovation framework and an enhanced awareness of innovation were suggested. A fundamental aspect was comprehending how to facilitate and establish connections among individuals.

Norton and Toohey (2011) claimed that poststructuralist notions concerning vocabulary, personality, and authority provided novel perspectives on language and educational matters. An exploration was undertaken into sociocultural theories of language learning, the development of investment, FORMED GROUP IDENTITIES, conventional qualitative research methodologies, and global investigations of identity and language education. Furthermore, poststructuralist concepts of location, subjectivity, and language were scrutinized. Moreover, the focus was on the identities of linguistic learners and the impact of consumer resistance on language learning. Subsequent studies should emphasize the creation of conditions and procedures that were more autonomous and inclusive for language teaching and learning.

Loorbach (2010) argued that an innovative paradigm for governance, known as "transition management," was based on the principles of complex systems theory and novel approaches to governance. It provided a platform for rationally addressing long-term societal changes and offered an analytical perspective on them. Empirical testing was conducted in the Netherlands and Belgium, but further research was needed to adapt it to different situations and cultural norms. The study described the transition management approach for environmentally friendly development governance. Around 2000, in the Netherlands, the distinction between four primary categories of administrative operations and their respective contributions to social change was established through a combination of deductive and inductive development. In this section, the theoretical foundations of transition management were exemplified by showcasing the Dutch national energy transition project.

Moulaert et al. (2005) examined alternative models of local innovation. The study discovered that SI played a role in governing urban communities. The study's main goal was to understand the importance of practical advancements within the theoretical structure of social science and how they could be employed to thoroughly analyze local governance and economic expansion. Special emphasis was given to SI in neighborhood development and its various applications in different social science disciplines. The findings revealed that alternative models for local innovation were employed as analytical tools for empirical research. Furthermore, the study highlighted the need for further exploration into the realm of SI.

S. no.	Year	Author	Locale	Major findings
01	2005	Moulaert et al.	UK	This paper explored different models of local innovation of the past 20 years to grasp the significance of tangible progressions in social science and their application in analyzing local governance and economic growth. It emphasized the necessity for additional investigation in the field of SI.
02	2010	Loorbach	Netherlands, the USA, and Belgium	This paper explored transition management as an innovative paradigm for governance, drawing upon complex systems theory and advanced governance methodologies. Empirical testing was conducted in the Netherlands and Belgium, yielding valuable insights. However, additional research was required to modify it to suit diverse contexts and cultural norms.
03	2011	Norton and Toohey	Canada	This paper examined poststructuralist concepts of vocabulary, personality, and authority in language and educational affairs. It concentrated on sociocultural theories of language learning, investment, FORMED GROUP IDENTITIES, traditional qualitative research approaches, and worldwide studies of identity and language education.
04	2012	Edwards-Schachter et al.	USA	The study explored the notion of SI, exploring its goals and defining features. A living-lab approach was introduced to foster collaborative place-based innovation, shedding light on the disparities between the requirements of elderly individuals and the income resources at their disposal. Furthermore, a framework for socio-technical innovation was proposed, contributing to a deeper comprehension of innovation. The capacity to connect individuals and serve as a bridge was deemed essential.

(Continued)

(Continued)

S. no.	Year	Author	Locale	Major findings
05	2014	Cajaba-Santana	Europe	In the study conducted on technical foresight and social change, it was discovered that groundbreaking social technology acted as a driving force for societal transformation. The research underscored the importance of employing SI as a paradigm for subsequent investigations that focused on implementing social policies.
06	2016	Huenteler et al.	USA	This study has examined the technological life cycles of wind and solar electricity from 1963 to 2009. Wind power accompanied the development of advanced objects and systems, while solar PVs followed the trend of mass-produced goods. These results highlighted the need to adapt technology policy to reflect emerging technologies and creative and educational processes. They also helped conceptualize earlier contradictory data regarding the historical effects of technology initiatives.
07	2016	Hobson and Lynch	UK	This study has investigated a strategy for economic expansion and a sustainable future, the circular economy. They found that forms of participation through technical means were overvalued, and the role of the consumer was depoliticized. Alternative socioeconomic plans for a more radical CE were explored, but CE proponents asserted that their agenda was "radical" despite its incapacity to address consumer and consumption-related concerns. The CE needed to be open to more "radical" criticism and reassessment if it was to bring about substantial reforms.
08	2017	Loorbach et al.	UK	This study has conducted a study on sustainability transitions, which emerged as an independent field of research focused on the nonlinear dynamics of social change. This research has had significant implications for policies and societies in response to pressing societal concerns. It has fostered a culture of interdisciplinarity, with active research groups operating at the intersection of science and society.

(*Continued*)

(Continued)

S. no.	Year	Author	Locale	Major findings
09	2018	Li	China	This study has examined China's "Industry 4.0" strategy and "Made-in-China 2025" plan to assess its position in the plan. Evidence showed an increasing trend in investment in human capital, dedication to scientific and technological advancements, and production capacity. This study contributed to understanding the link between technological innovation and socioeconomic changes in developing nations.
10	2019	Wittmayer et al.	USA	This study has examined the descriptions of transformation provided by four socially innovative initiatives. It highlighted the role of NoC in developing social and individual identity and concluded that NoC tested the model of change advocated by socially innovative initiatives.
11	2019	Pan et al.	China	This study has examined the internal dynamic relationship between environmental government control, scientific advancement, and power efficiency. In order to analyze the data, they utilized directed acyclic graph methods and VAR. The findings have revealed that market incentives stimulated technical advancement and had a direct influence on energy efficiency. The notion that there existed no noticeable disparity in the short term between environmental policies that granted market incentives for energy efficiency and those that were command-based was corroborated by SVAR-model-based decomposition of expected error variance.
12	2020	Terstriep et al.	Europe	This study has examined SI ecosystems, with a specific emphasis on wicked problems. They utilized data from SIMPACT and SI-DRIVE to analyze the dynamics of the SI ecosystem. The study applied regional innovation as a lens to investigate the ecosystem, revealing that rural self-organization strategies and autonomous collectives played a significant role in fostering SI.

(*Continued*)

(Continued)

S. no.	Year	Author	Locale	Major findings
13	2021	Sun et al.	USA, France, Netherlands, and Swiss nation	This study discovered a noteworthy connection between knowledge transfer and a nation's energy efficiency performance from 1994 to 2013. The investigation examined data from the Triadic Patents Persons database of the Organizational for Economic Development, encompassing 24 inventive nations. The USA, France, the UK, the Netherlands, and the Swiss nation were recognized as some of the most economically efficient countries, even though all nations demonstrated a consistent upward trend in efficiency. These discoveries underline the significance of nurturing domestic renewable energy development.
14	2022	Siregar	UK	This study employed discourse relation analysis to investigate correlations between variables and distinguish each context-specific component. The findings carried implications for predicting and portraying social situations before and after conflicts or other social changes occurred.

So, the gap identified in the literature is the significance of tangible innovation and their application in analyzing the economic growth and energy efficiency. Also empirical testing was conducted in the Netherlands and Belgium, yielding valuable insights in this empirical testing of impact of growth rate and potential of renewable power on innovation index. In the literature it is also found that the VAR model was used as a robust econometric method to test this relationship.

Thus, the objective of our study is to investigate the impact of growth rate and potential of renewable power on innovation index in Indian context.

3   Methods

3.1   Data and Model Specification

Literature with respect to interaction between technological, economic, and social changes explained that there is a positive relationship between innovation index, growth rate, and potential of renewable power. This study empirically validates this relationship, taking all the states of India for which the data of three indicators of innovation index are available on Niti Ayog. The data on renewable power and growth rate has been taken from MoSPI. All the data are available for the year 2021–2022. The dependent variable in our study is the innovation index and the independent variables are growth rate and potential of renewable power. This study investigates the possible impact of innovation index on growth rate and potential of renewable power. The independent variables are carefully chosen, based on previous literature and availability of data for the selected period. We have used VAR model to test this relationship.

The equation of the model is

$$IID = \beta + \beta_1 PRP + \beta_2 GR$$

Where IID (innovation index) is the dependent variable; PRP (potential of renewable power) and GR (growth rate) are independent variables; and β_1 and β_2 are coefficients of PRP and GR.

4   Results and Discussion

4.1   Descriptive Statistics

IID has a mean of 14.64, a median of 13.76, a standard deviation of 3.32, a skewness of 1.84, a kurtosis of 7.54, and a Jarque–Bera test p-value of 0.000. This indicates that the data is slightly positively skewed and has heavy tails. GR has a mean of 3.93, a median of 7.29, a standard deviation of 6.94, a skewness of –0.68, a kurtosis of 2.02, and a Jarque–Bera test p-value of 0.169. This indicates that the data is slightly negatively skewed and has a mesokurtic distribution.

PRP has a mean of 3.34, a median of 1.15, a standard deviation of 4.51, a skewness of 1.75, a kurtosis of 5.37, and a Jarque–Bera test p-value of 0.000. This indicates that the data is slightly positively skewed and has very high tails. In the Table 5.1 of descriptive statistics, the standard deviation of all the three selected variables is in the range of 3.3 to 6.9, which shows that there is not a very high difference between the standard deviations of all the three variables.

TABLE 5.1 Descriptive statistics

Variables	IID	GR	PRP
Mean	14.636367	3.928233	3.343333
Median	13.760000	7.285000	1.150000
Maximum	27.00000	11.43000	18.20000
Minimum	10.97000	–10.34000	0.100000
Std. deviation	3.315481	6.936041	4.514703
Skewness	1.843037	–0.684356	1.745595
Kurtosis	7.541635	2.018110	5.371733
Jarque–Bera	42.76699	3.546849	22.23691
Probability	0.000000	0.169751	0.000015
Sum	438.7100	117.8470	100.3000
Sum – sq. dev.	318.7801	1395.151	591.0937
Observation	30	30	30

Source: Authors' calculations.

Abbreviations: GR, growth rate; IID, innovation index; PRP, potential of renewable power.

In general, the data for all the three variables are spread out fairly evenly, with no outliers. However, the PRP variable has the most extreme values.

5 Stationarity Tests

The stationary condition has been tested using Augmented Dickey–Fuller (ADF) and Phillips–Perron (PP) test statistics. The unit root test results on the individual data series are shown as below:

The findings show that all the three variables are stationary. According to the ADF test statistic and PP test statistic at the first difference, the parameters of innovation index, growth rate, and potential of renewable power are estimated to be –5.176488, –5.699087, and –6.672519, respectively. The null hypothesis is rejected since the test statistics are higher than the critical values at 1%, level of significance. As a result, IID, GR, and PRP are all considered stationary variables.

TABLE 5.2 Unit root test results for innovation index at first difference

Null hypothesis: D(IID) has a unit root		
Exogenous: Constant		
Lag length: 0 (Automatic – based on AIC, maxlag = 7)		
Augmented Dickey–Fuller test statistic	t-Statistic: -5.176488	Prob. *: 0.0002

Source: Authors' calculations.

Abbreviation: AIC, Akaike information criterion.

*MacKinnon (1996) one-sided p-value

TABLE 5.3 Unit root test results for growth rate at first difference

Null hypothesis: D(GR) has a unit root		
Exogenous: Constant		
Lag length: 0 (Automatic – based on AIC, maxlag = 7)		
Augmented Dickey–Fuller test statistic	t-Statistic: -5.699087	Prob. *: 0.0001

Source: Authors' calculations.

*MacKinnon (1996) one-sided p-value.

TABLE 5.4 Unit root test results for potential of renewable power at first difference

Null hypothesis: D(PRP) has a unit root		
Exogenous: Constant		
Lag length: 0 (Automatic – based on AIC, maxlag = 7)		
Augmented Dickey–Fuller test statistic	t-Statistic: –6.672519	Prob.*: 0.0000

Source: Authors' calculations.

*MacKinnon (1996) one-sided p-value.

TABLE 5.5 Unit root test results for innovation index at first difference

Null hypothesis: D(IID) has a unit root		
Exogenous: Constant		
Bandwidth: 0 (Newly West Automatic – based on Bartlett Kenel)		
Phillips–Perron test statistics	t-Statistic: -5.176488	Prob. *: 0.0002

Source: Authors' calculations.

*MacKinnon (1996) one-sided p-value.

TABLE 5.6 Unit root test results for growth rate at first difference

Null hypothesis: D(GR) has a unit root		
Exogenous: Constant		
Bandwidth: 0 (Newly West Automatic – based on Bartlett Kenel)		
Phillips–Perron test statistics	t-Statistic: -5.699087	Prob. *: 0.0001

Source: Authors' calculations.

*MacKinnon (1996) one-sided p-value.

TABLE 5.7 Unit root test results for potential of renewable power at first difference

Null hypothesis: D(PRP) has a unit root		
Exogenous: Constant		
Bandwidth: 0 (Newly West Automatic – based on Bartlett Kenel)		
Phillips–Perron test statistics	t-Statistic: −6.672519	Prob. *: 0.0000

Source: Authors' calculations.

*MacKinnon (1996) one-sided p-value.

6   Vector Autoregression

To anticipate systems of linked time series and to examine the dynamic effects of random disturbances on the system of variables, VAR is frequently utilized. By considering each endogenous variable in the system as a function of all the endogenous variables in the system and their lag values, the VAR method avoids the necessity for structural modeling.

The coefficients for lagged indicators of potential of renewable power and growth rate are statistically significant at 5% and 1%, respectively, and innovation index had the desired sign. The growth rate was unaffected significantly by the innovation index. Although growth rate did not significantly affect IID, the coefficient of lagged GR and PRP had a negative sign. The regression analysis reveals a positive correlation between the dependent variable and GR, with a rise in GR correlated with a rise in the dependent variable. No significant correlation was found between PRP and the dependent variable, IID (–1) and GR(-I), and PRP (–1). However, a positive intercept was observed, indicating that even if all independent variables were 0, the dependent variable would still have a positive value. Overall, the findings suggest a favorable connection between GR and the dependent variable IID, with no significant effect from GR. In conclusion, the VAR

TABLE 5.8 VAR results

	ID	GR	PRP
IID (-1)	-0.084243	0.325323	0.072053
	(0.20603)	(0.44234)	(0.27630)
	[-0.40889]	[0.73546]	[0.26077]
GR(-I)	-0.098115	0.014821	0.184542
	(0.09807)	(0.21055)	(0.13152)
	[-1.00048]	[0.07039]	[1.40315]
PRP (-1)	0.152282	-0.035047	-0.303470
	(0.15969)	(0.34286)	(0.21416)
	[0.95360]	[-0.102221]	[-1.41700]
c	19.63277	2.524571	-2.148431
	(4.39388)	(9.43364)	(5.89269)
	[4.46821]	[0.26761]	[-0.36459]
R-squared	0.217228	0.128441	0.211682
Adj. R-squared	-0.006421	-0.120576	-0.013551
Sum – sq. resids	247.6480	1141.558	445.4161
S.E. equation	3.434059	7.372916	4.605463
F-statistic	0.971291	0.515793	0.939834
Log likelihood	-7024754	-91.64150	78.46554
Akaike AIC	5.517681	7.045821	-7846554
Schwarz SC	5.580732	7.378873	6.437733
Mean dependent	14.64036	3.852393	3.282143
S.D. dependent	3.423088	6.964961	4.574572

Source: Authors' calculations.

Note: Standard errors in () and t-statistics in [].

Abbreviation: SC, Schwarz Criterion; VAR, Vector Autoregression.

results support the intriguing finding that there is substantial evidence that the potential of renewable energy has favorably affected India's innovation index in different states but not growth rate.

Figure 5.1 shows a visualization of the factors being considered right now. An impulse response function's graph demonstrates how a variable respond to a single shock to another variable. The amount of the reaction in each state, the sign of the response, the direction of the change (positive or negative), and the shape of the response curve all show how the response changes over states. There is undoubtedly some parallel trending behavior, which points to potential cointegration between the variables' innovation index, potential of renewable power, and growth rate. Although the question that the trend may be adequately captured by a deterministic linear function of time, in the following we'll assume that the conditions are met by allowing for unit roots with an intercept term that is capable of being absorbed into the cointegration relation. However, we could not do a temporal (over time) study due to non-availability of year-wise data set at the state level on the selected variables.

Several elements, such as the slowdown in the economy, the performance of the agricultural and primary sectors, the output of the industrial and manufacturing sector, public investment, employment and migration, fiscal management, natural disasters, and the

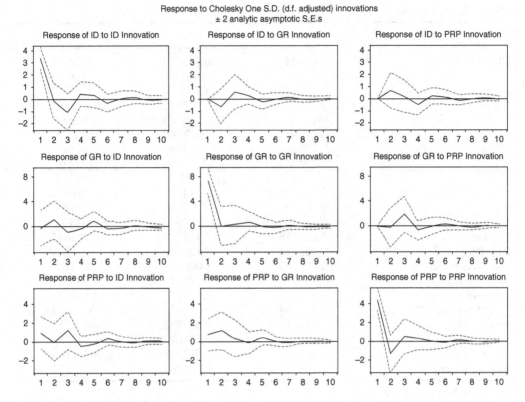

Response to Cholesky One S.D. (d.f. adjusted) innovations
± 2 analytic asymptotic S.E.s

FIGURE 5.1 Graph impulse response.

political climate, can be blamed for the declining growth rate in Chhattisgarh, Manipur, Nagaland, and Madhya Pradesh in 2019–2020. The economic development of these states may have been affected by variables including local problems, governmental policies, and global economic variables.

The government programs in Delhi, such as the startup environment and research and development, helped the innovation index rise in 2019–2020. Finding the major drivers requires validating data from trustworthy sources.

Progressive renewable energy policies, including feed-in tariffs, tax advantages, and financial incentives, have been adopted in Gujarat and Sikkim. Gujarat's geography and coastline make it perfect for offshore wind farms, while Sikkim's numerous rivers and water sources provide potential for hydropower. Governments at the state level promote environmental issues, infrastructural development, and renewable energy programs.

7 Conclusion

The SI paradigm has a significant impact on how much it costs to mitigate climate change. Conflict resolution, societal change, and sustainable transitions are all part of it. Global businesses and society have been touched by the COVID-19 pandemic, which has prompted study on sustainable transitions. Utilizing the idea of SI regimes, this study investigates SI ecosystems. Using information from Niti Ayog, the study confirms the association

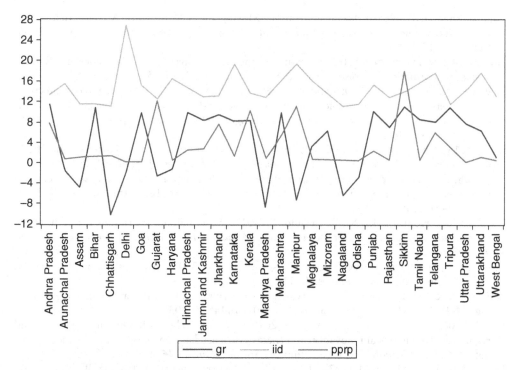

FIGURE 5.2   Graphical representation of growth rate, innovation index, and renewable of power in all the states of India.

between the innovation index, growth rate, and potential of renewable power in all Indian states. The growth rate is a stationary variable that has little effect on the innovation index. According to the regression analysis, the dependent variable (IID) and GR have a positive association, with an increase in GR being connected with a rise in the IID.

The surprising discovery that the potential of renewable energy has positively impacted India's innovation index in various states, but not growth rate, is supported by the VAR results. Growth rates of Chhattisgarh, Manipur, Nagaland, and Madhya Pradesh are expected to slow in 2019–2020 as a result of a number of factors, including the economy's slowdown, the performance of the agricultural and primary sectors, the industrial and manufacturing sector's output, public investment, employment and migration, fiscal management, natural disasters, and the political environment.

Delhi's government initiatives, including startup ecosystems and R&D, helped the innovation index increase in 2019–2020. Gujarat and Sikkim have enacted progressive renewable energy policies, including feed-in tariffs, tax breaks, and financial incentives. State governments support environmental causes, infrastructure improvement, and renewable energy programs.

References

Edwards-Schachter, M. E., Matti, C. E., & Alcántara, E. (2012). Fostering quality of life through Social Innovation: A living lab methodology study case. *Review of Policy Research, 29*(6), 672–692. https://doi.org/10.1111/j.1541-1338.2012.00588.x

Cajaiba-Santana, G. (2014). Social innovation: Moving the field forward. A conceptual framework. *Technological Forecasting and Social Change, 82*, 42-51. https://doi.org/10.1016/j.techfore.2013.05.008

Hobson, K., & Lynch, N. (2016). Diversifying and de-growing the circular economy: Radical social transformation in a resource-scarce world. *Futures, 82*, 15–25.

Huenteler, J., Schmidt, T. S., Ossenbrink, J., & Hoffmann, V. H. (2016). Technology lifecycles in the energy sector — Technological characteristics and the role of deployment for innovation. *Technological Forecasting and Social Change, 104*, 102–121. https://doi.org/10.1016/j.techfore.2015.09.022

Li, L. (2018). China's manufacturing locus in 2025: With a comparison of "Made-in-China 2025" and "Industry 4.0". *Technological Forecasting and Social Change, 135*, 66–74.

Loorbach, D. (2010). Transition management for sustainable development: A prescriptive, complexity-based governance framework. *Governance, 23*(1), 161–183. https://doi.org/10.1111/j.1468-0491.2009.01471.x

Loorbach, D., Frantzeskaki, N., & Avelino, F. (2017). Sustainability transitions research: transforming science and practice for societal change. *Annual Review of Environment and Resources, 42*, 599–626.

Moulaert, F., Martinelli, F., Swyngedouw, E., & Gonzalez, S. (2005). Towards alternative model (s) of local innovation. *Urban Studies, 42*(11), 1969–1990.

Norton, B., & Toohey, K. (2011). Identity, language learning, and social change. *Language Teaching, 44*(4), 412–446. https://doi.org/10.1017/s0261444811000309

Pan, X., Ai, B., Li, C., Pan, X., & Yan, Y. (2019). Dynamic relationship among environmental regulation, technological innovation and energy efficiency based on large scale provincial panel data in China. *Technological Forecasting and Social Change, 144*, 428–435.

Rittel, H. W. J. and Melvin M. (1973). Dilemmas in a General Theory of Planning. *Webber Source: Policy Sciences, 4*, 2, 155-169. http://www.jstor.org/stable/4531523

Siregar, I. (2022). The relationship between conflict and social change in the perspective of expert theory: A literature review. *International Journal of Arts and Humanities Studies, 2*(1), 9–16.

Sun, H., Edziah, B. K., Kporsu, A. K., Sarkodie, S. A., & Taghizadeh-Hesary, F. (2021). Energy efficiency: The role of technological innovation and knowledge spillover. *Technological Forecasting and Social Change, 167*, 120659. https://doi.org/10.1016/j.techfore.2021.120659

Terstriep, J., Rehfeld, D., and Kleverbeck, M. (2020). Favourable social innovation ecosystem(s)? – An explorative approach. *European Planning Studies, 28*(5), 881–905. https://doi.org/10.1080/09654313.2019.1708868

Weber, E., & Khademian, A. M. (2008). Managing collaborative processes. *Administration & Society, 40*(5), 431–464. https://doi.org/10.1177/0095399708320181

Wittmayer, J. M., Backhaus, J., Avelino, F., Pel, B., Strasser, T., Kunze, I., & Zuijderwijk, L. (2019). Narratives of change: How social innovation initiatives construct societal transformation. *Futures, 112*, 102433.

6

DIGITAL SKILLS DEVELOPMENT FOR INCLUSIVE DIGITAL TRANSFORMATION

Pankaj Kumar Ojha and Kalyan Ghadei

1   Introduction

In today's rapidly evolving digital landscape, the transformative power of technology is reshaping industries, economies, and societies. Digital transformation has become a ubiquitous term, representing the profound changes brought about by the integration of digital technologies into every aspect of our lives. As organizations and governments navigate this digital revolution, ensuring that individuals and communities are equipped with the necessary digital skills has emerged as a critical factor for achieving inclusive digital transformation.

Digital skills encompass a broad range of competencies that enable individuals to effectively navigate, understand, and leverage digital technologies. These skills are not limited to technical knowledge but also encompass critical thinking, problem-solving, creativity, and collaboration. In a world where digital literacy is increasingly becoming a prerequisite for meaningful participation, digital skills are essential for individuals to thrive in the digital age.

However, the digital divide persists, creating disparities in access to technology and inhibiting the development of digital skills. Marginalized communities, underserved populations, and individuals with limited resources face significant barriers in acquiring and honing digital skills. This digital divide exacerbates existing social and economic inequalities, as those without access to digital skills are left behind in an increasingly digitalized world.

To bridge this divide and foster inclusive digital transformation, there is a growing recognition of the need to develop comprehensive strategies and initiatives for digital skills development. These efforts aim to empower individuals with the knowledge, competencies, and confidence to harness the potential of digital technologies. By equipping individuals with digital skills, we can unlock opportunities for education, employment, entrepreneurship, and civic engagement, leading to improved livelihoods and enhanced social inclusion.

DOI: 10.4324/9781003433743-7

This chapter delves into the multifaceted landscape of digital skills development for inclusive digital transformation. It explores the importance of digital skills, the challenges faced in their development, and the strategies employed to promote inclusive digital transformation through skills development initiatives. Through an analysis of case studies, best practices, and emerging trends, this chapter seeks to provide a comprehensive understanding of the role of digital skills in driving inclusive digital transformation.

Ultimately, this chapter aims to serve as a valuable resource for policymakers, educators, researchers, and practitioners involved in digital skills development efforts. By highlighting the significance of digital skills and providing insights into effective strategies, it aims to inspire collective action and inform the design and implementation of inclusive digital skills development programs. Only through comprehensive and inclusive approaches to digital skills development can we ensure that no one is left behind in the digital transformation journey, creating a more equitable and prosperous future for all.

2   The Importance of Digital Skills for Inclusive Digital Transformation

In today's interconnected and technology-driven world, digital skills have become essential for individuals to navigate and thrive in the digital era. These skills play a pivotal role in driving inclusive digital transformation by empowering individuals, bridging socioeconomic gaps, and fostering economic growth. Understanding the importance of digital skills is crucial for realizing the full potential of digital technologies and ensuring that the benefits of digital transformation are accessible to all.

a Empowering Individuals: Digital skills empower individuals with the ability to effectively utilize digital tools, platforms, and resources. They provide individuals with the confidence and competence to navigate the digital landscape, access information, communicate, and engage with digital technologies. By acquiring digital skills, individuals can unleash their creative potential, solve complex problems, and adapt to the rapidly evolving digital environment. Digital skills empower individuals to become active contributors and participants in the digital economy, society, and civic life.

b Bridging Socioeconomic Gaps: One of the significant challenges in achieving inclusive digital transformation is the digital divide – the gap between those who have access to digital technologies and those who do not. The lack of digital skills exacerbates this divide, leading to unequal opportunities and social exclusion. Digital skills development plays a vital role in bridging these socioeconomic gaps by providing individuals with the tools to participate in the digital world. By equipping marginalized communities, underserved populations, and disadvantaged individuals with digital skills, we can empower them to overcome barriers, access educational resources, pursue employment opportunities, and improve their overall quality of life.

c Fostering Economic Growth: Digital skills are a catalyst for economic growth and innovation. As digital technologies continue to disrupt traditional industries and reshape the economy, individuals with digital skills are better positioned to adapt to changing job requirements and seize new opportunities. Digital skills enable entrepreneurship, facilitate the growth of digital startups, and drive innovation in established organizations. By fostering a digitally skilled workforce, countries can enhance their competitiveness in the global digital economy and stimulate economic growth.

d Enhancing Digital Literacy and Citizenship: Digital skills go beyond technical competencies; they also encompass digital literacy and digital citizenship. Digital literacy involves the ability to critically evaluate and effectively use digital information, while digital citizenship refers to responsible and ethical behavior in the digital realm. Digital skills development promotes digital literacy, enabling individuals to discern reliable sources of information, evaluate online content, and protect their privacy and security. Additionally, digital skills cultivate digital citizenship by promoting responsible digital behavior, respectful online communication, and awareness of digital rights and responsibilities.

Digital skills are essential for inclusive digital transformation as they empower individuals, bridge socioeconomic gaps, foster economic growth, and enhance digital literacy and citizenship. By recognizing the importance of digital skills and investing in comprehensive digital skills development initiatives, governments, educational institutions, and private sector organizations can ensure that individuals and communities are equipped with the competencies necessary to participate fully in the digital age. By prioritizing digital skills development, we can create a more inclusive and equitable digital society where everyone has the opportunity to benefit from the advantages of digital transformation.

3   Digital Skills Development: Challenges and Barriers

While the importance of digital skills development for inclusive digital transformation is widely recognized, numerous challenges and barriers hinder the acquisition and utilization of these skills. Understanding and addressing these challenges is crucial to ensure effective and equitable digital skills development initiatives. This section explores the key challenges and barriers faced in digital skills development and provides insights into strategies to overcome them.

a Access to Technology and Infrastructure: Access to technology and reliable internet connectivity is a fundamental requirement for digital skills development. However, many individuals, particularly those in underserved communities and rural areas, face limited access to affordable and reliable technology infrastructure. The lack of access to computers, high-speed internet, and digital devices hinders their ability to acquire and practice digital skills. Addressing the digital divide by expanding access to technology and broadband connectivity is crucial to fostering inclusive digital skills development.
b Affordability and Digital Divide: The affordability of digital devices and internet services is a significant barrier to digital skills development, particularly for individuals from low-income backgrounds. The cost of purchasing and maintaining devices, as well as access to high-speed internet, can be prohibitive for marginalized communities. Bridging the affordability gap through subsidized programs, community technology centers, and initiatives to reduce the cost of digital devices and internet services is essential to ensure equal opportunities for digital skills development.
c Digital Literacy and Awareness: Digital literacy serves as the foundation for digital skills development. However, a lack of basic digital literacy skills poses a barrier to individuals attempting to acquire more-advanced digital skills. Many individuals,

particularly older adults and individuals from disadvantaged backgrounds, lack basic digital literacy and struggle to navigate digital platforms and tools. Addressing digital literacy gaps through targeted training programs, community outreach, and public awareness campaigns is crucial to ensure comprehensive digital skills development.

d Gender and Socioeconomic Disparities: Gender and socioeconomic disparities persist in digital skills development. Women, girls, and individuals from marginalized communities often face additional barriers and social norms that limit their access to digital skills development opportunities. Addressing gender and socioeconomic disparities requires targeted interventions that promote inclusivity and equal access to digital skills development programs. Initiatives focused on bridging these gaps should provide mentorship, scholarships, and support networks to foster participation and engagement.

e Evolving Technological Landscape: The rapid pace of technological advancements presents a challenge for digital skills development. As new technologies emerge and existing technologies evolve, the skills required to effectively navigate and utilize them also change. Ensuring that digital skills development programs are agile and responsive to evolving technology trends is crucial. Continuous training, upskilling, and lifelong learning initiatives can equip individuals with the ability to adapt to emerging technologies and remain competitive in the digital age.

f Quality and Relevance of Training: The quality and relevance of digital skills training programs play a critical role in their effectiveness. Inadequate curriculum design, outdated teaching methods, and a lack of industry collaboration can lead to a mismatch between the skills taught and the skills demanded in the job market. Ensuring that digital skills training programs align with industry needs, incorporate hands-on learning experiences, and offer opportunities for real-world application is essential to enhance the employability and practical proficiency of individuals.

To address these challenges, effective strategies can be implemented:

- Developing comprehensive digital inclusion policies and strategies that prioritize digital skills development and address the barriers faced by marginalized communities.
- Establishing public–private partnerships to leverage resources and expertise in digital skills development initiatives.
- Creating community-based digital skills training centers and programs to reach underserved populations.
- Offering digital skills training in diverse formats, including online platforms, blended learning approaches, and flexible scheduling to accommodate different learning styles and needs.
- Encouraging collaboration between educational institutions, industry stakeholders, and civil society organizations to align digital skills training programs with industry requirements.
- Promoting digital mentorship programs that connect experienced digital professionals with individuals seeking to develop their skills.
- Engaging employers to create work-based learning opportunities, apprenticeships, and internships to bridge the gap between digital skills training and employment.

By addressing the challenges and barriers to digital skills development, societies can foster inclusive digital transformation and bridge the digital divide. These strategies, when implemented with a focus on equity and inclusivity, can empower individuals and communities to acquire the digital skills necessary for active participation in the digital age.

4   Strategies for Promoting Digital Skills Development

To promote digital skills development and foster inclusive digital transformation, a range of strategies and approaches can be employed. These strategies aim to address the barriers and challenges individuals face in acquiring digital skills and ensure equal access to opportunities for all. This section explores various effective strategies for promoting digital skills development.

a Formal Education and Curriculum Integration: Integrating digital skills into formal education systems is crucial for equipping students with the necessary skills for the digital age. This includes incorporating digital literacy, computational thinking, coding, and other relevant digital skills into school curricula at all levels. By integrating digital skills into education, students can develop a solid foundation and understanding of digital technologies, fostering their ability to adapt and learn new skills throughout their lives.

b Professional Development for Educators: Providing professional development opportunities for educators is essential for ensuring they have the knowledge and skills to effectively teach digital skills. Professional development programs can equip teachers with the necessary pedagogical approaches and technical expertise to deliver high-quality digital skills training. By investing in the continuous professional development of educators, institutions can enhance the overall digital skills development ecosystem.

c Blended Learning and Online Platforms: Blended learning approaches, combining both online and offline components, have proven effective in promoting digital skills development. Online platforms offer flexible and accessible learning opportunities, allowing individuals to learn at their own pace and from anywhere. These platforms can provide interactive tutorials, online courses, and collaborative learning environments, enabling individuals to acquire digital skills in a self-directed and engaging manner.

d Community-Based Learning: Community-based learning initiatives play a crucial role in reaching individuals who may not have access to formal education or online learning platforms. Community centers, libraries, and non-profit organizations can serve as hubs for digital skills development, providing resources, mentorship, and training programs tailored to the specific needs of the community. By engaging with the local community, these initiatives can address the unique challenges individuals face and foster a supportive learning environment.

e Public–Private Partnerships: Collaboration between public and private sectors is essential for promoting digital skills development. Public–private partnerships can leverage resources, expertise, and networks to create comprehensive digital skills initiatives. This collaboration can involve co-designing training programs, offering internships or apprenticeships, providing funding for digital skills projects, and fostering mentorship programs. By working together, governments and private sector organizations can ensure that digital skills development aligns with industry needs and addresses the demands of the job market.

f Targeted Programs for Marginalized Communities: To address the digital divide and promote inclusive digital skills development, targeted programs should be implemented to reach marginalized communities. These programs should consider the specific challenges faced by disadvantaged groups, including women, rural populations, individuals with disabilities, and ethnic minorities. Providing scholarships, mentorship programs, and tailored training initiatives can help bridge the gaps and empower these communities to develop the necessary digital skills.

g Lifelong Learning and Continuous Upskilling: Digital skills development is an ongoing process, considering the rapid pace of technological advancements. Encouraging lifelong learning and continuous upskilling is essential to ensure that individuals remain relevant and adaptable in the digital era. Providing opportunities for individuals to refresh their skills, acquire new competencies, and stay updated with emerging technologies is crucial for their professional growth and long-term employability.

h Collaboration with Industry and Industry-Recognized Certifications: Collaboration with industry stakeholders is crucial for aligning digital skills development with the needs of the job market. Engaging employers, industry associations, and professional certification bodies can help design training programs that equip individuals with the skills and knowledge required by employers. Recognized industry certifications can provide individuals with a competitive edge and increase their employability in the digital job market.

These strategies, when implemented in a coordinated and inclusive manner, can contribute to the effective promotion of digital skills development. By addressing the barriers and challenges individuals face in acquiring digital skills, societies can ensure that all members have the opportunity to participate in and benefit from the digital transformation.

5   Case Studies: Effective Digital Skills Development Initiatives

Examining successful digital skills development initiatives provides valuable insights into strategies and approaches that have yielded positive outcomes. The following case studies highlight effective initiatives that have made significant contributions to promoting digital skills development and fostering inclusive digital transformation.

a Digital Skills for Africa: The "Digital Skills for Africa" initiative, launched by Google, aims to provide digital skills training to young people in Africa, equipping them with the necessary tools to thrive in the digital economy. The initiative offers online training programs and offline training sessions conducted by local partners. By partnering with various organizations, Google has reached millions of individuals, empowering them with digital skills and supporting entrepreneurship and job creation in the region (Google, n.d.).

b Skill India: The "Skill India" campaign, launched by the Government of India, focuses on providing digital skills training to the country's workforce. The initiative offers a wide range of training programs, including the "Pradhan Mantri Gramin Digital

Saksharta Abhiyan," which aims to make rural citizens digitally literate. Skill India leverages partnerships with industry stakeholders, vocational training providers, and educational institutions to ensure that the training programs are aligned with industry needs (Skill India, n.d.).

c Digital Skills for All: The "Digital Skills for All" initiative, led by the World Bank, focuses on providing digital skills training to vulnerable and underserved populations in developing countries. The initiative employs a blended learning approach, combining online courses with face-to-face training sessions. It aims to bridge the digital divide by addressing the challenges of access, affordability, and relevance. The initiative also emphasizes the importance of fostering digital entrepreneurship and supporting women and girls in acquiring digital skills (World Bank, n.d.).

d Digital Skills Partnership: The "Digital Skills Partnership" in the United Kingdom is a collaborative effort between the government, private sector, and non-profit organizations. The partnership aims to address the digital skills gap by creating training programs tailored to specific industries and sectors. It focuses on upskilling existing workers and providing opportunities for individuals from disadvantaged backgrounds to acquire digital skills. The initiative promotes apprenticeships, coding boot camps, and online learning platforms to facilitate skills development (Department for Digital, Culture, Media & Sport, 2018).

e Generation: Generation, a global youth employment organization, offers digital skills training programs in partnership with employers. The programs focus on providing young individuals with job-specific digital skills required by industries such as healthcare, technology, and customer service. Generation combines intensive training, mentorship, and job placement support to ensure that graduates are equipped with the skills necessary to enter the workforce successfully (Generation, n.d.).

These case studies highlight the effectiveness of various approaches in promoting digital skills development. They demonstrate the importance of public–private partnerships, industry collaboration, targeted training programs, and inclusive approaches to reach marginalized communities.

6   Assessing the Impact of Digital Skills Development

Assessing the impact of digital skills development initiatives is crucial to understand the effectiveness of these programs and identify areas for improvement. By evaluating the outcomes and impact of digital skills development, policymakers, organizations, and educators can make informed decisions and optimize resource allocation. This section explores different methods and approaches for assessing the impact of digital skills development initiatives.

a Surveys and Self-Reports: Surveys and self-report questionnaires are commonly used to assess the impact of digital skills development. These tools gather data directly from individuals who have participated in training programs, capturing their self-perceived improvements in digital skills, confidence levels, and employability. Surveys can also assess changes in individuals' attitudes towards technology and their ability to utilize digital tools effectively.

b Performance Assessments: Performance assessments involve evaluating individuals' practical application of digital skills in real-world scenarios. These assessments can include tasks such as completing digital projects, problem-solving exercises, or demonstrating proficiency in using specific software or tools. Performance assessments provide objective measures of individuals' acquired digital skills and their ability to apply them effectively.

c Case Studies and Interviews: Case studies and interviews offer qualitative insights into the impact of digital skills development initiatives. Through in-depth interviews with program participants, trainers, and employers, researchers can gather rich data on the experiences, challenges, and outcomes of digital skills training. Case studies provide a holistic understanding of the broader impact on individuals' lives, including employment opportunities, income levels, and personal growth.

d Longitudinal Studies: Longitudinal studies involve tracking the progress of individuals over an extended period to assess the long-term impact of digital skills development. By measuring outcomes such as employment rates, career progression, and income levels over time, researchers can evaluate the sustained benefits of digital skills training. Longitudinal studies provide insights into the long-term effects on individuals' socioeconomic status and their ability to adapt to evolving digital technologies.

e Employer Feedback and Performance Indicators: Engaging employers in assessing the impact of digital skills development initiatives is essential. Employers can provide feedback on the performance and productivity of employees who have acquired digital skills through training programs. Monitoring performance indicators, such as productivity levels, digital innovation, and job retention rates, can help determine the impact of digital skills on organizational success.

f Economic Analysis: Conducting economic analyses can help assess the broader societal impact of digital skills development. Economic indicators, such as job creation, income growth, and return on investment, provide insights into the economic benefits generated by a skilled workforce. Cost-benefit analyses can compare the costs of implementing digital skills development initiatives with the economic gains resulting from increased productivity and reduced unemployment rates.

g Comparative Studies and Benchmarks: Comparative studies and benchmarks allow for comparisons between different digital skills development initiatives or across regions or countries. By establishing benchmarks and performance standards, policymakers and organizations can gauge the relative effectiveness of their programs and identify areas for improvement. Comparative studies provide valuable insights into best practices and effective strategies for digital skills development.

Utilizing a combination of these assessment methods can provide a comprehensive understanding of the impact of digital skills development initiatives on individuals, organizations, and society as a whole. It is important to tailor the assessment approach to the specific objectives and context of each initiative.

7 Future Trends and Emerging Technologies in Digital Skills Development

Digital skills development is an ever-evolving field influenced by the rapid advancements in technology. To ensure individuals are prepared for the future of work and digital transformation, it is essential to anticipate and adapt to emerging trends and technologies. This section explores some of the future trends and emerging technologies that are shaping digital skills development.

a Artificial Intelligence (AI) and Machine Learning: AI and machine learning technologies are transforming various industries and creating new opportunities for digital skills development. These technologies can be utilized in personalized learning platforms that adapt to individual learners' needs, providing tailored content and feedback. AI-powered chatbots and virtual assistants can also support learners in their digital skills journey by answering questions, providing guidance, and facilitating interactive learning experiences.

b Data Science and Analytics: As organizations increasingly rely on data-driven decision-making, data science and analytics skills are becoming highly sought after. Future digital skills development initiatives will likely emphasize data literacy, statistical analysis, and data visualization. Individuals will need to understand how to collect, analyze, and interpret data to derive insights and drive informed decision-making.

c Cyber security: As the digital landscape expands, cyber security skills will be crucial for individuals to protect themselves and organizations from cyber threats. Future digital skills development initiatives will likely focus on training individuals in cyber security practices, including identifying and mitigating risks, implementing secure practices, and responding to cyber security incidents. This will help individuals navigate the evolving cyber security landscape and contribute to maintaining a secure digital environment.

d Internet of Things (IoT): The proliferation of IoT devices presents new opportunities and challenges in digital skills development. Individuals will need to understand how to interact with and leverage IoT devices effectively. Future digital skills initiatives may focus on IoT-related skills, such as device connectivity, data management, and IoT application development. This will enable individuals to harness the potential of IoT technologies and contribute to the development of innovative solutions.

e Augmented Reality (AR) and Virtual Reality (VR): AR and VR technologies offer immersive and interactive learning experiences, creating new possibilities for digital skills development. These technologies can simulate real-world scenarios, allowing individuals to practice and apply digital skills in a virtual environment. Future digital skills initiatives may incorporate AR and VR to enhance hands-on learning, collaboration, and skill acquisition in fields such as design, engineering, and healthcare.

f Automation and Robotics: Automation and robotics are reshaping the workforce, leading to the emergence of new job roles and skill requirements. Digital skills development initiatives will need to prepare individuals for a future where automation and human–machine collaboration are prevalent. This includes skills such as programming robots, managing automated systems, and understanding the ethical implications of automation.

g Blockchain Technology: Blockchain technology has the potential to revolutionize various industries, including finance, supply chain management, and healthcare. Future digital skills development initiatives may focus on blockchain literacy, smart contract development, and decentralized application (dApp) development. These skills will enable individuals to leverage blockchain technology and contribute to its implementation and advancement.

h Continuous Learning and Adaptability: As technology continues to evolve, the ability to learn continuously and adapt to new tools and platforms will be essential. Future digital skills development initiatives will emphasize the development of learning agility, critical thinking, problem-solving, and adaptability. Individuals will need to cultivate a growth mindset and embrace lifelong learning to stay relevant in the ever-changing digital landscape.

As digital skills development evolves, it is important for stakeholders, including educators, policymakers, and organizations, to monitor these trends and align their strategies and resources accordingly. Anticipating future trends and embracing emerging technologies will ensure that digital skills development initiatives remain effective and relevant in preparing individuals for the digital era.

8 Best Practices and Recommendations for Effective Digital Skills Development

Effective digital skills development initiatives require careful planning and implementation to maximize their impact. Drawing on best practices and recommendations can help guide the design and delivery of programs. This section presents key best practices and recommendations for effective digital skills development.

a Needs Assessment and Targeted Training: Conducting a thorough needs assessment is essential to identify the specific digital skills gaps and requirements of the target audience. This assessment should take into account regional, industry, and individual needs. Based on the assessment, training programs can be tailored to address the identified gaps, ensuring that the content and delivery methods align with the learners' needs and learning preferences.

b Holistic Approach: Digital skills development should go beyond technical skills and encompass a holistic approach. This includes fostering critical thinking, problem-solving, creativity, and collaboration. Emphasizing digital literacy, digital citizenship, and ethical considerations is also important to empower individuals to navigate the digital world responsibly.

c Collaboration and Partnerships: Collaboration among various stakeholders, including government, educational institutions, industry, and community organizations, is crucial for effective digital skills development. Partnerships can facilitate resource sharing, expertise exchange, and the creation of comprehensive programs that align with industry needs. Public–private partnerships, in particular, can leverage the strengths of both sectors to bridge the digital skills gap more effectively.

d Blended Learning and Flexibility: Blended learning approaches, combining online and offline learning, offer flexibility and accessibility. Online platforms, video tutorials, and interactive modules can enhance self-paced learning, while in-person workshops, mentoring, and project-based activities foster collaboration and hands-on experience. Providing flexible learning options accommodates different learning styles and ensures wider access to digital skills development opportunities.

e Continuous Learning and Lifelong Learning: Digital skills development should emphasize the importance of continuous learning and lifelong learning. Encouraging individuals to embrace a growth mindset and pursue ongoing skill enhancement enables them to adapt to evolving technologies and industry demands. Promoting access to learning resources, micro-credentialing, and recognition of prior learning can support lifelong learning journeys.

f Trainers and Facilitators: Well-trained and skilled trainers and facilitators play a crucial role in effective digital skills development. They should possess both technical expertise and pedagogical skills to deliver engaging and interactive training sessions. Continuous professional development for trainers can ensure they stay up-to-date with emerging technologies and teaching methodologies.

g Evaluation and Feedback: Regular evaluation and feedback mechanisms are essential to monitor the effectiveness of digital skills development initiatives. Collecting feedback from learners, trainers, and employers helps identify areas for improvement and refine the programs. Tracking the outcomes and impact of the training programs allows stakeholders to measure the success and make data-driven decisions.

h Inclusion and Diversity: Digital skills development initiatives should prioritize inclusion and diversity. Efforts should be made to ensure equal access to training opportunities for marginalized groups, including women, persons with disabilities, and underserved communities. Providing targeted support, mentorship, and scholarships can help overcome barriers and promote equal participation.

By following these best practices and recommendations, digital skills development initiatives can better meet the needs of individuals and contribute to inclusive digital transformation.

9 Conclusion

The development of digital skills is paramount for fostering inclusive digital transformation in today's rapidly evolving world. This chapter has delved into the significance of digital skills, the challenges and barriers that hinder their development, strategies for promoting their cultivation, and the assessment of their impact. We have also explored case studies exemplifying effective digital skills development initiatives and discussed future trends and emerging technologies in this domain. Lastly, we provided best practices and recommendations for ensuring the efficacy of digital skills development programs.

The importance of digital skills cannot be overstated. They empower individuals to participate actively in the digital society, bridge the digital divide, and enhance their economic and social well-being. It is crucial to recognize that digital skills encompass not only technical expertise but also digital literacy, critical thinking, collaboration, and adaptability. However, numerous challenges and barriers hinder the development of digital skills, such as unequal access to resources, limited awareness, and the rapid pace of technological advancements. Overcoming these obstacles requires targeted interventions, comprehensive strategies, and collaboration among stakeholders from the public, private, and educational sectors. To promote digital skills development effectively, various strategies have been identified, including integrating technology in education, fostering public–private partnerships, and embracing lifelong learning approaches. These approaches facilitate personalized and flexible learning experiences, cater to diverse needs, and ensure the continuous acquisition and refinement of digital skills.

The impact of digital skills development programs can be assessed through a range of methods, including surveys, performance assessments, case studies, and economic analysis. By evaluating the outcomes and impact, policymakers and organizations can fine-tune interventions, allocate resources efficiently, and adapt to the evolving demands of the digital era. Throughout the chapter, we examined case studies that showcased effective digital skills development initiatives from different sectors and regions. These examples illustrate the transformative power of targeted interventions, collaboration, and innovative approaches in empowering individuals and communities to thrive in the digital world.

Looking ahead, it is essential to acknowledge the future trends and emerging technologies that will shape digital skills development. AI, data science, cyber security, the IoT, and other advancements will require individuals to continuously adapt and up skill to stay relevant in the digital landscape. To ensure the effectiveness of digital skills development programs, best practices and recommendations should be embraced. These include conducting thorough needs assessments, fostering collaboration and partnerships, promoting flexibility and inclusivity, investing in well-trained trainers and facilitators, and establishing mechanisms for continuous evaluation and improvement.

In nutshell, digital skills development is a fundamental driver of inclusive digital transformation. By equipping individuals with the necessary digital competencies, we can empower them to seize the opportunities presented by the digital age, bridge societal gaps, and foster sustainable development. It is through concerted efforts, collaboration, and a commitment to lifelong learning that we can build an inclusive digital society for all.

References

Department for Digital, Culture, Media & Sport. (2018). UK Digital Strategy. Retrieved from https://www.gov.uk/government/publications/uk-digital-strategy

Generation. (n.d.). Our Approach. Retrieved from https://www.generation.org/approach/

Google. (n.d.). Digital Skills for Africa. Retrieved from https://digitalskills.withgoogle.com/digitalskillsforafrica/

Skill India. (n.d.). About Skill India. Retrieved from https://www.skillindia.gov.in/about-us

World Bank. (n.d.). Digital Skills for All. Retrieved from https://www.worldbank.org/en/programs/digital-skills-for-all

World Economic Forum. (2020). The Future of Jobs Report 2020. Retrieved from https://www.weforum.org/reports/the-future-of-jobs-report-2020

7

APPLYING DESIGN SPRINT METHOD TO CREATE A MINIMUM VIABLE PRODUCT WITH MACHINE VISION

Kajal Bhandari, Jaakko Palokangas and Ville Ojanen

1 Introduction

In a dynamic landscape of technological innovation, every industry is indulging into innovative product development strategies to make their products efficient and optimum. Minerals processing is one of the areas that has the potential to develop its products and services with new-age technologies. In this chapter, we will take an iterative and collaborative approach to product development exploring the optimization need and the value provided by the minimum viable product (MVP). Minerals processing uses various types of filtration equipment depending on the operation's requirement such as vacuum filters, pressure filters and centrifugal (Rushton, 1997). The choice of the filtration technology depends on the parameters and requirements such as type of feed, cake moisture, solid content in filtrate and process data (Schoenbrunn et al., 1984). Due to the high residual moisture of the product passing to the dryers in the process, traditional filters such as rotary filters are not suitable in the mining industry data (Schoenbrunn et al., 1984) and so the popularity of pressure filters have increased over the years. The focus of this chapter is on pressure filtration with horizontal plates. Pressure filters are used for slurries that use pressure above 15 psig and release sufficient cake thickness permitting cake washing (Fuerstenau & Han, 2003). Pressure filters are inherently batch process, which means the filtration process must stop to load the slurry and unload the dry cake data (Schoenbrunn et al., 1984). Batch filtration process includes separating solids and liquid from the pumped slurry with the help of a medium (screen, woven cloth, paper, etc.) (Rushton, 1997). Pressure filters can be divided into three types of filter presses: vertical-plate filter press, horizontal-plate filter press and belt filter press data (Schoenbrunn et al., 1984). In this chapter we will concentrate on horizontal filter press that operates with horizontal plates. Horizontal filter plates are fully automatic filters that have horizontal chambers in the filter frame and are designed to operate with large capacity and to produce low-moisture-content data (Schoenbrunn et al., 1984). This kind of filter is designed for flexibility. They are structured in such a way that the plates can be added on top of each other, so over the course of operation it allows to increase the filtration area data (Schoenbrunn et al., 1984).

DOI: 10.4324/9781003433743-8

There are certain areas in the design of filters that could be optimized in order to make the filter more digital and sustainable. The filter's architecture isn't inherently flawed, but there is room for improvement by transforming it into a data-driven digital system that automates and optimizes the process. Thus, we began this effort in order to close this gap. In filters, filter cloth or the filter medium has a crucial role in the process. The problem with filter cloth is that, there hasn't been much research done on its effect on the filtration process. But we believe that the enhancement of the filter cloth will bring value to the process. The purpose of this research is to provide a MVP that addresses the design issues of the existing product. The design issue focusing on the filter cloth and solving customer problems such as "When can we know whether the filter cloth needs to be changed?", "When can we patch or change the filter cloth?", "Which process erodes the filter cloth the most?", "What is the lifecycle of the filter cloth?" and "What are the types of filter cloth suitable for certain processes?". To tackle these issues, we have formulated this research and created a MVP. The fusion of real-time monitoring system with machine vision (MV) provides a compelling intersection of efficiency, digitalization and sustainability. MVP addresses the problems in the existing product. In addition to this, the research also focuses on the possible benefits of the MVP over the existing system. The research has taken into account that the product should allow the users to use the intelligent system to their benefit and collaborate with the system rather than replacing the current users. The research is done with a human-centric approach that does not neglect the human factors that are needed to operate the system in the most efficient way.

A case study was developed on machine learning (ML) system with MV technology, in relevance to the filtration process. The chapter focuses on a case study done between 2020 and 2021. This research is not intended to generalize the importance of a particular technology in filtration but focuses on the advantages and importance of use of data in health monitoring of a product. The remainder of the chapter is structured as follows: In the Methods section, the methodology and case description used in the chapter is detailed, along with the factors that led to the choice of this problem. The case description will be followed by the research framework. The MVP will then be presented and explained in the Results section. The potential advantages of the product will next be discussed. A conclusion is provided at the end.

2   Background

The following section explains the background of the topic. With a focus on digital technology and sustainability, the study is conducted for the minerals processing industry. The MVP created should ultimately contribute to the development of digitally sustainable products and methods of operation. First, a brief description of the theories behind the minerals processing is presented. Then, the theory of digitalization and sustainability in the context of minerals processing is explained, together with an analysis of the associated challenges and connections.

2.1   Minerals Processing

Minerals processing processes ores and other materials to yield a concentrated product (Fuerstenau & Han, 2003). A typical minerals process starts by extracting the ore, followed by physical processing of the ore, followed by low-temperature processing, and refining, which results to a concentrated form of metal, ideally pure metal (Fuerstenau & Han, 2003). Filtration is an integral part in minerals processing. It is the process of separating solids from liquid through a medium. One of the most common types of filtration processes in minerals processing is cake filtration (Wills & Finch, 2016). In cake filtration process, a slurry is processed by the filter and it goes through the medium and results in filtrate and cake. Filtrate is the liquid that comes out of the filtration process and cake is the remaining solid particle that is blocked by the filter medium. The rate of filtration is calculated by the volume of filtrate per unit time (Wills & Finch, 2016). In a filtration process, there are variables that should be considered before testing. These factors determine how the necessary test should proceed, which will give an idea of the efficiency of the process. The following formula shows the filtration rate and the factors affecting it. It is based on the Darcy and Poiseuille theory of filtration (Wills & Finch, 2016).

$$v = \frac{1}{A}\frac{1dV}{dt} = \frac{\Delta p}{\mu(\alpha\omega\frac{V}{A})} \qquad (1)$$

where, v = filtrate flow rate
  A = area of the filter
  V = filtrate volume
  t = time
  ΔP = pressure drop across cake and filter medium
  μ = liquid velocity
  α = specific cake resistance
  w = slurry concentration

Equation 1 illustrates how the filtration rate changes across the filtration area in direct proportion with pressure drop (Wills & Finch, 2016) and filter medium. In the past decade, mining industry has come under huge pressure to improve its different aspects because of which the new research, technologies and business practices surrounding the industry are leaned towards the sustainability goals (Tuazon et al., 2012). In minerals processing, various digital instruments, such as sensors, cameras and other monitoring devices, have enabled the collection of data that can be used in health monitoring, fault detection, production decisions, maintenance and servicing, etc. (Kumar et al., 2020). The research (Dindarloo & Siami-Irdemoosa, 2017) used classification and clustering techniques to investigate the shovel failure behaviour and patterns to extract information on the availability, maintainability and reliability of the equipment. Not only this, the prediction of next shovel failure in the mining site was also predicted with more than 75% accuracy (Dindarloo & Siami-Irdemoosa, 2017).

2.2 *Digitalization and Sustainability in Minerals Processing*

Digitalization and sustainability together have a high potential to help industries to reach optimum in terms of their technological advancements and achieving their sustainability goals. Together they can also help to reduce the negative impact of people and processes on the environment (Seele & Lock, 2017). The complexity of our society and the environment, and its deep connection with each other, big data and Information and Communication Technology (ICT) can help to contribute to the promotion of sustainability (Gijzen, 2013; Hampton et al., 2013). Digitalization has great impact on transparency and accountability, which creates new opportunities for development, sharing and governance for sustainability (Heemsbergen, 2016).

In filtration technologies, sensors can be installed in various parts to gather data and optimize the process accordingly. While developing a product, it is important to understand and take into consideration the users of the technology. Keeping people in the loop and making a system user-centric allows the integration of any system smoothly. This type of collaborative approach is called Human–Machine Collaboration (HMC) (Bhandari et al., 2021). HMC is a concept that focuses on creating value by combining human ingenuity and the Artificial Intelligence (AI) aiming to answer a key question of how to bring the complementary skills of both systems together (Bhandari et al., 2021). It has today become an integral part of the businesses, and various industries are adopting the concept in applications such as human robotics (Desai et al., 2013), modern manufacturing (Johannsmeier & Haddadin, 2017), aviation (Cummings et al., 2007), and process control (Hu & Chen, 2017; Lee & Moray, 1992). This collaboration not only aims to find the best of both worlds but also focuses on how to create an environment for digitally enhanced and sustainable future. Minerals processing and sustainability are interlinked with each other at many different levels. The optimal use of mining products affects many different areas such as use of raw materials, environmental impact (e.g., energy use and emissions), wastewater management, recycling, control of toxic materials and lifecycle assessment (Van Berkel et al., 2004) along with social responsibility, workers health and well-being and governance responsibilities. Hence, a sustainable processing along with design and eco-efficient operations utilizes technologies in order to positively impact the areas mentioned above (Van Berkel et al., 2004).

In terms of visual data collection and processing, minerals businesses have used MV for sizing, sorting, ore fragmentation and flotation froth monitoring, etc. (McCoy & Auret, 2019). Utilization of visual data has in the past helped to automate tasks and now with the merger of ML with MV along with developments in AI, the capabilities of MV has come very close to human vision (Smith et al., 2021). MV is one of the application techniques of ML that generates image data presenting the complexity and challenges of any analytical technique (McCoy & Auret, 2019). It generates high-dimensional images that can be processed and analyzed to form a knowledge pool over a period of time that can be used for predicting the process parameters (McCoy & Auret, 2019). It has the potential to increase efficiency by continuously monitoring and adjusting parameters in real-time. This means that the use of a continuous monitoring aids to predictive maintenance reducing downtime for the filters. MV also provides optimized insights by leveraging analytics, which helps to make data-driven decision making. As an example, Figure 7.1 shows a user interface of Beltguard. It is a MV system that warns users of damages in a steelbelt used in sintering. It is continuously monitored, analyzed and sends feedback to the users to act on the situation according to the prompts. In the beginning, the system needs to be taught about what are the correct prompts and what kinds of situations or types of behaviour of the belt are a warning sign along with the degree of

FIGURE 7.1   User interface of a beltmap view. Courtesy of Company A.

severity. After teaching the system, it runs on its own and learns over time precisely when to send out warning signals.

MV has been used in industries to aid in cost reduction, efficiency and reduce human errors in the system (Smith et al., 2021). The information analysis in MV systems can be defined by five steps: image acquisition, pre-processing, segmentation, feature extraction and classification/interpretation (Smith et al., 2021). The first step requires the developers to design, position and obtain hardware and software, such as camera, lens and lightning arrangements. The three steps before the interpretation step include the MV solution, where developers work the most to process the data images, translation of the data, experimentation of the solution, filtering and reduction of data to viable and sensible information. The output of all these steps results into the last step that provides reports, guidable instructions that can be then turned into actions (Smith et al., 2021).

In textile and fibre-reinforced materials, MV has been used for various purposes, such as pattern recognition (Dindarloo & Siami-Irdemoosa, 2017), defect detection (Li & Zhang, 2016), quality control (Heleno et al., 2002), automated positioning of structures (Schmitt et al., 2008), to name a few. Li and Zhang (2016) express the advantages of automatic inspection of the fabric quality on the manual human inspection. Their research proposes a hybrid model of inspecting the defects of the textiles, which combines Gabor filters for images followed by Pulse Coupled Neural Network (PCNN) segmentation with an accuracy rate of 98.6% (Li & Zhang, 2016). Similarly, to tackle quality control in manufacturing industry, elimination of routine manual inspection in different production line was possible by INFIBRA MV system (Heleno et al., 2002). Fibre-Reinforced Plastics are among the important materials in industries to make the product lightweight and increase resistance (Schmitt et al., 2008). One of the research projects focused on inspecting textile structure during the manufacturing process with MV system concluded that the combination of image processing sensor and light section sensor allowed the optimization of inspection process in time and accuracy (Schmitt et al., 2008). Taking this concept into account, we investigated the current issues prevailing in minerals processing that could be resolved with this research. One of the issues that repeats in various applications in minerals processing comes with the continuous use of the filter cloth. Filter cloth is used continuously during the usage of the filter and thus it also bears a significant amount of strain in the system. Although this is an integral part of the process, there hasn't been much integration of any intelligent systems that help to elevate the product and get the most out of the system. Digitally enhancing the filter cloth involves improving the system to reduce costs, minimize the use of natural resources, and decrease manual labor, thereby lowering the overall resource requirements at the site. Apart from this, the system would provide useful data that could be analyzed and projected for upcoming minerals processing operations that use comparable characteristics. Hence, we researched on the used cases in the minerals processing industry that has used and solved similar problems.

3   Research Methods

The research approach employed in the study is explained in this section. The research's design framework is covered in the first part, and the research's case is explained in the second part. The Design Framework section provides an explanation of the research methodology, data collection and analysis procedures, and the rationale behind their selection. The case-selection process, issues and reasons for selecting the case are discussed in the second section.

3.1   Design Framework

This study was planned to follow an action research methodology. Action research is a qualitative research methodology that addresses immediate problems or improves existing systems with a practical outcome (Adelman, 1993). It is an adaptive method that facilitates change in the existing system. Action research follows a cycle of planning, taking action, observing and reflecting in cycles. It is a reflective process whose action directly affects the process of transformation (Hur et al., 2013). In both social science and design disciplines, it is regarded as a potent human-centred design strategy (Baum et al., 2006; Hur et al., 2013). To cater the action research to this research, design sprint methodology was used. The design sprint methodology is originally developed by Google Ventures as a "unique 5-day process of answering crucial questions through prototyping and testing ideas with customers" (Knapp et al., 2016). Because the process aids in active learning in engineering requirements and facilitates collaborative and hands-on learning on the subject in addition to theoretical discipline (Ferreira & Canedo, 2019), it has been used in various prototyping projects. One of such research was done by Keijzer-Broers and de Reuver (2016) to develop a health and well-being platform that follows design sprint methodology in action design research. As problem solving and implementing the plan

TABLE 7.1 Research framework

Days	Task	Description
Plan: Day 1	Map	Understand long-term goals
		Risks
		Build a map
	Sketch	Lightning demo
		Sketches of the various solutions
	Decide	Voting and deciding the best suited solution
Action: Day 2	MVP	Creating the MVP
Reflect: After	Test	Laboratory testing
		Customer testing

Abbreviation: MVP, minimum viable product.

are the foundations of each of these approaches, they appear to work best together in this context. Hence, the following research framework was designed as shown in Table 7.1. The framework consists of planning, taking action (making a MVP) and testing the MVP in one cycle. For this research, the design sprint for this problem was conducted in two days. This is because of the difficulty to get everyone included in the process to clear up the schedule for five days. For this reason, we optimized the first three days of the sprint, which is mapping, sketching and deciding. This has limited the process to a very tight schedule.

The problem chosen for the research is practical or an existing problem prevailing in industries and hence a practical way of solving the issue was needed in order to reach to a conclusion. Additionally, during the initial phase of research, due to several restrictions, such as time, research agenda of Company A and participants in the research, a modified version of action research was necessary to adapt. For these reasons, a combination of action research with design sprint was necessary in the research process. In design sprint, the participants in the research were involved, gathered in one space and took time to map, sketch, decide, build and test the prototype (Knapp et al., 2016). Action research in combination with design sprint method allowed the research to be flexible, time efficient and curate the research specifically to the problem in hand. Here in this chapter, we follow the same principle and have designed the exercise as a participatory action research.

Before starting the sprint days, a proper planning is necessary. First, the design challenge was selected in accordance with the need of Company A. Then, a design sprint team was selected representing various departments, such as engineering, designing, product management, testing, technology experts and automation expert. All together, a team of 8 persons were selected, and a facilitator. A decider among the team members is also chosen. The first day started off with defining long-term goal, followed by sprint questions. Long-term goal refers to the optimal scenario for project, assuming that everything will go according to the plan and yield in a positive outcome. Next, sprint questions were put forward by the team. The sprint questions give us the chance to think and ask what can go wrong. With these questions, all the risks of the research are also listed. Subsequently, the mapping of the users, their experience and opportunities for them within this project is drawn. This defines the actors and their journey throughout the process. With these in place, the next step is to ask the experts.

In this step, the experts were interviewed on different areas of the problem with "How might we…?" questions. The experts during this interview would take individual notes and all the questions that arise during the session were written and posted on the board. These questions were then categorized and labelled. After categorization, the questions were voted and the most relevant questions according to the users were then selected. Based on these questions, the most critical path of the user's journey is selected. This provides the target for the sprint.

Before the sketches are drawn for the solution, lightening demo is also done. Lightning demo is a real-life example that is related to our problem in hand. After this, the sketching of the solution starts. A simple hand-drawn sketch of the possible solution keeping in mind the target map and long-term goal is drawn by each user. Sketching includes taking notes on goals, opportunities and inspiration, after which rough ideas are written down, followed by rapid sketching of the ideas and finally the best idea with all details is sketched. This final idea would have a title and a storyline. Finally, a storyboard with all the solutions is prepared. Keeping in mind the goal of the exercise and target for the sprint, all the users voted on the best solution. Then, the next action steps were created, which is called storyboarding. During storyboarding, the next actions and steps are posted on the board to clarify what needs to be done after the sprint is finished. During the sprint days, the problem definition and possible viable solution were created.

3.2   Case Description

The research was done in collaboration with Company A. Company A is one of the largest companies in the world to provide filtration technologies all over the world. In this research, we are focusing on digitalizing a part of a filter in order to optimize the use, cost and overall monitoring of the filter. The part of the filter we are focusing on is the filter cloth. In vertical pressure filters, filter cloths are between each chamber and are stacked on top of each other. The filter cloth is continuous, which means there are no individual cloths in the filter but rather one cloth that is running in between the chambers (Wills & Finch, 2016). The cake is formed in the chambers of the filter plates, and upon completion of the process, the press is opened and the filter cake is discharged, followed by washing of the filter cloth.

Filter cloth is one of the major cost components in the process and often the most important component to assure an efficient operation of the filter (Wills & Finch, 2016). There are many parameters of the process that lead us to choose different kinds of filter cloth. The parameters such as clay content, fines content, particle size and abrasiveness for the slurry are few of the parameters that need to be considered while choosing a filter cloth type for a process as described in Table 7.2. If chosen incorrectly, then it can cause the cloth or medium to go blind to wear and tear prematurely, which in turn adds to the unforeseen cost of the media. For example, if there is slime in the filter slurry that is fed into the process, then the filter cloth tends to blind very easily (Wills & Finch, 2016). This will not only add to the cost of the material but also additionally labour cost, engineering hours, loss in production and filter availability. After choosing a filter cloth type, during the run time, filter cloth needs to be regularly stitched, changed or the type of filter cloth also may be needed to change. It needs a constant check whether the cloth has been

TABLE 7.2 Filter cloth terms (Schoenbrunn et al., 1984)

Term	Description
Blinding	The plugging up of a filter fabric, resulting in reduced flow rates and filtration efficiency.
Cake release	The ability of a filter cloth to completely discharge the cake from the cloth.
Monofilament	A single, long, continuous strand of a synthetic fibre extruded in fairly coarse diameter.
Multifilament	A smooth yam consisting of two or more monofilaments twisted tightly together.
Needled felt	A fabric (felt) made by the mechanical interlocking of individual fibres in a random orientation.
Nylon	A synthetic fibre manufactured from aliphatic or semi-aromatic polyamides. Has good resistance to alkalis but is affected by strong acids and solutions in the pH range of 1 to 6. Maximum operating temperature is 107°C.
Oxford weave	A modified plain weave where both warp and weft yarns are multiple yarns but not of equal number.
Plain weave	The simplest and most common weave produced by passing the weft thread over and under each successive warp thread. Offers low permeability and excellent particle retention; however, it is susceptible to blinding.
Polyester	A synthetic fibre manufactured from terephthalic acid and ethylene glycol; the resulting polymer has excellent resistance to most mineral acids and solutions in the pH range of 1 to 8. Maximum operating temperature is 140°C.
Polypropylene	A synthetic fibre manufactured from a petroleum industry by-product. Excellent resistance to full pH range and has maximum operating temperature of 32°C. It is affected by oxidizing agents.
Porosity (permeability)	The rate of flow of air under differential pressure through a cloth. Generally measured in litres per minute (at 12.7 mm water pressure).
Satin (or sateen) weave	A weave in which warp yarns are carried uninterruptedly over many weft yarns to produce a smooth-faced fabric. Offers superior cake release and excellent resistance to binding.
Spun (staple)	Yarns made from filaments that have been cut into short lengths, then twisted together. Staple fibres offer good particle retention; however, cake release may suffer due to the hairiness of the yarns.
3 × 1 Double weave	A special weave in which both sides of the cloth show a smooth 3 × 1 broken twill surface. Offers excellent stability, retention and cake-release properties.
Twill weave	A weave in which the weft threads pass over one and under two or more warp threads to give the look of diagonal lines. Offers medium retention and blinding properties with high abrasion resistance and good flow rates.
Warp	The yarns that run lengthwise in cloth as they are woven on a loom.
Weft	The yarns that run width wise in cloth as they are woven on a loom. Also known as filling yarns.

damaged to keep the filter availability and get the required output from the system. In the context of this research, these terms are important to note because the system should in theory be able to distinguish and see how the cloth type affects the filtration cycles, whether it is the type of weave or material or different parameters of the filter cloth such as permeability and porosity.

Hence, to lessen the manual task, reduce the above-mentioned costs and digitalize the process, adding a digital form of data collection to monitor and analyze the conditions of the cloth is necessary. This kind of digital solution would not only add value to the company but would also support company's sustainability strategy. With the addition of this product to the filter, it has the possibility to reduce the number of filter cloth that needs to be changed, reducing the filter cloth waste and increasing the life expectancy of the filter cloth, it optimizes the process and it has the potential to aid in using less energy and water consumption. Another issue with the current process is that the filter cloth is chosen after start-up of the filters; operators will closely monitor the filter cloth and with the help of suppliers, the best cloth type is chosen based on various parameters of the feed. The type of filter cloth can be chosen according to the need of the process. Few parameters that are considered during selection process of the filter cloth are shown in Table 7.2. This process is currently a manual process. The condition of the filter cloth is manually inspected; there is no data available from the filter cloth and so there are no analytics available from the filter cloth. The solution that will come out of this exercise will centre on all these issues and will aim to find a smart solution that serves as a sustainable approach which is empowered by digitalization.

In 2020, the above-mentioned problems with the existing product were discussed with different stakeholders in Company A. The decision to work on the design issues in the product was a strategic-level decision to encourage digitalization and sustainability in Company A products. Hence, this research aims to offer a practical solution to this problem with a MVP and the possible benefits it can bring to the process. The goal of the research was to create a MVP that can provide feedback to the users hence allowing the users to monitor and track the condition of the filter cloth. After the MVP is designed, possible benefits, testing and future research ideas will also be presented in this chapter. To fulfil the goal of this chapter, a modified action research methodology was chosen as defined in Section 3.1.

4   Results and Discussion

As a result of the research and sprint exercise, a MVP was created. The MVP uses MV and ML on pressure filters to monitor the filter medium in order to track, monitor and maintain the filter cloth, contributing to the overall health monitoring of the filter. The MVP uses ML to identify the abnormality in the filter cloth and its severity. The system first must be taught what is normal, while the filter is in use, and what is abnormal. With the start of the MVP, the product was able to identify various aspects of the filter cloth such as small holes and seam. The system had to be taught that the seam is a part of the filter cloth and alarming when a seam comes around is not necessary. Similarly, the system also noted small holes that were poked in the filter with different dimensions to see whether it would detect it as seen in the figure below.

The system can provide the size and exact position of the holes in the filter cloth. As shown in Figure 7.2, the MVP is showing where the smallest wear and tear is occurring with the red dot on the right-hand side. It can provide exact position of where the cloth needs to be checked with the degree of severity. As seen in the above figure, the red dot that is appearing is not a hole and does not need to be repaired soon, so it reads no holes. But this indicates that there is a small wearing happening, which might develop into a hole

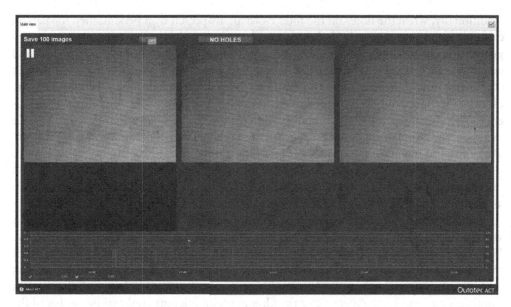

FIGURE 7.2 Minimum viable product concept for Company A.

and affect the overall output of the filter. It can also provide the size and exact position of the holes in the filter cloth which in turn lets the maintenance know where to repair the cloth. This kind of information helps to predict the health of the filter and allows to understand whether the output of the filter is being affected by the filter cloth. This early detection of any wear and tear allows the users to fix it before it gets to the point that the holes cannot be stitched and the whole cloth needs to be changed. This unnecessary changing of the filter cloth leads to extra cost and disposal of the filter cloth, which is not sustainable. The MVP also can detect the seam of the cloth so that the system knows it is a seam and not something else that is hampering the filter cloth. Additionally, it also tracks the alignment of the filter cloth. During a cycle, if the cloth moves horizontally, then the total area of filtration will reduce, which reduces the output of the cycle. Hence, it is very important to keep track of the alignment of the filter cloth. There is an alignment system available in most of the pressure filters, but tracking is not available. With this tracking system integrated, we can gain the benefit of knowing how often the filter cloth gets out of the range and whether there is a reason other than normal shifting, that the cloth is moving.

Along with the hole detection, seam detection and alignment of the filter cloth, it also tracks the cloth consumption per cycle. This kind of information helps the users to understand the number of clothes needed for a filter within a certain amount of time reducing unnecessary wastage of the cloth. This could possibly prevent the number of filter cloths that are thrown away. This also aids in to manage the warehouse in the sites and to determine the need of the filters available. With the MVP, we were able to get a visual data of error in the system, which means that we can get the visualization of even the smallest holes in the filter cloth. This eliminates manual checking of filter cloth by the maintenance workers and in turn reducing hours from the workers time changing from active checking to alert-based checking at a particular area of the filter cloth. This increases the possibility to manage resources in the site and decrease the number of manual hours.

Additionally, when the holes on the filter cloth are inspected by a person, then the person can either chose to stitch the hole or to replace the whole cloth. This collaboration of people and the intelligent machine within the system helps to optimize the process and create an efficient way of working. The intelligent machines work on a repetitive task along with providing large amount of data to the system, and alongside people are using that data to figure out the best possible solution that fits the problem with their experience. The aligning of filter cloth and seam detection in the filter are automatic without using any additional appendages. It tracks any changes in the condition of the cloth. This allows to maintain the quality of the product with a smooth-running process. Since it is helping the product to run smoothly in a more efficient way, theoretically, it would improve the loss of product in the process and to ensure the efficient use of resources such as water and electricity reducing the impact on the environment.

The above-mentioned benefits are of the immediate value provided by the MVP but with the installation of product over time, there are many other benefits that come along. First, the product has high possibility to integrate to an automation system that most of the minerals processing industries use today. The data that we get from the system can provide valuable information to the process owners, such as the kind of cloth that is most suitable for a process, the lifecycle of the filter cloth in different applications, index of the washing quality, and resource allocation. From technology perspective, its software and hardware can be upgraded, and new services can be introduced by expanding its applications. It can be further developed to adapt into other filter types, given the requirements are similar. Hence, the possibility of such technology has opportunities ahead to integrate and improve the efficiency of the processes. This kind of technology keeps the individuals involved in the process in the loop where they are excluded from routine tasks but rely on them as an expert within the system.

5   Conclusion

Our exploration of applying design sprint method to create a MVP for a real-time monitoring system was completed at the end of the research. The goal of the research was to provide a MVP that aids to contribute to a more digitalized and sustainable product. As a result of the sprint exercise, the MVP of the solution was created. A hole- and seam-detection MVP was demonstrated during the sprint exercise. A functional MVP was installed on the existing product and tested to get feedback from the laboratory users. After creating a MVP, a laboratory test was done few months later to test the viability of the MVP on a real product. The two problems with the product were solved in the process: aligning the filter cloth in place while the filter is running and the incapability of the system to alarm when the cloth is being teared or damaged. Apart from using a digital element to address the aforementioned issues, the solution aims to enhance the sustainability of resources and work practices as explained in the Results and Discussion section.

We have observed the methodical development of concepts from conception to prototyping via the lens of collaborative and iterative design. Throughout this chapter, the connections between design sprint concept and the complexity of creating a MVP that is suited for real-time data and machine-driven insights have been demonstrated. The product was scheduled to be tested on a client site following the laboratory test, but the test has been paused and rescheduled for several reasons. One of the limitations was that the research effort was put on hold for two years because of the COVID epidemic that began in 2020. The research was impacted by additional factors, such as the pandemic's effects on the economy, which made the project take longer than anticipated. Design sprint method has provided a structured and flexible framework to design and create a MVP. The research is based on one case for a company, and it not meant to be generalized in different scenarios. However, the conceptualization and the process behind the product can be adaptive to different products and processes. Looking forward, the MVP should be tested in a customer base so that the real benefits can be known over a period of time. After the testing in customer base, we can get the actual tangible and non-tangible benefits of the solution, which can be reflected to the possible benefits of the solution provided in this chapter.

References

Adelman, C. (1993). Kurt Lewin and the Origins of Action Research. *Educational Action Research*, *1*(1), 7–24. https://doi.org/10.1080/0965079930010102

Baum, F., MacDougall, C., & Smith, D. (2006). Participatory Action Research. *Journal of Epidemiology and Community Health*, *60*(10), 854–857. https://doi.org/10.1136/jech.2004.028662

Bhandari, K., Xin, Y., & Ojanen, V. (2021). Understanding Human-Machine Collaborative Systems in Industrial Decision-making. *2021 IEEE International Conference on Industrial Engineering and Engineering Management (IEEM)*, Singapore, pp. 1402–1406. https://doi.org/10.1109/IEEM50564.2021.9673073

Cummings, M., Bruni, S., Mercier, S., & Mitchell, P. (2007). Automation Architecture for Single Operator, Multiple UAV Command and Control. *The International C2 Journal*, *1*(2), 1–24. https://oai.dtic.mil/oai/oai?verb=getRecord&metadataPrefix=html&identifier=ADA478338

Desai, M., Kaniarasu, P., Medvedev, M., Steinfeld, A., & Yanco, H. (2013). Impact of Robot Failures and Feedback on Real-time Trust. *ACM/IEEE International Conference on Human-Robot Interaction*, Tokyo, Japan, pp. 251–258. https://doi.org/10.1109/HRI.2013.6483596

Dindarloo, S. R., & Siami-Irdemoosa, E. (2017). Data Mining in Mining Engineering: Results of Classification and Clustering of Shovels Failures Data. *International Journal of Mining, Reclamation and Environment*, *31*(2), 105–118. https://doi.org/10.1080/17480930.2015.1123599

Ferreira, V. G., & Canedo, E. D. (2019). Using Design Sprint as a Facilitator in Active Learning for Students in the Requirements Engineering Course: An Experience Report. *Proceedings of the ACM Symposium on Applied Computing, Part F*, 147772, 1852–1859. https://doi.org/10.1145/3297280.3297463

Fuerstenau, M. C., & Han, K. N. (Eds.). (2003). *Principles of Minerals Processing*. Metallurgy, and Exploration, Inc. ISBN 0-87335-167-3

Gijzen, H. (2013). Big Data for a Sustainable Future. *Nature*, *502*(7469), 38. https://doi.org/10.1038/502038d

Hampton, S. E., Strasser, C. A., Tewksbury, J. J., Gram, W. K., Budden, A. E., Batcheller, A. L., Duke, C. S., & Porter, J. H. (2013). Big Data and the Future of Ecology. *Frontiers in Ecology and the Environment*, *11*(3), 156–162. https://doi.org/10.1890/120103

Heemsbergen, L. (2016). From Radical Transparency to Radical Disclosure: Reconfiguring (In) Voluntary Transparency through the Management of Visibilities. *International Journal of Communication*, *10*, 138–151. https://ijoc.org

Heleno, P., Davies, R., Brazio Correia, B. A., & Dinis, J. (2002). A Machine Vision Quality Control System for Industrial Acrylic Fibre Production. *Eurasip Journal on Applied Signal Processing*, *2002*(7), 728–735. https://doi.org/10.1155/S1110865702204114

Hu, B., & Chen, J. (2017). Optimal Task Allocation for Human-Machine Collaborative Manufacturing Systems. *IEEE Robotics and Automation Letters*, *2*(4), 1933–1940. https://doi.org/10.1109/LRA.2017.2714981

Hur, E., Cassidy, T., & Thomas, B. (2013). Seeding Sustainability through Social Innovation in Fashion Design. *10th European Academy of Design Conference – Crafting the Future*, April, Sweden, pp. 1–18.

Johannsmeier, L., & Haddadin, S. (2017). A Hierarchical Human-Robot Interaction-Planning Framework for Task Allocation in Collaborative Industrial Assembly Processes. *IEEE Robotics and Automation Letters*, 2(1), 41–48. https://doi.org/10.1109/LRA.2016.2535907

Keijzer-Broers, W. J. W., & de Reuver, M. (2016). Applying Agile Design Sprint Methods in Action Design Research: Prototyping a Health and Wellbeing Platform. In *Lecture Notes in Computer Science (Including Subseries Lecture Notes in Artificial Intelligence and Lecture Notes in Bioinformatics): Vol. 9661 LNCS* (pp. 68–80). Springer Verlag, Canada. https://doi.org/10.1007/978-3-319-39294-3_5

Knapp, J., Zeratsky, J., & Kowitz, B. (2016). *The Design Sprint - The Sprint Book*. Simon & Schuster (March 8, 2016). ISBN13: 9781501121746.

Kumar, A., Dimitrakopoulos, R., & Maulen, M. (2020). Adaptive Self-learning Mechanisms for Updating Short-term Production Decisions in an Industrial Mining Complex. *Journal of Intelligent Manufacturing*, 31(7), 1795–1811. https://doi.org/10.1007/s10845-020-01562-5

Lee, J., & Moray, N. (1992). Trust, Control Strategies and Allocation of Function in Human-machine Systems. *Ergonomics*, 35(10), 1243–1270. https://doi.org/10.1080/00140139208967392

Li, Y., & Zhang, C. (2016). Automated Vision System for Fabric Defect Inspection Using Gabor Filters and PCNN. *SpringerPlus*, 5(1), 1–12. https://doi.org/10.1186/s40064-016-2452-6

McCoy, J. T., & Auret, L. (2019). Machine Learning Applications in Minerals Processing: A Review. *Minerals Engineering*, 132, 95–109. https://doi.org/10.1016/j.mineng.2018.12.004

Rushton, A. (1997). Batch Filtration of Solid—Liquid Suspensions. In *Handbook of Batch Process Design* (pp. 153–192), P.N. Sharratt (Eds.), Springer Dordrecht. ISBN: 978-94-010-7150-5

Schmitt, R., Pfeifer, T., Mersmann, C., & Orth, A. (2008). A Method for the Automated Positioning and Alignment of Fibre-reinforced Plastic Structures based on Machine Vision. *CIRP Annals – Manufacturing Technology*, 57(1), 501–504. https://doi.org/10.1016/j.cirp.2008.03.128

Schoenbrunn, F., Laros, T., Henriksson, B., & Arbuthnot, I. (1984). *Solid and Liquid Separation* (pp. 44–52). Chichester: Ellis Harwood.

Seele, P., & Lock, I. (2017). The Game-changing Potential of Digitalization for Sustainability: Possibilities, Perils, and Pathways. *Sustainability Science*, 12(2), pp. 183–185. https://doi.org/10.1007/s11625-017-0426-4

Smith, M. L., Smith, L. N., & Hansen, M. F. (2021). The Quiet Revolution in Machine Vision - A State-of-the-Art Survey Paper, Including Historical Review, Perspectives, and Future Directions. *Computers in Industry*, 130, 103472. https://doi.org/10.1016/j.compind.2021.103472

Tuazon, D., Corder, G., Powell, M., & Ziemski, M. (2012). A Practical and Rigorous Approach for the Integration of Sustainability Principles into the Decision-making Processes at Minerals Processing Operations. *Minerals Engineering*, 29, 65–71. https://doi.org/10.1016/j.mineng.2011.10.017

Van Berkel, R., van Berkel, R., & Narayanaswamy, V. (2004). *Sustainability as a Framework for Innovation in Minerals Processing*. www.csrp.com.au

Wills, B. A., & Finch, J. A. (2016). Dewatering. In Finch J. (Eds.), *Wills' Mineral Processing Technology* (pp. 417–438). Elsevier. https://doi.org/10.1016/b978-0-08-097053-0.00015-7

8

DEVELOPING A DIGITAL SUSTAINABLE DEVELOPMENT GOAL PASSPORT FOR POSTGRADUATE MANAGEMENT STUDENTS IN A UK BUSINESS SCHOOL

Helen Millward and Becky Snelgrove

1 Introduction

1.1 *United Nations' Sustainable Development Goals and Principles of Responsible Management Education*

The premise of this chapter is to discuss the rationale behind, and arguments for, the development and introduction of a digital sustainable development goal (SDG) passport for postgraduate-level management students.

Foregrounding the SDG passport project, the ambitions of the SDGs and the introduction of the Principles of Responsible Management Education (PRME) United Nations (n.d.b) help to set the scene in which the project is situated.

Based on the eight Millennium Development Goals scheduled for implementation by 2015 (Chiba and Katsuma, 2022), the SDGs represent 'a set of international norms adopted at the 2015 United Nations (UN) Sustainable Development Summit' as a 'blueprint to achieve a better and more sustainable future for all by 2030' (Chiba and Katsuma, 2022: 3). The 2030 agenda for sustainable development suggests the SDGs as a highly interconnected 'plan of action for people, planet and prosperity' comprised of 17 goals and 169 targets, with the aim of balancing 'the three dimensions of sustainable development: the economic, social and environmental' (United Nations, 2015). Indeed, recent descriptors note the SDGs as 'the universally-agreed road map to bridge economic and geopolitical divides, restore trust and rebuild solidarity' (United Nations, 2023).

The United Nations' SDGs cover a broad range of priorities, including, for example, with goals related to poverty, education, energy, climate action, and so forth. PRME, on the other hand, lends focus directly to business and management education. Developed in 2007 by an 'international task force' from a range of leading academic institutions and Business Schools United Nations (n.d.c), PRME notes its mission as to 'transform management education and [to] develop the responsible decision-makers of tomorrow to advance sustainable development' United Nations (n.d.b). Traditionally based on a set of six principles including 'Purpose' [Principle (P) 1], 'Values' (P2), 'Method' (P3), 'Research'

DOI: 10.4324/9781003433743-9

(P4), 'Partnership' (P5) and 'Dialogue' (P6), PRME's remit covers a range of objectives encompassing elements such as curriculum enhancement, interaction with organizations and other stakeholders, and research United Nations (n.d.d). In 2023, PRME launched a 'refreshed' set of seven principles so as to be aligned with more contemporary business education practice. These include 'Purpose' (P1), 'Values' (P2), 'Teach' (P3), 'Research' (P4), 'Partner' (P5), 'Practice' (P6) and 'Share' (P7). As of 2023, PRME has more than 800 signatory members across 96 countries, with 17 regional chapters and a number of working groups having also been established United Nations (n.d.b) since PRME's inception.

2   Sustainability for Profit or Planet?

Via discussion of the extant literature, the chapter explores how traditional Business School module content leverages the notion of profit as a key component in organizational success (Cicmil et al., 2017; Kopnina, 2020; Scheyvens et al., 2016), much in juxtaposition with many of the principles introduced by the United Nations' SDGs United Nations (n.d.a). Equally, this chapter suggests that contemporary employers are often keen to connect with graduates who have a solid awareness and understanding of the SDGs (Edie, 2022; Forbes, 2020; Insightful Environments, n.d.), providing a rationale for the introduction of the SDG passport to showcase students' recognition of the link between the SDGs and organizations.

3   Methodological Considerations

The project team, comprised of the Business School's PRME lead and a University Learning Experience Designer, deemed an interpretivist action research approach to be the most suitable. This was due to the need to understand student interactions with the SDGs from the perspective of each student participating in the project, suggesting the 'truth' of the matter as a social construct (Bedeian, 2004; Burrell and Morgan, 1994). The project asks participants to upload written evidence of their interactions with the SDGs during the course of their programme, and to complete Likert scales to indicate their confidence levels with each of the SDGs. Equally, participants are also asked to complete an end-of-programme online questionnaire to further gage any benefits and limitations of the pilot SDG passport project. As such, both qualitative and quantitative data collection were deemed appropriate, ultimately resulting in the need for both content and statistical forms of analysis.

4   Project Aims

Initially introduced as a year-long pilot study, the SDG passport held two key aims:

1 To understand how the SDGs were represented by the Business School's current curriculum, and where further opportunities to introduce SDG-related content might be feasible.
2 To identify opportunities to increase student understanding and awareness of how the SDGs were connected to their studies and the wider environment.

The pilot project was also concerned with the secondary aims of exploring students' level of confidence in terms of their understanding of the SDGs, with check points positioned at both the start and end of the period, in which the students could edit their personal SDG passport via a learning journey platform. Equally, emphasis was also placed on the benefits that the SDG passport might hold in facilitating students' demonstration of their knowledge of, and experiences with, the SDGs to potential future employers. With this in mind, a cornerstone benefit for students in taking part in the SDG passport project was the ability to be able to show to, and hopefully discuss with, potential future employers.

5   Looking Ahead

While for the purpose of this study we refer to higher education as related to Postgraduate UK Business School MSc Management students, we hope that via outlining our approach to this pilot study, we might showcase the beginnings of a roadmap via which other education for sustainable development (ESD) practitioners may gain further inspiration for their own initiatives in this area.

The following section explores the extant literature surrounding the SDGs and Business Schools, paying specific attention to the arguably contradictory notion of business and business education for societal good, rather than purely for profit.

6   Literature Review

6.1   Profit-Oriented Organizations vs. the SDGs

The higher education landscape is adorned with multiple frameworks and benchmarks designed to foster action and progress around the broad theme of sustainability. For example, the gathering of world leaders in 2015 to endorse the SDGs (Scheyvens et al., 2016) marked a significant accord in world sustainability ambitions. The PRME (unprme, n.d.), on the other hand, are more specifically focused on the work of Business Schools, and along with other initiatives, it 'aims to develop a new generation of managers characterized by a deeper understanding of the world and their own selves' (Anninos, 2017: 30). Further aims might be seen in PRME's emphasis on sustainable growth, environmental awareness, and an understanding of society, ethics, responsible business practice, and so forth (Anninos, 2017).

The responsibility of instilling such characteristics and awareness within our students is a significant challenge 'and as a result of such initiatives, educators must question how they might best teach such a complex, multifaceted and often disputed topic' (Cicmil et al., 2017: 46). In line with this school of thought, ESD provides students with 'the knowledge, skills, attributes, and values required to pursue sustainable visions of the future' (Advance HE, 2023), arguably taking place using 'active pedagogies' to support learners in tackling 'wicked problems' and in identifying how they can contribute to solutions that address environmental integrity, social injustice and economic prosperity' (Advance HE, 2023).

However, if one of the primary functions of business is indeed how to make a profit and therefore sustain on-going organizational survival, then must we also not consider ESD from the perspective of organizations themselves? Arguably, the link between profit-driven organizations and the SDGs can at times be difficult to grasp, with both concepts often appearing at odds with one another. This may push us to question whether for-profit organizations can really make a genuine, sustained, and 'meaningful contribution' to achieving the SDGs (Scheyvens et al., 2016: 372), or, whether we will only see a token effort for surface appearances sake. In such instances, we might link back to PRME's mission for a 'new generation of managers' with a more ethical focus (unprme, n.d.), again considering the role and responsibilities of the higher education landscape in instilling students with considerations of profit vs. the planet.

Further salient questions of a similar vein may also arise, as 'If economic sustainability remains the priority, what distinguishes sustainability education from the topics that have always been taught' in the business and management school arena (Cicmil et al., 2017: 46). This wicked problem is further compounded by the notion of the SDGs as irreconcilably interlinked, both progressing and often limiting one another's progress much as with traditional educational streams in which 'economic priorities are being taught at the expense of ecological considerations' (Kopnina, 2020: 282). Indeed, how might an individual or organization 'reconcile this tension in his/her mind and then be in a position to make an effective contribution to progress towards a sustainable society?' (Cicmil et al., 2017: 46).

In the contemporary education and business landscape, there is 'a new urgent request' from businesses and business students to move away from corporate-centric models, towards 'purpose-driven business', or in other words, towards a model in which society is the key beneficiary rather than the individual organization (Morsing, 2022: 4). This, however, has implications for the higher education landscape and how educators teach business in challenging 'the basic ethical standards for norms of trust, responsibility and fairness that guide managerial practice' (Morsing, 2022: 5), in addition to challenging what might be viewed as success and responsible leadership (Morsing, 2022). As ESD practitioners, we must recognize that regardless of our intent, we are communicating 'social and behavioural expectations to our students ... for ethical and social interactions in the classroom and beyond' (Morsing, 2022: 8). As such, we might begin to question 'what is or should be the aim of education?' (Kopnina, 2020: 281), arguably resulting in the conclusion that there is a critical role for educators to play in instilling a 'more holistic understanding of business and its role in sustainable development' (Mihov, 2022: 18) as we recognize that the business education students receive in our classrooms is being 'put into practice [in] business reality everyday' (Morsing, 2022: 3).

It is here that we hope the introduction of an SDG passport for students may help in marrying the two perspectives. Learning might be seen as a 'critical parameter' in creating both individual and collective change (Anninos, 2017: 31), with significance being placed upon the role and responsibility of the academic world 'in training the' current and future generations of leaders' (Weybrecht, 2022: 1).

While the previous discussion related to whether we might reasonably expect genuine efforts to help to advance and reach the United Nation's SDGs from profit-oriented organizations' stands, it is clear there are some genuine factors that may encourage organizational efforts. For example, research suggests employee willingness to reskill for a sustainability-focused job role, or to accept a job with a lower rate of pay as not to compromise an individual's sustainability principles, therefore making sustainability focus key in organizational efforts to attain and retain sought-after employees (Edie,

2022; Forbes, 2020; Insightful Environments, n.d.). Indeed, as Business Schools are being challenged to instil a 'beyond-the-bottom-line mindset' (Buono, 2017: 131), the SDG passport hopes to encourage students to view sustainability holistically, facilitating students in the creation of a valuable record via which they can evidence their engagement with the SDGs to potential future employers.

The following section sets out the process of idea generation to implementation of the pilot project for the SDG passport.

7 Methodology: Considerations and Practice

7.1 Education for Sustainable Development

As part of the commitment to ESD, members of the Business School's senior executive group identified the need to map the SDGs to individual modules.

While a short-term mapping activity would perhaps have allowed, for example, for the inclusion of the relevant SDG connections to be illuminated within each module's information, this would not, however, have provided a route by which students could meaningfully engage with the SDGs. In efforts to solve this problem, the notion of the SDG passport was born, with the intention of encouraging students to engage at a deeper level and to reflect on their own connections, in addition to those garnered via their taught modules.

As a result, the SDG passport project held two key objectives:

1 To help the Business School to understand which SDGs were being explored by current teaching and where improvements might be made to the curriculum in efforts to incorporate the remaining SDGs.
3 To identify opportunities to increase student understanding and awareness of how the SDGs are connected to their studies and the wider environment.

The next issue for exploration was how to make the SDG passport concept a reality. In particular, this led to discussions of who needed to be in the proverbial room. This meant a consideration of the practicalities as to how the SDG passport might be created, and how it might appear visually. Due to the desire for students to be able to access and use the SDG passport throughout and across their various modules and beyond, the decision was taken to create a digital version of the SDG passport, with it not being tied to any one module. This decision suggested that a range of skills would be required in creating the SDG passport, and ultimately, a partnership between the Business School's PRME lead and a University Learning Experience Designer was formed. It was felt that this alliance would provide a strong mix of skills in support of activities varying from mapping the SDGs to modules to the creation of a digital space for the passport.

8 Action Research and Reflexivity

The project team determined that action research would be the most appropriate research approach for the SDG passport project, due to its proclivity for the inclusion of multiple stakeholder perspectives and progressive adaptations via various research phases and cycles (McNiff and Whitehead, 2006). Figure 8.1 demonstrates the various action

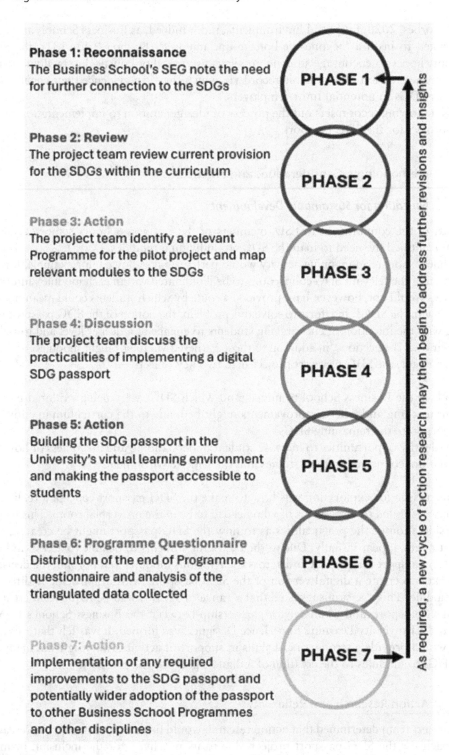

Phase 1: Reconnaissance
The Business School's SEG note the need for further connection to the SDGs

Phase 2: Review
The project team review current provision for the SDGs within the curriculum

Phase 3: Action
The project team identify a relevant Programme for the pilot project and map relevant modules to the SDGs

Phase 4: Discussion
The project team discuss the practicalities of implementing a digital SDG passport

Phase 5: Action
Building the SDG passport in the University's virtual learning environment and making the passport accessible to students

Phase 6: Programme Questionnaire
Distribution of the end of Programme questionnaire and analysis of the triangulated data collected

Phase 7: Action
Implementation of any required improvements to the SDG passport and potentially wider adoption of the passport to other Business School Programmes and other disciplines

As required, a new cycle of action research may then begin to address further revisions and insights

FIGURE 8.1 Action research model demonstrating the pilot project's key phases.
Source: The Authors, 2023.

research phases involved with the pilot project, also noting the potential for future cycles of action research to be undertaken to allow for further developments and insight in extending the reach of the SDG passport to further programmes, and potentially, to other disciplines. Due to such phases being interspliced with action, the potential for insights garnered throughout the duration of the project to be applied was both desirable and feasible, thus providing incremental development for the SDG passport project in real time as appropriate. Due to its focus on 'professional learning' (McNiff and Whitehead, 2006: 7) via which practitioners might reflexively explore their work for the purpose of challenging established practice, the selection of action research further serves as a valuable basis from which the SDG pilot project might evolve to encompass further programmes and disciplines in the future.

Underpinned by the interpretivist paradigm as comprised of a subjective ontology and epistemology, the SDG passport project accounts for differing viewpoints and experiences from multiple participant perspectives (Burrell and Morgan, 1992). As such, understandings of the SDGs and how various student experiences might connect to the SDGs may present the 'truth' of participant interactions with the SDGs as 'a product of social definition' (Bedeian, 2004: 199). Or, in other words, as illuminating connections to the SDGs as seen from the perspectives of students themselves as insiders of the phenomena under review (Oldfather and West, 1994), rather than those suggested purely by module-mapping efforts.

In returning to notions of 'professional learning' (McNiff and Whitehead, 2006: 7), action research facilitates natural stopping points for reflexivity throughout its various phases of implementation and action. With particular reference to the PRME leads' job role in relation to ESD and as a teaching member of faculty, an awareness was required of the project teams 'necessary connection' to the project in order to limit the colouring of results (Aull Davies, 2008: 7). Reflection was also required from the project team in considering how the team themselves might impact the project (Holland, 1999). While in typical forms of research it would, of course, be frowned upon to colour research with one's own input (Beck et al., 2011: 688), in the case of this pilot project, the ability to make changes to the digital passport might perhaps be taken in a positive light, particularly when considered in line with action research's proclivity for stages of alteration within its cycles.

9   Data Collection Methods

While still in its early stages, the pilot project aims to gather both qualitative and quantitative data via students reflections of their interactions with the SDGs as noted within the evidence section of the passport, via the Likert scales also completed within the passport as to garner information with regards to elements such as student confidence with the SDGs and via an online end-of-programme questionnaire designed to evaluate the project's success.

Student reflections will be explored as a form of documentary analysis, due to their having been written by students via their normal course of study engagement throughout the duration of the SDG passport. Documentary analysis can prove a useful way to interpret data collected without the direct intervention of the researcher, holding a host of benefits in terms of timesaving and availability of data, however, with the caveat that documentation may include limitations, such as insufficient detail of the phenomena under exploration (Bowen, 2009). Likert scales, on the other hand, assume latent variables, such as confidence, upon which participants can self-report using a ratings scale. Such scales are typically viewed as quick and easy for participants to complete, while also being relatively simple for researchers to interpret (Tanujaya et al., 2022). Finally, the use of an online questionnaire serves to provide additional information as to participant experiences at the end of the year-long engagement period, enabling data triangulation and as such, allowing for the project team to be more confident of their results (Jick, 1979).

The use of mixed methods determines the need for both content and statistical analyses to be conducted once all relevant data has been collected. It is also salient to note that, from an ethical standpoint, all students on the MSc Management Programme regardless of their agreement to participate in the pilot project will have access to the SDG passport. It is only via their agreement to participate in the study that the data will be used for research purposes.

10   After the Pilot Project: Next Steps

Following the completion of the pilot project, the project team plans to evaluate to what extent the project has been successful, and whether any further improvements might be made. If successful, then the project will be scaled up to include additional programmes and modules, eventually covering all taught provision within the Business School.

Following a previous presentation by the project team to members of the University's Institute for Sustainable Futures Community of Practice group, interest in rolling the project out across the wider university was also apparent. Indeed, there is also perhaps scope to include colleagues within the SDG passport initiative, allowing each individual connected with the university to create their own SDG passport and, therefore, their own record of connection to the SDGs.

11   A Road Map: Module Identification and Mapping

As previously noted, the initial problem was concerned with exploring where the SDGs might be seen within the Business School's current curriculum, and how to facilitate student interaction with, and consideration of, the SDGs. While time consuming, it would have been relatively straightforward to map content within modules to the SDGs; however, this arguably would not have increased student engagement and understanding to any significant extent. Nor, would a simple mapping exercise have provided students with any evidence from which they might draw in future interactions with potential employers.

The initial stage of the project required modules to be mapped to the SDGs. As the Business School has a multitude of modules, a pilot project in which the modules from one programme would be mapped to the SDGs and run for one academic year to determine the sustainability of the SDG passport appeared most achievable. The PRME lead also held the role of MSc Management Programme Director, meaning that a number of appropriate modules could be easily identified, allowing for them to be mapped to the SDGs.

While the PRME lead had existing insight into how some of the programme's modules might link to the SDGs, the decision was taken to back up this knowledge using Open SDGs (OSDG), which is an 'open-source tool that assigns SDG labels' to any text inserted via the online tool (osdg, n.d.). This was a time-consuming process, as it required the collection of multiple descriptors for each of the modules identified, to allow the OSDG tool enough text from which to accurately map to the SDGs. Equally, some module information did not produce any SDG connections, requiring input from various module leads as to whether there were indeed any connections to the SDGs within their module content. This process resulted in 22 modules being mapped to the SDGs; however, 1 module was confirmed to currently hold no links to the SDGs by the relevant module lead. In mapping the modules, SDGs 4, 8, 9, 12, and 16 were predominantly present, with some modules having strong links to more than 1 SDG.

12   Digital Creation of the SDG Passport

Once the appropriate modules had been mapped, the next challenge was to create the digital space in which the SDG passport would be housed and through which, it would eventually become accessible to students. The Learning Experience Designer opted to create this space via the PebblePad learning journey platform, providing graphics, and uploading information for students as to provide an initial explanation of the SDG goals and the issues that they cover United Nations (n.d.a). Figure 8.2 shows the cover page of the SDG passport, which students see when they access the digital materials.

This left further decisions as to the remainder of the content. Here, the project team considered the primary purpose of the SDG passport: to encourage students to showcase evidence of their learning and how this links to the 17 SDGs. While the modules mapped during the pilot study do not cover the entire range of the SDGs, additional mapping will take place once the pilot project has concluded, therefore likely demonstrating links to additional SDGs. Equally, the space is not designed only to assess students' relationships with the SDGs within their modules, but for them to consider wider implications and connections, meaning that all SDGs may in theory be linked to by the students through their wider experiences.

However, for the purpose of the pilot study, the project team decided that it would be useful for students to initially rate their awareness and confidence in understanding for each of the SDGs, in addition to their view as to how useful the SDG passport might be in considering future career advancement and perceptions value to potential employers. Achieved via the completion of Likert scales, this aims to provide insight for the students as to where they may wish to further their understanding, and for the Business School, as to where further improvements might be made in mapping module content to the SDGs.

The next stage in the process was to ensure that students held a good working knowledge of the SDG passport and how they might access and engage with the system. An initial introduction to the SDG passport was provided to students on the MSc Management Programme by the project team during induction week. However, at this point, a significant number of students were unable to join the talk on the University's campus, for reasons outside of the project team's control. This resulted in the project team's decision to run three further introductory sessions to the SDG passport, with two sessions taking place virtually via Microsoft Teams and one session taking place on campus. The

FIGURE 8.2 Sustainable development goal passport cover image, as included on the learning journey platform.

Source: The Authors, 2024.

aim of the sessions was to provide students with one-to-one support in accessing the SDG passport on the learning journey platform, and to provide information as to its purposes for those who may have missed the initial talk within induction week. In addition, the project team completed a demonstration of how to access and use the SDG passport at the start of a core module lecture for MSc Management students. This was well received and resulted in several students verbally demonstrating a keenness to use the passport, along with students from other programmes, who were also in attendance at the lecture, indicating their desire to use the SDG passport. While it was not possible to accommodate the inclusion of students external to the MSc Management Programme within the pilot study, this in itself indicates that students are eager to use the SDG passport, arguably showing that they can see the benefits of doing so.

MSc Management students were asked to begin their interaction with the SDG passport by completing the rating activities as detailed above, and equally, will be asked to complete the activity again at the end of their programme, potentially providing insights into how well the identified modules are supporting students in their learning and understanding of the associated SDGs. In addition, students will be asked to submit evidence from their work against the SDGs in order to create a portfolio of evidence that might be shared with potential employers upon graduation, demonstrating their learning against the SDGs. Students can upload evidence at any point throughout their programme of study. This evidence might include pieces of assessed or non-assessed work, reflections of learning or other experiences, and so on. There is also space for students to provide further details as to how the evidence uploaded links to the SDG(s) in question.

Once students move towards the completion of their programme, their efforts in completing the passport will be checked and signed off by the Programme Director. Students will then be able to use the passport in providing evidence of their knowledge, confidence and experiences with the SDGs to potential and current employers.

13 Discussion and Results

13.1 Potential Benefits: The SDG Passport

While the project is still in its pilot phase, it is possible to consider the potential benefits should the project prove successful. The project team sees such potential benefits as related to three specific stakeholder groups: students, the wider university and potential employers.

In a tough job market, graduate-level positions can be highly competitive, with the 'average number of applications of graduate schemes in the UK' on the rise (Milkround, n.d.). Students being able to accurately showcase their past engagement with and understanding of the SDGs may therefore provide them with an additional advantage over those who are not able to demonstrate the same level of awareness. As the extant literature notes, business skills are required to 'support growth in a green economy' (HM Government, 2011: 8), suggesting that students being able to demonstrate their experiences with the SDGs are a valuable resource for organizations attempting to increase sustainability-related activities, focus and goals. From the organizational perspective, it is clear that while profit remains important, organizations still require access to graduates who are able to 'reconcile' the 'tension[s]' between profit and making an 'effective contribution to progress towards a sustainable society' (Cicmil et al., 2017: 46). Equally, from the wider university perspective, the SDG passport may prove a valuable tool in helping the institution to meet its civic responsibilities, along with ESD ambitions (Weybrecht, 2022), via further mapping of its module content to the SDGs.

14 Potential Challenges: Module Selection, Mapping, Digitalization and Responsibility

As previously noted, the selection of the MSc Management Programme was primarily due to convenience, with a member of the project team serving as Director of the programme. This was also convenient as postgraduate programmes tend to have a smaller number of module options due to their typically shorter duration than, for example, undergraduate programmes, meaning that less time was required in the initial stages of the project. While the Programme Director had a reasonable understanding of the contents of each module mapped, this was not always extensive, meaning that mapping was at times difficult in understanding the connections between module content and the SDGs. This implicit understanding was bolstered by both the use of the OSDG checker tool (osdg, n.d.) and the input of relevant module leads as required.

However, in considering how the pilot project might be scaled up going forwards, further consideration of mapping efforts will be imperative. We might wish to question whether it is reasonable or even sensible for the Programme Director alone to undertake the required mapping activities. Module leads would arguably hold a more in-depth understanding of where content connects to the SDGs and as such, their undertaking of module mapping would perhaps be a more thorough approach. Equally, this would help to tackle the significant time burden that would be associated if only Programme Directors were to attempt to map modules to the SDGs, particularly where large undergraduate programmes might be concerned.

We may also wish to consider the digital aspect of the SDG passport in future iterations of the module, particularly if the initiative is to become available to a wider number of students across programmes and potentially, across disciplines. From lessons learnt during the pilot project, a digital SDG passport appears to remain preferable to a physical copy, with the perhaps obvious sustainability arguments as relates to the use of resources also being at play. However, it is also important to consider the background systems in place to be able to add students to the passport initiative, and the need for a faculty member (in the case of the pilot project, the Programme Director) to 'sign off' the passport in checking that students have engaged with the initiative. Again, scaling up the initiative may prove problematic here, as it might be seen as unrealistic to expect one individual to check and sign off passports for programmes with large cohorts. This, we suggest, is an issue to which further consideration is required before any efforts to scale up the use of the SDG passport commence.

15   Conclusions

15.1   Key Ambitions Revisited

This chapter details the introduction of a pilot project designed to create and launch an SDG passport for Postgraduate Management students within a UK Business School. The pilot project held two key aims: understanding where the Business School's current curriculum links to the SDGs and where further future connections might be feasible, along with ambitions of increasing student awareness, and understanding and engaging with the SDGs throughout students' studies and beyond. The project was further concerned with providing a platform for students through which they might demonstrate their engagement with, and knowledge of, the SDGs to potential future employers.

Foregrounded within the work of PRME and the broader United Nation's SDGs, the profit vs. planet debate takes central stage within the chapter in line with considerations of ESD practice. In particular, the somewhat 'wicked' problem of aligning traditional business school taught module content and sustainability ambitions often appears at odds with one another. However, it remains clear that contemporary organizations do recognize the need for sustainability literate graduates within the workforce, and in a similar vein, for emphasis on sustainability within working practices if high performing gradate staff are to be retained. As the chapter suggests, this places onus on Business Schools and their faculties to consider taught content and the ways in which this is delivered to students if we are to ensure that graduates leave university with a truly holistic view of sustainability.

16   Successes and Limitations

From anecdotal feedback provided by students during the project team's introductory sessions to the SDG passport, it appears that there is much interest in the project from the student's perspective. This in itself suggests that students are interested in engaging with the initiative, and that they can see the value and benefits that might be gained via their participation. From the university's perspective, student use of the SDG passport arguably helps to further ESD efforts to instil a holistic view of sustainability within future graduates, in addition to increasing student reflexivity on issues and experiences connected to sustainability. As discussed above, strong connections with sustainability and the SDGs are also likely to constitute a positive impression when considered by potential future employers.

The inclusion of an interpretive action research methodology provided further usefulness in terms of its ability to recognize multiple perspectives throughout the project, and in allowing discussions of reflexivity as to the project team's involvement. This approach appears particularly useful given that a key limitation of the project included the ways in which (and by whom) module identification and mapping was undertaken. Notably, this represented a high time cost burden for the project team, which would arguably be untenable in its current format were the SDG passports to be made available to multiple programmes and cohorts across the Business School and beyond. Indeed, we suggest that a wide scale roll out of the SDG passport would ideally require delegation to the directors of any programmes wishing to use the SDG passport, and/or the relevant module leads.

17   Future Ambitions

As previously noted, there is the potential to, and considerable interest in, scaling up the pilot project to include students across all Business School programmes, and potentially, across the wider university for both students and colleagues. However, before such efforts might begin, the final two phases of the action research project require completion. While much has been learnt during the completed (as much as one *can* complete a phase within action research) 1 through 5 phases, phases 6 and 7 are still to take place. As detailed within Figure 8.1, these respectively pertain to the distribution of the end-of-programme questionnaire and its subsequent analysis, and to the implementation of any required adaptation based on the data collected before any wider adoption of the SDG passport might take place. It is from the vantage point of a 'completed' phase 7 that we hope to include any further learnings from the pilot project within our approach to the SDG passport in the next academic year for MSc Management students and beyond.

References

Advance HE (2023) *Education for Sustainable Development in Higher Education*. The Quality Assurance Agency for Higher Education and Advance HE.

Anninos, L. N. (2017) 'A Responsible Business Education Approach: Insights from Neuroscience', in Flynn, P. M., Tan, T. K. and Gudić, M. (eds.). *Redefining Success: Integrating Sustainability into Management Education*. Routledge, pp. 29–44.

Aull Davies, C. (2008) *Reflexive Ethnography: A Guide to Researching Selves and Others*. Second Edition. Routledge.

Beck, J. L., Belliveau, G., Lea, G. W. and Wager, A. (2011) 'Delineating a Spectrum of Research-Based Theatre', *Qualitative Inquiry*, 17(8):687–700.

Bedeian, A. G. (2004) 'Peer Review and the Social Construction of Knowledge in the Management Discipline', *Academy of Management Learning and Education*, 3(2):198–216.

Bowen, G. A. (2009) 'Document Analysis as a Qualitative Research Method', *Qualitative Research Journal*, 9(2):27–39.

Buono, A. F. (2017) 'Beyond the Classroom: Embedding Responsible Management Principles, Practices, and Possibilities in Our Business Schools', in Flynn, P. M., Tan, T. K. and Gudić, M. (eds.). *Redefining Success: Integrating Sustainability into Management Education*. Routledge, pp. 131–144.

Burrell, G. and Morgan, G. (1994) *Sociological Paradigms and Organisational Analysis*. Ashgate Publishing Limited.

Chiba, M. and Katsuma, Y. (2022) 'The Sustainable Development Goals (SDGs) as International Norms', in Bacon, P., Chiba, M. and Ponjaert, F. (eds.). *The Sustainable Development Goals: Diffusion and Contestation in Asia and Europe*. Taylor and Francis Group.

Cicmil, S., Ecclestone, R. and Collins, K. (2017) 'Responsible Education in a Complex Content of Sustainable Development: Co-creating a Pedagogic Framework for Participatory Reflection and Action', in Flynn, P. M., Tan, T. K. and Gudić, M. (eds.). *Redefining Success: Integrating Sustainability into Management Education*. Routledge, pp. 45–57.

Edie (2022) 'Survey: Half of UK Professionals Would Consider Working in Sustainability'. Available at: www.edie.net/survey-half-of-uk-professionals-would-consider-working-in-sustainability/. Accessed 13/10/23.

Forbes (2020) 'The Power of Purpose: The Business Case for Purpose (All the Data You were Looking for pt 2)'. Available at: www.forbes.com/sites/afdhelaziz/2020/03/07/the-power-of-purpose-the-business-case-for-purpose-all-the-data-you-were-looking-for-pt-2/. Accessed 13/10/23.

HM Government (2011) 'Skills for a Green Economy Report'. Available at: www.assets.publishing.service.gov.uk/media/5a74c5c2ed915d502d6cae02/11-1315-skills-for-a-green-economy.pdf. Accessed 13/10/23.

Holland, R. (1999) 'Reflexivity', *Human Relations*, 52(4):463–484.

Insightful Environments (n.d.) 'Why a Sustainable Workplace is Key to Attract & Retain the Best Talent'. Available at: www.ie-uk.com/blog/sustainable-workplace-attract-retain. Accessed 13/10/23.

Jick, T. D. (1979) 'Mixing Qualitative and Quantitative Methods: Triangulation in Action', *Administrative Science Quarterly*, 24(4):602–611.

Kopnina, H. (2020) 'Education for the Future? Critical Evaluation of Education for Sustainable Development Goals,' *The Journal of Environmental Education*, 51(4):280–291.

McNiff, J. and Whitehead, J. (2006) *All You Need to Know about Action Research*. Sage Publications.

Mihov, I. (2022) 'PRME's Role in Advancing the Broad View of Business as a Force for Good', in Morsing, M. (ed.). *Responsible Management Education: The PRME Global Movement*. Routledge, pp. 17–23.

Milkround (n.d.) 'How Competitive Are Graduate Schemes'. Available at: www.milkround.com/advice/how-competitive-are-graduate-schemes. Accessed 27/10/23.

Morsing, M. (2022) 'Principles for Responsible Management Education: Towards Transforming Leadership Education', in Morsing, M. (ed.). *Responsible Management Education: The PRME Global Movement*. Routledge, pp. 3–12.

Oldfather, P. P. and West, J. (1994) 'Qualitative Research as Jazz', *Educational Researcher*, 23(8):22–26.

OSDG (n.d.) Available at: www.osdg.ai/. Accessed 27/10/23.

Scheyvens, R., Banks, G. and Highes, E. (2016) 'The Private Sector and the SDGs: The Need to Move beyond "Business as Usual"', *Sustainable Development*, 24:371–382.

Tanujaya, B., Prahmana, R. C. I. and Mumu, J. (2022) 'Likert Scale in Social sciences Research: Problems and Difficulties', *FWU Journal of Social Sciences*, 16(4):89–101.

United Nations (n.d.a) *PRME*. Available at: www.unprme.org. Accessed 27/10/23.

United Nations (n.d.b) *PRME: History of PRME*. Available at: www.unprme.org/history-of-prme/. Accessed 15/11/23.

United Nations (n.d.c) *PRME: The Six Principles*. Available at: www.unprme.org/what-we-do/. Accessed 15/11/23.

United Nations (n.d.d) *The 17 Goals*. Available at: www.sdgs.un.org/goals. Accessed 27/10/23.

United Nations. (2015). 'Transforming our world: The 2030 Agenda for Sustainable Development'. Resolution adopted by the General Assembly on 25 September 2015 (A/RES/70/1). Available at: https://sdgs.un.org/sites/default/files/publications/21252030%20

United Nations. (2023). 'The Sustainable Development Goals Report: Special Edition'. Available at: https://unstats.un.org/sdgs/report/2023/The-Sustainable-Development-Goals-Report-2023.pdf.

Weybrecht, G. (2022) 'Business Schools Are Embracing the SDGs – But Is It Enough? – How Business Schools Are Reporting on their Engagement in the SDGs', *The International Journal of Management Education*, 20:1–10.

INDEX

Note: **Bold** page numbers refer to tables and *italic* page numbers refer to figures.

Printed in the United States
by Baker & Taylor Publisher Services